CW01497785

St Antony's Series
General Editor: **Richard Clogg** (1999–), Fellow of St Antony's College, Oxford

Recent titles include:

Geoffrey Wiseman
CONCEPTS OF NON-PROVOCATIVE DEFENCE
Ideas and Practices in International Security

Pilar Ortuño Anaya
EUROPEAN SOCIALISTS AND SPAIN
The Transition to Democracy, 1959–77

Renato Baumann (*editor*)
BRAZIL IN THE 1990s
An Economy in Transition

Israel Getzler
NIKOLAI SUKHANOV
Chronicler of the Russian Revolution

Arturo J. Cruz, Jr
NICARAGUA'S CONSERVATIVE REPUBLIC, 1858–93

Pamela Lubell
THE COMMUNIST PARTY DURING THE CULTURAL REVOLUTION
The Case of the Sixty-One Renegades

Klaus Gallo
GREAT BRITAIN AND ARGENTINA
From Invasion to Recognition, 1806–26

Peter Mangold
SUCCESS AND FAILURE IN BRITISH FOREIGN POLICY
Evaluating the Record, 1900–2000

Mohamad Tavakoli-Targhi
REFASHIONING IRAN
Orientalism, Occidentalism and Historiography

Louise Haagh
CITIZENSHIP, LABOUR MARKETS AND DEMOCRATIZATION
Chile and the Modern Sequence

Renato Colistete
LABOUR RELATIONS AND INDUSTRIAL PERFORMANCE IN BRAZIL
Greater São Paulo, 1945–60

Peter Lienhardt (*edited by Ahmed Al-Shahi*)
SHAIKHDOMS OF EASTERN ARABIA

John Crabtree and Laurence Whitehead (*editors*)
TOWARDS DEMOCRATIC VIABILITY
The Bolivian Experience

St Antony's Series
Series Standing Order ISBN 0–333–71109–2
(*outside North America only*)

You can receive future titles in this series as they are published by placing a standing order.
Please contact your bookseller or, in case of difficulty, write to us at the address below with
your name and address, the title of the series and the ISBN quoted above.

Customer Services Department, Macmillan Distribution Ltd, Houndmills, Basingstoke,
Hampshire RG21 6XS, England

Success and Failure in British Foreign Policy

Evaluating the Record, 1900–2000

Peter Mangold
Senior Associate Member
St Antony's College
Oxford

in association with
St Antony's College, Oxford

© Peter Mangold 2001

All rights reserved. No reproduction, copy or transmission of
this publication may be made without written permission.

No paragraph of this publication may be reproduced, copied or
transmitted save with written permission or in accordance with
the provisions of the Copyright, Designs and Patents Act 1988,
or under the terms of any licence permitting limited copying
issued by the Copyright Licensing Agency, 90 Tottenham Court
Road, London W1T 4LP.

Any person who does any unauthorised act in relation to this
publication may be liable to criminal prosecution and civil
claims for damages.

The author has asserted his right to be identified
as the author of this work in accordance with the
Copyright, Designs and Patents Act 1988.

First published 2001 by
PALGRAVE
Houndmills, Basingstoke, Hampshire RG21 6XS and
175 Fifth Avenue, New York, N.Y. 10010
Companies and representatives throughout the world

PALGRAVE is the new global academic imprint of
St. Martin's Press LLC Scholarly and Reference Division and
Palgrave Publishers Ltd (formerly Macmillan Press Ltd).

ISBN 0–333–80448–1

This book is printed on paper suitable for recycling and
made from fully managed and sustained forest sources.

A catalogue record for this book is available
from the British Library.

Library of Congress Cataloging-in-Publication Data
Mangold, Peter.
    Success and failure in British foreign policy : evaluating the
    record, 1900–2000 / Peter Mangold.
        p. cm. — (St. Antony's series)
    Includes bibliographical references and index.
    ISBN 0–333–80448–1
    1. Great Britain—Foreign relations—20th century. I. Title.
    II. Series. III. St. Antony's series (Palgrave (Firm))

    DA566.7 .M36 2001
    327.41'009'04—dc21
                                                    2001034498

10   9   8   7   6   5   4   3   2   1
10   09 08 07 06 05 04 03 02 01

Printed and bound in Great Britain by
Antony Rowe Ltd, Chippenham, Wiltshire

To the memory of my Mother

We are a very empirical people. We try to deal with facts as we see them. Nothing is permanent in the world.

(Harold Macmillan, 1955)

The British are emotionally and ideologically committed to the belief that they are unemotional and strangers to ideology. They have the same conviction as the fat man who thinks that he is thin or the pretty girl who is convinced that she is plain.

(Peter Unwin, Hearts, Minds and Interests, *1998)*

Contents

Acknowledgements

My great thanks are due to Dr Geoffrey Edwards, Dr John Hughes, Professor Michael Lee and Sally Morphet for their very helpful comments on parts of the original draft. Clare Brown and John Eidinow were kind enough to read complete drafts, and I owe much to their patience and promptings. I am of course alone responsible for the text as it has finally emerged.

I would also like to thank the Warden and Fellows of St Antony's College, Oxford where much of this book was written, for their hospitality, and to acknowledge a very old debt to the late Philip Windsor, under whose original supervision at the London School of Economics, I first became interested in the inconsistencies of British pragmatism.

PETER MANGOLD

Lines from Philip Larkin's *Homage to a Government* appear by permission of Faber & Faber.

1
The Scope of the Possible

It may be well to emphasise at the outset the cardinal difference between our foreign policy and that of many other countries. Obviously the ultimate, if not the immediate, aim and object of the foreign policy of countries such as Germany, Hungary and Russia is to recover the territory lost in the war. Italy has her eye on the Aegean Islands and parts of Asia Minor. Japan may well hope some day to absorb Manchuria. We, on the other hand, have no territorial ambitions nor desire for aggrandisement. We have got all that we want – perhaps more. Our sole object is to keep what we have and live in peace. Many foreign countries are playing for a definite stake and their policy is shaped accordingly. It is not so in our case. To the casual observer our foreign policy may appear to lack consistency and continuity, but both are there. We keep our hands free in order to throw our weight into the scale on behalf of peace. The maintenance of the balance of power and the preservation of the *status quo* have been our guiding lights for many decades and will so continue.[1]

This summary of British foreign policy was written in 1926, during the last unchallenged phase of British pre-eminence. Britain's rivals had been defeated in the First World War. With the collapse of Germany and the Ottoman Empire, British imperial power had extended to its furthest point. The Soviet Union had retreated into revolution, the United States back into isolation. Britain had been left as the sole superpower.[2] According to the Foreign Secretary, Austen Chamberlain, it occupied a unique position to 'do what no other nation on the face of the earth can do' and decide the great questions of war and peace.[3]

Judged against these exalted, and fundamentally overambitious standards, the British foreign policy record in the twentieth century must seem a failure. Within fifty years, Britain had lost almost all of its empire and had ceased to be a Great Power. The country which was so anxious for peace had to fight a Second World War and was engaged in a forty-year long Cold War. The 'free hand' had finally been abandoned with the establishment of the North Atlantic Treaty Organisation (NATO) in 1949 and membership of the European Economic Community (EEC) in 1973. Although the 1926 memorandum made no reference to national sovereignty, by the end of the century this was being increasingly eroded.

The impression of failure is reinforced by a series of high-profile errors and misjudgements. These included the miscalculation of German intentions in July 1914, the 1919 Versailles settlement which failed to establish the basis for a long-term peace in Europe and the 1938 Munich agreement with Hitler. After the war came the refusal in the wake of the 1955 Messina conference of the offer of founder membership of the EEC, and the failure, once Britain did join, to maximise the advantages of membership. On the imperial front there were the long succession of errors and evasions in the Far East which culminated in the surrender of Singapore in 1942, the abandonment of the Palestine Mandate in 1948, Suez and the messy withdrawal from Aden in 1967. Britain failed to prevent Rhodesia unilaterally declaring independence in 1965 or Argentina invading the Falkland Islands in 1982.

Foreign policy also compares unfavourably with the domestic record. For, while much went wrong on the home front, the Depression of the 1930s, the long history of bad labour relations and slow economic growth, the stubborn survival of class differences and social inequalities, the overall record across the century is one of progress and achievement. Between 1900 and 2000, Britain became a more prosperous, fairer, more democratic society, whose citizens came to enjoy, particularly during the second half of the century, increasingly high standards of education, welfare and living. The contrast with foreign policy, a story of contraction and decline, is striking.

Cumulatively, these can be read as a formidable indictment, belying any claim that foreign policy is a British strength.[4] But there are other perspectives on the large and complex canvas of British foreign policy, which quite literally spanned the globe. However much went wrong, the fact remains that, in a violent and unstable century, Britain succeeded in protecting its vital interests. 'The ultimate aims of any Government in the United Kingdom,' an official report of 1960 noted, 'must always remain the security of these islands from foreign domination or attack, the prosperity of the British people and the protection of our individual freedom and liberty.'[5] This Britain achieved. It ended the world's largest empire with good grace and at least relatively little violence. Although it lost Great Power status it retained both its self-respect and a good deal of its international reputation. At the end of the century it was still an *active* power, with an instinct to lead and a sense of responsibility for the maintenance of international order. And while it had lost around a quarter of its pre-war wealth between 1939 and 1945 – some £7300 million[6] – and was subsequently to slip down the international league tables, it remained one of the world's richest countries.

Success and failure in foreign policy are thus by no means simple or self-evident propositions. Historical perspectives alter over time. The diplomacy of the 1930s is today judged in much more nuanced fashion than it was in the immediate aftermath, when the talk was of 'guilty men'. Similarly, it has now become possible to take a more understanding view of the policy of the decades when policy makers fought a rearguard action to maintain Britain's status as a Great Power than it was in the dogdays of the 1970s when the inevitability of decline had come to seem self-evident. Perspective also reflects values and points of view. British policy towards the European integration process looks very different to a Eurosceptic than it does to one committed to the European idea. Few judgements on foreign policy questions are entirely value-free, particularly where it comes to the larger questions of national purpose, the role the country should play in the world, or where sentiment is otherwise engaged.

An evaluation of the foreign policy record must therefore begin by establishing a set of criteria by which judgement should be made. First and foremost there is the issue of objectives. Were these appropriately set in terms of protecting and promoting long-term interests, and were they achievable? The latter is particularly important in the case of a declining power. The scope of what was possible was contracting for much of the period, at least until the early 1980s, and success depended heavily on the ability of officials and ministers to judge their residual latitude of action, and to set, or more often adjust, objectives accordingly. This is not to suggest that it was always wrong to pursue risky or even apparently unrealisable objectives. Few would dispute that it was right to continue fighting in May 1940, and there is little criticism of the decision to send a task force to the south Atlantic to retake the Falklands Islands in 1982. The operation, after all, ended in a victory. Churchill and Macmillan's peace diplomacy of the 1950s illustrate a somewhat different point – that policy can achieve useful ends even if the immediate declaratory aims are not met. The prospects of initiating *détente* with the Soviet Union at this relatively early point in the Cold War were slim, and the rationale for their attempts is open to question. But there was a need to demonstrate to an anxious public that the government was doing something to try to reduce international tensions. These, however, are exceptions. For the most part the pursuit of overambitious goals proved a recipe for failure and frustration, if not worse, the hallmark of a policy which has failed to adjust ends to means.

The instances where policy makers overplayed their hand are relatively easy to identify. Assessing where residual freedom of action was underestimated is by contrast often very difficult. The point can be illustrated by the manner in which Britain adjusted to the emergence of the European integration movement. Writing in his memoirs of the refusal in 1950 to take part in the negotiations for the establishment of the European Coal and Steel Community (ECSC) Lord Plowden argued that the radical reorientation which membership of an exclusively European body, with a strong supranational element required of a country which had, since Elizabethan times, looked outward from Europe, was politically and psychologically impossible at the time. 'The beliefs engendered by four hundred years of history are not changed overnight by intellectual argument.'[7] There was 'no possibility of persuading the British people or any British government at that time to enter into the Coal and Steel Community on the terms laid down by the French.' This then 'was *an opportunity but not, in my view, a missed opportunity*'[8] (emphasis added).

This at least is the determinists' defence. But were the constraints always as great as decision makers believed, or later claimed that they were? Many years after the event, the former Chancellor of the Exchequer, Lord Butler, who had been quite openly bored by the negotiations which led to the formation of the Common Market, gave an interview for a radio documentary on the British relationship with Europe, which included the following, remarkably candid, exchange.

> *Interviewer.* Do you say that there was – in view of your own disarming confession that you were plainly wrong in 1955 – that there was a failure of the political class in this country? A failure to encourage the British people into a belief that their circumstances were totally different?
>
> *Butler.* Yes. When you say I make a disarming confession, I definitely do, because I now think I ought to have been more far-sighted. But

on the other hand, absolutely no force was urging me the other way, either in British public opinion or in British ministerial opinion. So it was not, so to speak, my fault. But I think that, being a prominent citizen and having a brain, I ought to have looked further ahead.[9]

As Lord Butler points out, it was the policy-makers', in particular the politicians' job to look ahead, just as it was their responsibility to keep their nerve in difficult situations and provide a lead to a public opinion which did not like, and often did not understand the need for change. What, however, politicians *should* have done, and what they were willing or able to do, were often two different things. The fact that the most senior ministers and officials were often the prisoners of their own prejudices or conventional thinking does not necessarily mean that no alternative courses were possible. Far-sighted or determined prime ministers could take actions which more conventional or narrow-minded colleagues could not. Churchill in 1940 is the most obvious example, but one might also cite Attlee's decision to withdraw from India, as indeed Macmillan's decision in the face of considerable Cabinet scepticism, to proceed with Britain's first application for EEC membership in 1961. The real distinction is often between the difficult and the impossible.

In seeking to make these fine judgements, the historian has only a limited number of advantages over the participants. Hindsight, and knowing what was happening on the 'other side of the hill', are the two most obvious. The historian has a vital knowledge of what was happening in Berlin and Vienna in the summer of 1914 which was denied to the Foreign Secretary, Sir Edward Grey. But just as hindsight is a privilege which can easily be abused, so too the detachment afforded by time and distance can lead to an underestimation of the wide and often subtle range of pressures under which decision makers were operating, and a consequent oversimplification of the problems which they faced. While it can certainly be argued that policy makers were imprudent to have dismissed the possibility of the emergence of a Common Market, and unperceptive not to have picked up the growing political will among the Six to make the enterprise succeed, the fact that it would do so was not self-evident at the time. Similarly, it would be wrong to underestimate the extent of the pressures militating against early membership. Here, as on other occasions, the impact of intangibles, the influence of history, prejudice in the literal sense of the word, and method, the way in which policy making was approached, on limiting the options is easy to underestimate.

A second crucial set of criteria for evaluating success and failure, which are fortunately relatively easier to evaluate, are those of cost. At what price were outcomes achieved? Was it proportionate to the ends? Might different policies or prompter action have achieved the same aim at lower outlays of blood, treasure or diplomatic opportunity? These are important to any country, especially when it comes to the strategic dimension of policy, where human lives are at stake. The bloodletting of the trenches is the single most terrible failure of the period. But the resource issue is particularly sensitive in the case of a power which seemed constantly to be operating at or near the limits of its economic potential, and where economy of means was therefore at a premium.

Finally, and again more briefly, there is the ethical dimension. Were actions in conformity with national values and prevailing international rules and norms? If the answer is simple in the case of Suez, which was in clear breach of international law, it is much more complex in the case of the 1999 NATO-led Kosovo operation where strong moral arguments for military action had to be weighed against the absence of a United Nations mandate. Conversely, the absence of action in cases where human rights are being grossly abused may constitute a failure of policy.

Four criteria are therefore critical to any assessment of the success or failure of policy. How realistically did policy makers set goals and exploit their freedom of action? Were interests and national purposes effectively protected and promoted? Was policy 'efficient' in the sense of achieving its aims in a timely and economic fashion? Was it morally and legally defensible? If the answers to these questions are rarely simple, it is nevertheless possible to identify *patterns* of relative success and failure, and the periods, as also the areas of policy, in which they were concentrated. This in turn may suggest the kind of issues which tended to be well or less well handled, as too the major strengths and weaknesses which the small groups of ministers and officials involved brought to the making of British foreign policy.

The term should be briefly defined. Foreign policy here is understood to mean the exercise of power (including imperial power) and influence in the international arena in the promotion of British purposes and interests. While the latter has come to cover an increasingly wide range of economic, environmental and social issues, particularly during the latter half of the century, the main focus will be on 'high policy'. Issues of war and peace are thus central, as are the ways in which Britain responded to complex adjustments demanded of her by loss of power and the pressure of external events. Many of the more detailed issues of foreign policy, some of which involved a great deal of ministerial time, are also excluded.

The problems facing policy makers in the difficult and dangerous conditions of the twentieth century were formidable. 'My world began in war,' wrote Anthony Eden in the autobiography he published in 1960. 'It has been spent in war, its preparation and its aftermath.'[10] Two of those wars had been against Germany. The first, aptly know at the time as the 'Great War', in which Eden fought as a subaltern, cost Britain and its empire some 744 700 lives.[11] During the Second World War, which this time extended to the Far East, Britain was threatened with invasion and subjected to first bomber and later rocket attack. Although Singapore which had been lost in 1942 was eventually re-taken, the prestige on which empire depended had been irrevocably undermined, and with Indian independence in 1947 the process of decolonisation was under way. Already, however, a new global conflict was developing in the form of a 'cold' war. While the Soviet Union was a much more prudent adversary than Germany, this new conflict, which lasted until the late 1980s, was expensive and uniquely dangerous. It accelerated the erosion of British security which had been under way since the advent of the aeroplane at the beginning of the century. The only defence against nuclear or thermonuclear missile attack was deterrence. Beyond a rudimentary civil defence system, there was nothing by way of reinsurance.

Britain's most obvious disadvantage in coping with this succession of threats was material – the fact that for much of the century, certainly until the early 1980s, it was losing power, that is the ability to impose its will *vis-à-vis* other major states or nationalist movements. The lead it had established by pioneering the industrial revolution in the late eighteenth and the early nineteenth century was being undermined as other powers with stronger geographical and larger population bases industrialised, and British growth rates slowed. Between 1900 and 1938, the British share of world manufacturing output slipped from 18.5 per cent (compared with Germany's 13.2 per cent and America's 23.6 per cent) to 10.7 per cent (compared with Germany's 12.7 per cent and America's 31.4 per cent).[12] In 1950, its gross national product (GNP) was still the third highest in the world, 71 billion dollars, compared with France's 50, Germany's 48 and Japan's 32 billion.[13] Thirty years later, the British GNP of $443 billion was dwarfed by Japan's $1157, Germany's $838 and France's $633 billion.[14]

Power of course does not correlate simply with GNP. It is a function of skill, will and prestige, and thus can linger after the economic trends have turned down. But Britain was in a particularly exposed position since it had built its position of international primacy on very narrow military margins. This situation had only been sustainable because for much of the nineteenth century, after the defeat of Napoleon, no other state challenged her position. However, once newly industrialised countries began to plough wealth into navies, as they did at the end of the century, Britain had to retrench. Hence the abandonment of the so-called 'splendid isolation' heralded by the Anglo-Japanese treaty of 1902 and the withdrawal of British forces from the western hemisphere. When in the mid-1930s Britain suddenly appeared to be threatened by a combination of German, Italian and Japanese power, it found itself in an impossible position. The Treasury pessimists who warned Britain could not afford to fight a second world war were right.[15] Within less than eighteen months of its declaration of war against Germany, the country faced bankruptcy, saved only by American 'Lend-Lease', and the formidable military power deployed by the USA and the Soviet Union.

Thereafter the milestones of decline are set closer. By 1945, Britain was no longer a power of the first rank, the achievement of its vital interests dependent on the support of allies, primarily the USA. More ominously for its ambitions of hanging on to its position as the world's third most powerful state, economic weakness now became one of the permanently dominant factors conditioning policy. In the words of an official paper completed only weeks before the nationalisation of the Suez Canal in July 1956, 'ever since the end of the war we have tried to do too much – with the result that we have only rarely been free from the danger of economic crisis. This provides no stable basis for policy in any field'.[16] In 1960, Britain was forced to accept that it could not afford to build its own strategic missile, Blue Streak. A series of major economic crises in the mid-1960s, culminating in the devaluation of sterling in November 1967, led to the withdrawal of British forces East of Suez. The claim to Great Power status, which had hitherto been resolutely defended but was by now manifestly at odds with the facts, was finally and reluctantly abandoned. Indeed, in his 1979 valedictory despatch, the retiring British ambassador in Paris, Sir Nicholas Henderson, wrote that 'today we are not only no longer a world power, but we are not in the first rank even as a European one'.[17]

Important as material weakness was, it is important to recognise the extent to which its practical impact was compounded by the disorientation which decline, vulnerability and the reaction to modern warfare engendered. Policy under these circumstances was constantly in danger of being thrown off balance. At its worst this meant panic and overreaction. This latter was largely resisted; the British avoided the expensive rearguard actions which the French conducted in Indochina and Algeria. For the most part nerve held, reinforced by realism and common sense. But not always; the nationalisation of the Anglo-Iranian Oil Company in 1951 and the pressure to withdraw from the great base in the Suez Canal Zone had already produced growls of anger – not just from the right-wing Conservative 'Suez Group' which had Churchill's at least tacit support, but in the case of Iran also from Labour ministers. When Nasser nationalised the Canal, patience finally snapped, and the fear that retreat was turning into rout led to the ill-judged attempt to overthrow him by way of a large and clumsy military invasion.

At the other end of the spectrum were the risks of fatalistic inaction or procrastination. These were first evident in the uniquely difficult circumstances of the 1930s, when Britain found itself facing a potential combination of threats from Germany, Japan and Italy, while still suffering a form of delayed 'shell shock' from the terrible casualty lists produced by the First World War, in addition to the material and psychological effects of the much more recent Depression. Hence the slow pace of rearmament, and Appeasement. It was again evident in more low-key though more protracted form in the quarter century following the Second World War, when successive governments showed themselves reluctant to bring overambitious ends into line with the much more limited power which was now at the country's disposal. *The Economist* put its finger on the fundamental problems of the period, when it wrote in 1962 that 'the classic military predicament of declining Powers is to straddle ever more awkwardly between necessity and inclinations. Nothing is harder than to choose between them...The psychology of the declining power is not to choose, but to wait upon events'.[18]

Danger and decline had a further and equally insidious effect on policy; they helped promote evasion and a reluctance to face up to facts. Some diplomatic commentators, including Sir Ivone Kirkpatrick, Permanent Under-Secretary (PUS) at the Foreign Office in the mid-1950s, see wishful thinking as a specifically British trait. Kirkpatrick cites Samuel Pepys, George Meredith and Lady Hester Stanhope in support of this contention, the latter claiming, 'I cannot but lament a fault too common to most of our public men – that of seeing things in the light they wish them to be and not as they are.'[19] Harold Nicolson, writing a few months before the outbreak of the Second World War, appeared to take a similar view. 'The average Englishman,' he claimed, 'is by temperament optimistic; it comforts him to believe that what he wishes to happen is likely to occur. The average Englishman would adopt almost any expedient rather than face realities which might disturb his equanimity.'[20]

Yet the desire to avoid 'cerebral discomfort' and 'unpleasant mental effort', by which Nicolson explained this alleged national characteristic,[21] is, at best, part of the story. The prevalence of wishful thinking for much of the century is perhaps better explained by the way in which it helped to bridge the recurring gap between preference – what policy makers and nation wanted to do, or as often to avoid doing – and practicality, between the world as it was and as they wished that it was. This is already evident at the beginning of the century when, in the face of increasing competition from foreign navies, the government decided to limit the traditional two-power naval standard, (the principle that the Royal Navy should be as strong as its two main rivals) to European waters. Yet, as Aaron Friedberg notes, British policy makers

> continued to talk as if nothing of any significance had really changed, as if, in short, Britain's position was not very much different than it had been thirty years before. This was partly the result of habit and of the fact that the Royal Navy was still larger and more capable than any other in the world. But it was also the expression of conscious deception and, increasingly with the passage of time, self-delusion.[22]

Three decades later, wishful thinking facilitated and legitimised Appeasement, keeping alive the increasingly desperate hope of the generation which had lived through the trenches that there would not be another war. When the crowds cheered Neville Chamberlain's declaration of 'peace in our time' on his return from Munich, they did so because this was what they wanted to believe. Wishful thinking was again very much a temptation in the post-war years, as policy makers struggled to come to terms with Britain's reduced international status. Attlee's comment to Bevin after his visit to Washington in December 1950 that throughout the talks 'we were treated as partners, unequal no doubt in power but still equal in counsel', reflects what the Prime Minister, along with his successors, wanted to believe, more than it does the actual facts of the case.[23]

Danger and decline with their disorientating psychological as well as material effects are the two most familiar *leitmotifs* of twentieth century British foreign policy. But there was also a third, which could at times prove as, if not more, troublesome. The need for change was unrelenting. In the early part of the century the main focus had been strategic. Traditionally, Britain had relied on seapower and on the blockade to fight its continental wars. Now it had to learn first to fight a modern land war in which the machine gun at first seemed to predominate, and then to adjust both mentally and militarily to the revolution in airpower which rendered British cities vulnerable to attack. In the wake of the Second World War, the whole of British foreign policy had to be recast. Long entrenched ideas about Britain's place in the world, its commitment to the European mainland and the traditional distinction between domestic and foreign policy had to be reappraised. New alliances had to be made, new restrictions had to be accepted on the country's freedom of action. By the end of the century the international agenda had again changed substantially, with a quite new emphasis on transnational issues such as the environment, international terrorism and drug control, and the proliferation of weapons of mass destruction. The world Robin Cook dealt with in 2000 had not changed totally out of recognition from the one the first Foreign Secretary of the period, Lord Lansdowne, had handled a hundred years previously, but it was a much more complex, and in many respects very different place, in which the geography, as indeed much of the nature of power, had altered radically.

Change at such speed and on such a scale was not easy to cope with, even for a normally pragmatically-minded people such as the British. Pragmatism certainly helped and some developments, notably the process of decolonisation, were adapted to with relative ease. The guiding principles governing British policy to nationalism, as summarised in a 1952 Foreign Office paper, were 'to anticipate and, as far as possible, to forestall by adaptation of existing policies nationalist demands which may threaten our vital interests'.[24] On a number of other occasions, however, adaptation required far more than tactical flexibility, that 'ability to tack and turn as circumstances change' which decision makers regarded as one of their strengths.[25] The problem was not just one of changing policy, but fundamental readjustments to the way in which Britain saw its place in the world. Accepting 'the inevitable pleasantly', to use a phrase of Attlee's, was not however always easy.[26] This was partly a matter of pride, which was inevitably hurt by the prospect of contraction and withdrawal. But there was also the fact that Britain was a conservative country with a marked preference for evolutionary rather than radical change. Eden refers in his Memoirs to 'our English preference for taking our changes in doses rather than gulps'.[27] 'New ideas,' wrote Marshal of the Royal Air Force, Sir John Slessor six years earlier, 'seldom have a very strong appeal to Englishmen; it is one of our strengths that we look at them critically and measure their validity by empirical tests.'[28] But it could also be a source of weakness, increasing the risk that Britain might either lose opportunities for which it was not yet mentally prepared, or get into trouble by sticking to obsolete ideas and positions. In the words of a 1958 Chatham House Report on British interests in the Mediterranean and the Middle East, there could be 'no greater danger to Britain's real interests than to found her immediate policy on ways of thought which do not fit the circumstances of today'.[29]

The dangers posed by instinctive conservatism in an era of radical change raise a further issue which is central to any understanding of the foreign policy record – that of method. Account must be taken of certain characteristics, temperamental and cultural as much as organisational, of the British approach to foreign policy. A number of these constituted long-term handicaps, which restricted the options still open to the country over and beyond the limitations imposed by the loss of power and prestige. The normal emphasis of British policy, *pace* the assertion in the Foreign Office's 1952 paper on nationalism, was not on the anticipation of events, but rather the ability to respond and react, to the point where policy makers sometimes appeared to pride themselves in not having a policy at all. In a lecture given in 1965, the recently retired PUS, Lord Caccia, recounted a story told by one of his predecessors, who, in answer to the complaint by the German ambassador at the beginning of the century that he did not understand the policy of the British government, replied that 'he ought to know that we had not got a policy and worked from hand to mouth'.[30] Looking ahead on any kind of systematic basis came much less easily.

Planning in the unpredictable world of international politics is of course an error-prone business. It was by no means only British ministers and officials who were reluctant to take time off from the more pressing problems of day to day affairs to stare into a murky crystal ball, or make themselves foolish by forecasts which were likely to be rapidly overtaken by events.[31] What is striking about the British approach is a temperamental distaste, which at times seemed to amount to a taboo, for preparing 'precise schemes to meet an imprecise future'.[32] The suggestion by a junior official in late 1933 that Germany was likely to remilitarise the Rhineland and that Britain and France should think ahead what they would do in the circumstances, was rebuffed by the Foreign Secretary, Sir John Simon, on the grounds that 'We cannot consider hypothetical issues.' One of his successors, Lord Halifax is reported as distrusting 'anyone who foresees consequences and advances remedies to avert them'.[33]

This state of affairs gradually began to alter after 1945, as the pace of international change accelerated and the pressures on Britain's position as a Great Power increased. When in 1959 Macmillan launched a major review of overseas policy, at a conference at Chequers, its objectives, as outlined in his speaking notes were:

> To identify probable trends and developments which might be prejudicial to our national interests, so that we may try to check or modify these to our advantage.
>
> To adjust the direction of our own policies, so that we may be better able to meet the dangers which we cannot avert, and continue to play a significant part in world affairs.
>
> To make sure that our ambitions are kept in line with our resources; and to avoid a situation in which, by trying to do too many things, we fail to do any of them well enough.[34]

Good intentions, however, were not matched by results. While much work went into the 'Future Policy Study' which sought to look ahead over the next ten years, the review appears never to have been properly considered by ministers or followed up.[35] Nearly forty years later planning was still being hampered by the reluctance of ministers to engage in the process. Sir Percy Craddock, who was Foreign Policy Adviser to Mrs Thatcher and John Major, writes how, as the Balkan crisis developed in 1990, he found it impossible to get ministers

> to look at the likely outcome and to ask what we ourselves wanted and how best to attain it. This though we had been forecasting the violent disintegration of Yugoslavia since early 1990. Policy in these conditions was shaped less by longer-term aims than by a series of day-to-day decisions taken with little reference to a larger framework.[36]

The risk of being overtaken by events was increased by an empirical approach which was ill-suited to periods of rapid change.[37] There was, to use Andrew Shonfield's phrase, a 'penchant for the piecemeal',[38] a preoccupation with the immediate business in hand at the expense of the larger picture. Proceeding on an ad hoc basis, it was easy for ministers and officials to miss the trends and underestimate the scale of change. The tendency was reinforced by the problems, which were again by no means unique to Britain, of coordinating the various baronies responsible for policy overseas. In addition to the Foreign Office, there were the service ministries, each of which sometimes appeared to act as a law unto itself. A 1926 paper from the Committee of Imperial Defence baldly stated that the size of the British forces 'is governed by various considerations peculiar to each service, and it is not arrived at by any calculation of foreign policy, nor is it possible that they ever should be so calculated'.[39] It was not until 1964 that a centralised Ministry of Defence was finally established. On the imperial front there were (until 1947) the India Office, the Colonial Office and, until 1966 when it was merged with the Foreign Office, the Commonwealth Office. The Board of Trade, and above all the Treasury, were important players. With British entry into the EEC, the number of departments involved increased still further. Each department had its own, by definition partial, perspective on the problems. A larger view only emerged when a strong Prime Minister, or possibly Foreign Secretary, insisted on it.

This, however, was the exception far more than the rule. Policy making lacked breadth of vision. Individuals, Churchill, Keynes, Lloyd George, Lord Robert Cecil (the main ministerial proponent of the League of Nations) thought radically and imaginatively. So too did Edward Heath, the untiring proponent of British membership of the EEC, as indeed to some extent Macmillan. The majority did not. This may again be ascribed to the fact that Britain was both a satisfied power, which saw no need to make significant changes in the world, and a declining power which felt decreasingly able to make its mark. But it has also to do with temperament and character. 'Am I altogether wrong in thinking,' asked the Commander-in-Chief, India, Field Marshal Lord Chetwoode in his farewell address to the Quetta Staff college in 1934, 'that, to many Englishmen, to be independent in thought, to have imagination, to go outside the obvious, to be different to others, is to be almost un-English, or even that most frightful crime, "not sound"?'[40] The point is echoed in an amusing exchange recorded by a Belgian official, which took place in 1955 when Belgium and Holland were trying hard to interest Britain in the proposed Common Market. 'Have I been obscene?' the Belgian Foreign Minister, Paul-Henri Spaak demanded of his officials after a particularly unproductive meeting with the Chancellor of the Exchequer, R. A. Butler. 'Why obscene, sir?' they replied, taken aback. 'Well, I don't think I could have shocked him more when I tried to appeal to his imagination than if I would have taken my trousers off.'[41]

The example of the Common Market points to a less familiar but more damaging weakness. While danger, decline and the need for change placed a premium on objective and clear-headed judgement, policy making was often a less rational and unsentimental business than policy makers cared to admit. Officials prided themselves on their dispassionate approach. Their job was to record facts, however unpalatable, and look at problems from 'a practical and not an emotional or sentimental point of view.'[42] 'Don't get carried away by enthusiasms or antipathies, and don't espouse causes,' new recruits to the Foreign Office were advised in the early 1950s.[43] But as the cases of Sir Neville Henderson, the ambassador in Berlin in the late 1930s who strongly supported Appeasement, Sir Ivone Kirkpatrick, the PUS who championed Suez, and some of the officials who wrote off the prospects for European integration in the 1950s illustrate, they did not always adhere to these sound precepts.

These cannot simply be dismissed as aberrations, the disoriented response by individuals to particularly trying circumstances. As another former British diplomat, Peter Unwin, argues in a book entitled *Hearts, Minds and Interests*:

> The British think of themselves as an unemotional people who shy away from gestures and heroics and are driven by practical considerations. The political classes believe that their conduct of foreign relations is governed by their heads, not by their hearts or by unrealistic ambitions. Hence the pride they take in Palmerston's exaltation of British interests above British allies. The fact that there is much historical evidence to the contrary leaves the judgement unaffected. The British are emotionally and ideologically committed to the belief that they are unemotional and strangers to ideology. They have the same conviction of the fat man who thinks that he is thin or the pretty girl who is convinced that she is plain.[44]

One result was a series of 'philias' – the countries of the English-speaking world, not least the USA – and 'phobias', including the Germans, the French and Egyptians, which at various times biased policy.[45] The phobias extended more generally to relations with Continental Europe, where heart was often in conflict with head. In a revealing diary entry of 1907, the Director of Military Operations, Major General Stuart Ewart admitted to what he called 'an insular prejudice' against the Channel tunnel, not on military grounds for it is easy to exaggerate the danger – but on sentimental grounds. I am prepared to admit that with France friendly or in alliance it might be a Military advantage – but its completion will Europeanise us. I hate Cosmopolitanism. I stick to my insularity.[46]

Responding fifty-three years later to a Foreign Office paper arguing that Britain's long-term objective must be to join the EEC, the Head of the Diplomatic Service, Sir Frederick Hoyar-Millar was no less candid. While agreeing 'that the political arguments in favour of joining the community are strong, all my instincts are against doing so. Although one's mind thinks one ought to join, one's heart is against it'.[47] In addition to these anti-continental prejudices, pride, fear and anger were, as already noted, at various times exerting considerable influence on policy.

Equally unexpected in a country in which officials at least took a normally hard-headed view of the harsh world of international politics was a streak of naïveté sometimes evident in the approach to power. Policy makers, politicians in particular, could too easily assume that their benign view of human conduct was internationally widely shared. This was certainly one aspect of Sir Edward Grey's conduct of the vital crisis of July 1914. The fact that the Foreign Secretary did not realise that Germany was encouraging Austria to take military action against Serbia in July 1914 cannot simply be explained by German deception, poor intelligence, or indeed to Grey's dislike of the Balkans in general and Serbia in particular.[48] The Foreign Secretary had received at least one veiled warning from the German ambassador in London which, combined with subsequent additional evidence, might have led a more suspicious man to recognise more quickly that, as Grey later put it, 'some devilry' was afoot in Berlin.[49] But Grey, while on other occasions very chary of German intentions, shared that rational, liberal outlook, which as one foreign commentator put it in a book published two years before Hitler's advent to power in Germany, inclined English politicians to see their continental colleagues 'as gentlemen ... and forget that the ideal by which the latter is governed is that of the warrior'.[50] Speaking in a radio interview at the time of the Falklands invasion, the Chief of the Defence Staff, Lord Lewin, admitted that he 'just couldn't believe that one apparently civilised country would try and settle its dispute with another civilised country by going to war at this part of the century'.[51]

One final handicap should be mentioned at this stage: the 'correcting mechanisms' were limited. The key problems, particularly those of 'high policy', were heavily concentrated among a small elite of officials, responsible primarily for assessing situations, defining options and policy recommendations. Decisions, however, were the responsibility of politicians, above all the Prime Minister. Policy makers could and did argue, sometimes heatedly, about which course of action to take and how to adjust to change. But on those occasions where key pointers were missed or where 'groupthink' prevailed there was little which those not directly involved in the debate could do. The Cabinet provided a safety-net of sorts. It could sometimes force a Prime Minister who it believed to be acting unwisely to alter course. Chamberlain, who was very hostile to the Soviet Union, was pressured by his colleagues to take a somewhat more forthcoming approach to negotiations for on alliance with Moscow in the Spring of 1939. Churchill was forced to desist from pursuing the idea of an ill-prepared Summit with Soviet leaders in 1953. But collective Cabinet judgement was not necessarily superior to that of the Prime Minister. Alternatively, ministers could be reluctant to challenge an experienced Prime Minister who was strongly pushing a dangerous policy, as in the case of Eden over Suez .

Nor is there much evidence of criticism from other sources having an impact. Public opinion was on the whole unknowledgeable and uninterested, with major debates on foreign policy being relatively few and far-between. The successful public pressure for the abandonment of the 1935 Hoare–Laval Pact which proposed ceding most of Abyssinia to Italy, and of Appeasement in the wake of Hitler's 1939 takeover of Prague, are very much the exceptions. At the more informed level, the views of outsiders were not, at least until the very end of the century when the Labour government significantly widened the network of external consultation, particularly welcome. A book published as late as the early 1990s records a senior ambassador as saying that 'We are too convinced that only our information is really worth having and that outsiders don't know the score.'[52] The interested public was in any case small. Ideas developed in the academic world did not easily percolate into the Foreign Office. 'When working in government,' wrote Sir John Coles after his retirement from the Foreign Office in 1997, 'I was only dimly aware of academic and other criticisms of the policy-making process in Britain. I suspect that most of my former civil service colleagues were equally oblivious of them.'[53]

Cumulatively all this was damaging. It suggests a picture of a country which was in some respects imperfectly equipped to deal with the challenges and threats which it faced in the twentieth century. The predominant approach, reactive, pragmatic and tactical, was suited to a more stable and powerful age. Decision makers had a number of bad habits, of which the tendencies to wishful thinking and to allow heart to overrule head, along with the reluctance to embrace radical change, were perhaps the most damaging. These weaknesses, vices is a tempting if strong term, should not, however, be seen primarily as failings of the way in which the foreign policy elite operated, since for the most part they reflected attitudes and approaches which were more widely shared within national culture and society. This in turn suggests that the bias against the ability to exploit available opportunities is more entrenched than any assessment which focuses on the structures and the processes of the policy-making process might indicate.

There is, fortunately for British foreign policy, another part to the story. The impact of weaknesses was offset by a number of long-honed virtues or strengths which helped ensure that vital British interests were secured, and often allowed policy makers to play their cards above their value. The predominant British approach *was* empirical. It respected facts, and adjusted accordingly. The best officials changed their minds as circumstances developed. They understood power, knowing where to stand firm and where it was wiser to give way. To quote again from the 1952 Foreign Office paper on nationalism, 'We are bound to swim with the tide but we can hope to exert influence on the speed at which the tide runs, both in general and specific cases.'[54] There was in other words a considerable capacity for flexibility, which took the complexities and frequent inconsistencies of international politics in its stride. No less important, a liberal as well as a status quo power pursued a policy of moderation. Britain eschewed extremes and was rarely tempted to over-reach itself in the way in which Germany, Japan or the Soviet Union did. It understood the disciplines imposed by the larger international society of which Britain was part, and on the whole respected and upheld its rules. And British foreign policy enjoyed the advantages of a stable and united national base. If sometimes dangerously slow to react, this was a country which where necessary would fight long and hard, and whose armed forces lost battles rather than wars. Its diplomats were for the most part skilful and well-regarded. Overall 'virtues' outweighed 'vices'.

This goes a long way to explaining why Britain often had the policy-making capacity to make the most of opportunities, to 'punch above its weight' to use a familiar phrase of the 1990s, as indeed why Britain avoided the disasters which overcame so many other countries over the period. But the 'virtues' were by no means strong enough to neutralise the bias towards underpeformance represented by methodological and organisational 'vices'. Much depended on the issue in question and the extent to which it played to British strengths or weaknesses, as to an often contradictory set of values and traditions. Britain was an imperial, but also a liberal power, one of the world's leading democracies. A strong military tradition co-existed with a marked pacific streak. Ambitious in terms of their global role and desire to retain Great Power status, the British were also parsimonious, reluctant to spend the money which these objectives required. The reactive, short-term approach to problems co-existed with the kind of enlightened self-interest which funded a body like the BBC World Service, whose value depended on its reputation for impartiality and trustworthiness, rather than its direct support for British policy. Pragmatism was both a virtue and vice, making for realism and flexibility, while also militating against the long-term and the larger view. On issues such as strategic bases in the Middle East in the 1950s and relations with continental Europe, pragmatism vied with a conservative, sometimes reactionary face of policy which could lead the country into deep, and in the latter case prolonged, trouble. It vied too with a romantic and idealistic streak, as with a bloody-mindedness evident in the determination to fight on in 1940, and regain the Falkland Islands against the military odds.

Some of these contradictions were clearly accentuated by personality, though these too sometimes seem to have been split. Pragmatic instincts led Eden, as Foreign Secretary, to fight against Churchill's opposition to withdraw from the Suez Canal Zone base, yet it was Eden who as Prime Minister led the ill-considered attempt to regain the Suez Canal after its nationalisation in July 1956. Mrs Thatcher accepted the 1980 Rhodesian settlement against her instinctive preferences, and sought to work with the grain over President Reagan's Strategic Defence Initiative, which she disliked. Yet when it came to German reunification and the renewed impetus of European integration in the mid 1980s, she allowed heart to rule over head.[55]

This by no means exhausts the factors which explain the patterns of success and failure of the foreign policy of what is still an influential state, and which for the first half of the twentieth century was one of the world's leading powers. At issue after all is a remarkably disparate range of problems. Decisions such as how to contain Wilhelmine Germany, the wisdom of relaxing controls in the strategically vital protectorate of Egypt in the early 1920s, or the right time and rate at which to enter the Exchange Rate Mechanism, the ERM, in the 1980s, have little obvious in common. The reliability and clarity of information and intelligence varied, as did the effectiveness with which they were used by the governmental machine. The Whitehall committee system, which worked well in the Second World War, had functioned far less effectively in the 1930s.[56] Some prime ministers, foreign secretaries and senior officials were quite simply more competent than others, as at times were different deparments of state and different branches of the armed services. To take one of the most obvious examples, the RAF in 1940 was a much more effective force than the army. Fluctuations in national mood and self-confidence were at times also important. Occasionally, these helped precipitate unwise courses of action; Suez is a classic example; more often they inhibited policy. And there was the power of the so-called 'lessons' of history, the belief in the 1930s that secret assurances to France prior to 1914 had helped embroil Britain in the First World War, the analogy drawn in 1956 between Nasser and Mussolini. These, however, are essentially random variables which are primarily important in helping to explain individual cases on characterising particular periods, rather than identifying patterns.

What follows is in no way intended to represent a comprehensive history of British foreign policy over the twentieth century, nor at the risk of repetition, should it be read as offering any kind of definitive judgement of the overall record. The object, is rather to suggest a framework for judgement as a means of provoking argument and debate about an often controversial, as well as inconsistent record. In the process we hope to be able to explore in more detail the states of mind and mindsets which helped determine how effectively officials and ministers worked under the pressures created by change and decline, and the extent to which they were able to exploit their residual lattitude of action. Such issues are ill-suited to chronological treatment, (a chronology of the main events of the period, and a list of Foreign Secretaries can be found in appendixes 1 and 2) and the approach adopted in subsequent chapters is therefore thematic. Chapter 2 considers the problem of overstretch, as British imperial ends constantly outstripped the means the country was willing or able to make available. Chapter 3 shifts the geographical focuses to Europe and the reluctance to accept the need for closer military and, after the Second World War, economic and political ties with the continent. Britain's handling of its main alliance relationships, primarily with France and the USA, are considered in Chapter 4. The ability to adapt to changes in military technology, and later to more restrictive international attitudes towards force, were important factors in determining the success and failure of British foreign policy, and these provide the background for an evaluation of the use and the threat of force in Chapter 5. Chapter 6 considers how effectively Britain adjusted to the painful loss of Great Power status in the quarter century following the Second World War. Chapter 7 broadens the focus to consider the impact which British foreign policy had on the stability of the international system, and the contribution it made to the establishment of a more civilised international order. The final chapter seeks to draw the strands together and consider some of the implications of the analysis for British foreign policy in the early part of the twenty-first century.

2
Ends beyond Means

For slightly more than two-thirds of the century, Britain was an imperial or a world power; indeed, the expansion of empire only reached its apogee in the wake of the First World War.[1] As late as 1945, Britain governed some 480 million people, some 22 per cent of the world population.[2] In addition to the formal empire, there was after 1918 an extensive informal empire in the Middle East, partly held under League of Nations mandates, a series of treaty ports, concessions and settlements in China, as well as protectorates and spheres of influence in other parts of the world. This empire was important less by now in economic terms than for reasons of prestige and self-esteem. Britain's heart lay East of Suez. Here, as Kipling's verse suggests, was romance, adventure, an important part of national purpose. It was here that the British acquired that world view which distinguished them from other, notably European, states. And it was with the states of the old Commonwealth, with their 'kith and kin', that they felt most at home.

Yet there was a paradox. Despite the importance of the imperial enterprise, militarily it had always been undercapitalised.[3] This was an empire which had grown used to living beyond its means. Britain, as the Liberal leader, Sir Henry Campbell-Bannerman remarked in 1903, could not 'provide for a fighting Empire, and nothing will give us the power'.[4] 'Overstretch' was a structural condition of British imperial power. Britain was a rich but small island which relied largely on its own resources to defend its imperial interests. Significant help could only be expected from India and the Dominions in the case of war. The defence of global interests against Soviet pressure in the post-war era depended in the last resort on American protection. When in 1958 Britain sent paratroopers to Jordan, Eisenhower assured the British Foreign Secretary, Selwyn Lloyd, that 'we would of course not permit the British to get into a jam there'.[5] But the Americans were unwilling to participate directly in the operation, and American policy continued to be coloured by anti-colonialism well into the Cold War era. Britain therefore was largely dependent on the resources it was itself willing *and* able to make available.

The distinction, while often in practice blurred, is important. Britain did not spend generously on the defence of empire. It could not, and this was particularly true after 1945, afford to do so. During the Second World War, Britain had run up substantial debts to countries in the sterling area, and its post-war reserves were regarded as dangerously small. 'Whatever risks we may have taken since the war in other areas of policy,' an official report of 1956 noted, 'they are nothing compared with the risks we have taken, are taking and must for some time continue to take, in this vital sector.'[6] But if the problem of sterling was relatively recent, the underlying concern with economic overstretch was not. 'However reluctant we may be to face the fact,' the Chancellor of the Exchequer, Austen Chamberlain had warned his Cabinet colleagues in 1904, 'the time has come when we must frankly admit that the financial resources of the United Kingdom are inadequate to do all that we should desire in the matter of Imperial defence.'[7]

Such statements, however, need to be treated with a degree of caution since they easily elided economic and political constraints. 'The fact is,' as one official noted in 1960, 'that, if the public can be taxed in some way or another so that they have less money for television sets, then we will have more money for aid and other overseas expenditure.'[8] Politicians, by contrast, tended to be more chary. Empire had not been deliberately or consciously sought; it evoked pride rather than mass enthusiasm. There was a natural reluctance to take political risks by raising taxes to make good the recurrent gap between imperial ends and existing military means in a century in which the franchise became universal, and there were constantly increasing competitive demands from welfare spending and private consumption.[9] While ministers were rarely sure of the limits of public tolerance regarding overseas military expenditure, the tendency was to prefer to err on the side of political caution. When the large rearmament programme began in the wake of the Korean war, it appeared to threaten economic recovery and living standards, the politicians, in John Darwin's words, 'instinctively...began to make their way back to what they believed to be the levels of spending sanctioned by historical experience'.[10] Although the issue was rarely acknowledged so bluntly, and there was relatively little by way of public debate, the tension between ends and means reflected the desire of a country, with what by international standards was an underperforming economy, to have its cake as a Great Power and still eat it domestically. The limits of the possible in other words were thus both assumed by decision makers and to a degree self-imposed, a matter of priorities as well as a function of relative economic weakness.

Historically, the gap between ambition and parsimony had been bridged by economic strength, the absence of rivals and the skilful husbanding of scarce resources. Prestige was high, and bluff therefore worked. Indirect rule could be practised through local elites who were willing to collaborate.[11] There was a tradition of flexibility which made it relatively easy to make judicious, if limited, concession when necessary. The distinction between the substance and shadow of power was clearly appreciated, if only because Britain could not otherwise have afforded its immense imperial venture. The great challenge facing British policy in the twentieth century was to retain this flexibility in the face of decline, and avoid British power becoming stretched to the point that territory could be seized, and Britain forced into costly and damaging withdrawals. This it only partially succeeded in meeting.

Pragmatic realism got Britain through the majority of the challenges faced; in particular it facilitated three major sets of adjustments and retrenchments when the gap between ends and means threatened to become critical. The first occurred at the turn of the century when the world's greatest empire suddenly felt itself vulnerable. The Franco-Russian alliance of 1894 had seen a coming together of Britain's two major imperial rivals.[12] The Boer war had left it friendless. There was a need to reduce disputes which, if wrongly handled, might lead to war and to ease the economic pressure caused by an upsurge of international naval building. It was, as Lord Selborne, the First Lord of the Admirality, noted in 1903, 'a terrific task to remain the greatest naval Power, when naval Powers are year by year increasing in numbers and in naval strength and at the same time to be a military Power strong enough to meet the greatest military Power in Asia' (that is, Russia).[13]

In theory a solution might have been found by increasing defence expenditure. But this had already risen as a result of the Boer war, reaching a high point in 1901 of 7.1 per cent of net national product (subsequently, however, declining in the years up to 1913 to less than half this figure).[14] Ministers took the orthodox view that larger budgets and higher taxes would damage the economy and weaken the country's ability to raise large sums in the event of emergency, as well as causing them political trouble.[15] They therefore opted to make alliances after a period of so-called 'Splendid isolation' and cut back on commitments.[16]

Forces were withdrawn from the western hemisphere and disputes with the USA – over Venezuela, Alaska and the Panama Canal – were settled on American terms. Two years after signing a treaty in 1902 with Japan to bolster Britain's position in the Far East, Britain and France reached an understanding over colonial rivalries in Africa, in the form of the *Entente Cordiale*.

No less striking than the scale of these adjustments was the lack of difficulty which they entailed. Lord Lansdowne, the Foreign Secretary who negotiated the Anglo-Japanese alliance, has been described as a 'shrewd, pragmatic Whig aristocrat', without 'inflexible prejudices or unalterable conceptions about the conduct of foreign affairs'.[17] Lansdowne was certainly more flexible than the Prime Minister, Lord Salisbury, who was much more ideologically opposed to treaty commitments. But the Foreign Secretary was operating within a tradition of appeasement dating back to the mid-1860s, defined by Paul Kennedy as the settlement of quarrels 'by admitting and satisfying grievances through rational negotiation and compromise'.[18]

Under such circumstances pragmatism relatively easily prevailed. Policy makers would have preferred a Far Eastern treaty with Germany or the United States, but were perfectly prepared to accept one with Japan when the former proved unattainable. They accepted that British interests would be better served if, as the First Naval Lord put it, 'the US carry us with them instead of getting what they are sure to get in spite of us',[19] just as they accepted the fact that in the event of serious naval competition with the USA, the weight of American resources must eventually tell against Britain.[20] These particular concessions were eased by the absence of any sense of rivarly with the USA, whose political claims were limited to the western hemisphere. US economic competition did not hurt Britain in the way that German economic competition did. War with a fellow Anglo-Saxon state which was already beginning to be seen as a potential ally was unthinkable. Graceful political and military withdrawals were thus both politically sensible and, no minor consideration, emotionally relatively painless.[21]

Policy makers were broadly supported by public opinion as expressed in the press and parliament. The *Entente Cordiale* was widely welcomed.[22] Although there was opposition to the abandonment of 'splendid isolation', it was limited in extent and neither bitter nor prolonged. Lord Lansdowne's injunction that the treaty with Japan should be considered strictly on its merits, unhindered by 'any musty formulas or old-fashioned superstitions as to the desirability of pursuing a policy of isolation' was heeded.[23] 'Splendid isolation' – the term had in fact only entered the political currency as a term of irony in 1896 at the time of the Jameson raid – was not an inflexible dogma, and an alliance with a distant and relatively unknown country was not an unduly sensitive issue.[24] One further factor should also be taken into account. Although taken together these retrenchments mark a notable contraction of British power, politicians and public did not fully grasp the larger implications of what was happening. This may partly have reflected the discrete nature of the separate arrangements; the settlement of the Venezuelan dispute with the USA took place in 1895, the abandonment of Britain's treaty right to claim a half share in the construction of a Panamanian Canal in 1901, the treaty with Japan in 1902, and the *Entente Cordiale* in 1904. But there was also an element of official discretion. As the Secretary of the Committee of Imperial Defence, George Clarke privately wrote in 1905, 'It is best to recognise facts but not always to proclaim them from the housetop.'[25]

The second successful major exercise in bringing imperial ends and means back into a more manageable and stable equilibrium took place in the early 1920s. The problem this time was not rivals but nationalism and overambition. In seeking to exploit the opportunities for imperial expansion and security in the Middle East and the Caucusus created by the defeat of the Ottoman Empire in the First World War, the government overreached itself. The immediate result, against the background of rapid post-war demobilisation and acute economic stringency, was a series of local disturbances and revolts – in Egypt, Palestine, Iraq and Afghanistan. The army found itself grossly overstretched and overstrained.[26] Policy, as General Sir Henry Wilson warned the Cabinet, had to be brought 'into some relation with [the] military forces available to it . . . I cannot too strongly press on the Government the danger, the extreme danger, of His Majesty's Army being spread all over the world, strong nowhere, weak everywhere, and with no reserve to save a dangerous situation or avert a coming danger'.[27] The urgency of this warning was underscored by political pressures, and the Cabinet soon found itself out on a limb. Parliament and press saw little advantage in expensive commitments in remote regions which might be tenuously justified in terms of Indian security. With memories of the bloodletting of the First World War still fresh, there was no national disposition to incur yet more casualties by acting as what the Conservative leader, Bonar Law, described as the 'policeman of the world'.[28]

Appreciation of these pressures did not keep the government itself from disaster. Lloyd George had pursued an ambitious policy in Asia Minor, where he had incautiously supported the expansion of Greek power. The rise of Kemal Ataturk and the retreat of the Greek army brought British and Turkish forces into confrontation, and at Chanak on the Turkish Straits, in September 1922, the prospect of war suddenly seemed real. Although the crisis was peacefully resolved, it helped precipitate the fall of the Lloyd George government less than a month later. But Asia Minor apart, the broad message that the country would not support the politicians' ambitions had been registered. 'Everything else that happens in the Middle East is secondary to the reduction in expenses,' the Colonial Secretary, Winston Churchill noted in 1921.[29] There was talk of pulling out of Palestine and Iraq, two of the new League Mandate territories which Britain had just acquired.[30] Troops were withdrawn from Persia and Russia, where Britain had sought to intervene in the civil war which followed the Revolution of 1917. More striking was the withdrawal from Ireland, where Sinn Fein had mounted the first successful major military challenge to British colonial power. Ireland had been a net drain in manpower during the First World War when more troops were stationed than raised there. What mattered strategically were the Irish ports, and the 1921 Anglo-Irish treaty which accompanied the establishment of the Irish Free State left Britain in control of the coastal defences.[31]

British policy in two other areas at this period is of particular interest for what it tells us about its underlying flexibility and realism. China and Egypt occupy very different places in imperial thinking. British interests in the former were purely economic. Britain sought to protect its trade and maintain the 'Open Door' policy aimed at ensuring access to Chinese markets. Its interests in Egypt were strategic, and by implication therefore less negotiable. Yet in both countries policy makers showed themselves willing to adapt. They knew that the old nineteenth century arrangement in China was ceasing to be viable. International norms were changing and, as one official, perhaps prematurely, noted, with the establishment of the League of Nations gunboat diplomacy was no longer possible.[32] 'Times change and circumstances alter,' declared Sir Austen Chamberlain, now Foreign Secretary. 'We are ready, and our history shows it, to adapt ourselves to new conditions.'[33] A formal offer to modify the system was made two years later, which according to a 1930 Foreign Office memorandum, took

the sting out of the attack on Great Britain as protagonist of the old treaty position; and it has placed the Chinese in a quandary, since, when they come to work out the details for modification, they find that practical difficulties are very great and that there is more to be said in favour of the old arrangements than they could ever be brought to admit.[34]

Britain's power in the Far East was in decline. Its power in the Middle East was at its height. Egypt, which was central to the British position in the region, was not part of the formal empire. It was a protectorate where the British hand had become heavier and clumsier as a result of the First World War. Here, as elsewhere, the nationalist revolt of 1920 forced a reassessment of policy. The terms of the subsequent Milner mission, 'to reconcile the aspirations of the Egyptian people with the special interest which Great Britain has in Egypt',[35] summarise Britain's aims not only in Egypt, but in much of the imperial world for the next three decades. The circle could still be squared, though not by committing more troops or deeper involvement which, as Lord Allenby, the British High Commissioner in Cairo realised, was poor policy if Britain wished to retain the Canal.[36] There were cheaper and less provocative means of achieving British ends. They followed logically from Milner's realisation that Britain could not hope to extinguish Egyptian nationalism, but only 'seek to guide it into *reasonable* channels'[37] (emphasis added). The formula which thus emerged was to grant Egypt formal independence, while retaining the essential strategic right to maintain British forces in the country, along with a monopoly of foreign assistance in critical areas such as the army, wireless communication and aviation.

These concessions did not come easily. The timing was bad for a government which was already being criticised by Conservatives for giving way elsewhere – in Ireland and India (the Montagu – Chelmsford reforms) – as well as for its more moderate approach now being adopted towards the Soviet Union. There were doubts within the Cabinet about the risks which Milner's proposals entailed. How, as Elizabeth Monroe asks,

> were they to be sure that imperial communications would be safe if Britain were to agree to abolish the protectorate *before* signing a treaty with an infant of an independent government and monarchy, and would not British imperial security be jeopardised if Egypt were to enjoy diplomatic representation abroad, entailing reciprocity and the representation of unfriendly powers in Cairo?[38]

Precedents were being established. There was concern that, by bargaining with nationalist extremists, Milner was destroying the moral basis of imperial collaboration in other dependencies.[39] Yet in the end, as the Cabinet gradually came to realise, there was no sensible alternative. In Curzon's pithy phrase:

> Why worry about the rind if we can obtain the fruit? I take it that all we have in view is that Egypt would remain inside rather than outside the British Imperial system. If the best way to do this is to drop the word protectorate and conclude a treaty of alliance with her, as we did with the Indian princes a century or more ago...why not do it?[40]

The new approach worked. Britain retained effective power in Egypt over the next two decades with relatively little difficulty, although it was only in 1936, in the wake of Mussolini's Abyssinian adventure, that it was able to gain a treaty which formally legitimised its military presence in the country.[41] This involved further concessions; Britain withdrew its remaining advisers, the Residency's 'eyes and ears' from the government, and promised to end its military presence in Cairo and Alexandria as soon as barracks could be built in the newly-designated 'canal zone'. But with the beginning of the Arab Revolt in Palestine, there was concern about what the Prime Minister, Stanley Baldwin, described as a 'disorganized' Near East, and it was 'hoped', again Baldwin's word, that Britain's position in the Middle East would be 'very much stronger than it was today' when the treaty expired in 1956.[42]

The final and potentially most difficult period of successful retrenchment begins in the wake of the Second World War and continues until the withdrawal from East of Suez in 1971. It was at this point that the imperial system as a whole ceased to be viable. The problem was no longer as it had been in the inter-war years, one of local revolts, but of the end of the acquiescence on which it had ultimately depended. This did not mean that Britain gave up. On the contrary, it sought, as it had historically done, to retain influence by new, if by now much more informal, means.[43] Empire was transformed into Commonwealth. Treaties of protection such as the 1899 Anglo-Kuwaiti treaty were replaced or renegotiated. By the late 1960s, however, as the scale of British economic problems became critical and the role of force in defence of economic interests was increasingly coming into doubt, ambitions contracted in line with the unwillingness to fund an effective post-imperial role. Though policy makers did not realise or want to realise the fact, from 1947 onwards they were managing the process of terminal decline.

There is an obvious risk in any summary account of an extended and complex process – more than fifty British dependencies gained independence between 1947 and 1997, when the lease of Hong Kong expired – of glossing over the difficulties. Decolonisation was a disorganised, sometimes helter-skelter business in which the force of nationalism was constantly underestimated and crucial decisions were frequently taken late. In a lecture given in 1975, a senior Foreign Office official spoke of an impression of 'permanent improvisation – of constant surprise'. He cited the case of a paper written three years before the independence of an unnamed but 'large' African country in which the working hypothesis was that of a gradual move to limited autonomy over a ten-year period.[44] If Britain was rarely pushed, the margins between disaster and a successful handover of power could, on occasion, be very narrow. The record of the last few years of British rule in India seems as often to be testimony to the evasion of difficult and unwelcome decisions in the face of the loss of control over crucial areas of the administration, as of the hard-headed realism which ultimately resulted in independence and withdrawal.[45] In classic fashion, Britain muddled through.

Yet the fact remains that the overall process of withdrawal was conducted in a broadly orderly fashion, for this was the kind of sensitive political manoeuvre which Britain was relatively well equipped to conduct. The romantic dogmatism symbolised by Churchill, who had been singularly uncompromising over India during his wartime premiership, and at one stage spoke of 'the clattering down of the British empire with all its glories',[46] did not in the final analysis prevail. The Labour government of Clement Attlee recognised that the game in India and Burma was finally up, and that it was much better to make a virtue out of necessity and go before Britain was pushed.[47] There were neither the troops nor the political will to continue governing India against the opposition of the politically minded. When Bevin objected to fixing a date for withdrawal and warned of the wider implications for the future of the British Empire, the Prime Minister replied that, if he disagreed with what was proposed, the Foreign Secretary must 'offer a practical alternative. I fail to find one in your letter'.[48]

Macmillan, who oversaw the second major phase of decolonisation, took an equally hard-headed approach. Within less than a month of assuming the premiership in January 1957, he was calling for 'something like a profit and loss account for each of our Colonial possessions, so that we may be better able to gauge whether, from the financial and economic point of view, we are likely to gain or lose by its departure'.[49] He readily accepted the advice a few years later from a senior colonial administrator to give a territory independence immediately, even though the country would not be ready for it in less than fifteen to twenty years:

> If the fifteen or twenty years were to be applied in learning the job, in increasing their experience of local government, or of central administration, why then I should be all for it. But that is not what will happen. All the most intelligent men capable of government will be in rebellion. I will have to put them in prison. There they will learn nothing about administration, only about hatred and revenge. They will not be fruitful, but wasted years; so I say, give them independence now.[50]

By then, however, as policy makers realised, they had no realistic alternative. 'If General de Gaulle with a million men couldn't hold Algeria,' noted the radical new Colonial Secretary, Ian Macleod, who had been appointed in 1959, 'then we couldn't hold about a third of the Continent.'[51] To stand against the nationalist tide in Africa would impose an impossible and unnecessary range of strains – on an army which was in the process of ending conscription, on domestic politics where Macmillan felt himself vulnerable to criticism from both Left and Right, and on the 'special relationship' with the USA.[52] Britain could not afford to ignore the precedents set either by the French, who were granting independence to their West African territories, or by the Belgians, who were leaving chaos behind them in the Congo. It was concerned to retain influence with potential successor states and avoid conceding unnecessary advantage to the Soviet Union, which was becoming increasingly active in Africa. Much wiser therefore to acknowledge that, in the words of one of the most famous phrases of the whole post-war era, a 'wind of change' was blowing throughout Africa and that, 'whether we like it or not, this growth of national consciousness is a political fact. We must accept it as a fact and our national policies must take account of it'.[53]

Pragmatism helped Britain to control the process of decline. Liberalism offered to turn necessity into virtue. The British concept of empire was ultimately self-liquidating. The British 'did not conceive of themselves as having the right to govern in perpetuity'.[54] The principle of self government, which had long been proclaimed at least as an eventual objective, now offered a formula for peaceful hand-overs of power in which the country could take pride. It meant too that Britain was mentally prepared for change. The Dominions had after all been self-governing since the last century. The Commonwealth, into which a republican India and nearly all the newly independent states were admitted, dated back to 1926. The overall impact might be radical, but the process reflected the kind of evolutionary change which Britain was good at.[55]

A third factor, while less remarked, is probably as, if not more, important. Decolonisation was, or at least seemed to be, a reasonably painless process. There were certainly strategic and political costs. The loss of the critical manpower reserve which had long been provided by the Indian army was a major reverse, the full extent of which was probably not immediately registered. Similarly, the extent of the diminution of British power which decolonisation involved was not appreciated. This was perhaps as well, for the relative ease with which decolonisation was effected was in large part due to the assumption that influence could still be maintained by other means, and that Britain's status as a Great Power would remain unaffected. The key decisions were taken at a time when Britain still appeared able to remain the single most important source of development capital and economic aid, and confidence in Britain's long-term future was reasonably high. Policy makers thus overestimated their ability to retain the kind of influence which the French kept in their former colonies in West Africa. They also underestimated, whether because of lack of imagination or of wishful thinking, the determination of newly independent states to pursue their own foreign policies.[56] Had Attlee or Macmillan realised the significance of colonial independence as a milestone in Britain's decline as a world power, the process might have proved much more difficult.

On the economic front, too, and contrary to expectations expressed by ministers as late as 1946 that the fall of the empire would mean a considerable fall in the standard of living in Britain,[57] there was little by way of obvious damage. Key sterling holders, notably Malaya, remained within the sterling area, but few colonies were in fact of vital economic interest to Britain. As Lawrence James notes, 'No jobs were lost, factories closed or investment opportunities frustrated as a result of the loss of the colonies.'[58] Nor were there serious intangible hurts which might have prompted strong reaction in the UK. In contrast to other empires, British nationhood did not appear to have been altered by the imperial experience. Several decades later, when devolution and the growing powers of the European Union were bringing English and British national identity into question, a rather different case came to be argued. 'Imperial Britain,' wrote David Marquand, '*was* Britain. The iconography, the myths, the rituals in which Britishness was embodied, were, of necessity, imperial, oceanic, extra-European.... Empire was not an optional extra for the British; it was their reason for being British as opposed to English, Scottish or Welsh.... Deprived of an empire and plunged into Europe, "Britain" had no meaning.'[59] At the time, however, the falling away of the looser connections linking Britain to her colonies seemed to leave continuity of national existence unbroken.[60]

In key respects, therefore, decolonisation was easier for British prime ministers than it was for their continental European counterparts. In addition, they were not haunted by the ghost of defeat in the Second World War, or hamstrung by weak coalition governments, as were the French in dealing with Indochina and Algeria or the Dutch with Indonesia. Nor, with the exception of Rhodesia, and to a more limited extent Kenya, were they harried by angry settler colonists capable of stirring up political trouble back home. And they were fortunate in the sense that after 1947 they were building on what was in effect success. If the withdrawal from India had gone wrong, as at times it came very close to do doing, or if later withdrawals had been seen as humiliating, the whole process of decolonisation might have proved much more difficult. But Palestine apart, the main colonial insurgencies of the period – Malaya, Kenya and Cyprus – were successfully contained. Thus when in March 1959 Parliament debated the agreement which would provide independence for Cyprus, Enoch Powell could claim that 'Those [British] civilians, and those in the Queen's uniform, who died in Cyprus died no less certainly for Britain's honour than if they had fallen on the field of battle in our campaigns of imperial expansion.' 'It was in forging such a link,' writes Robert Holland, 'however artificially, between expansion and contraction, the beginning and the end, that the more reflective mind of British Conservatism was able to rationalize and make bearable the loss of empire.'[61]

This raises the final point of the way in which domestic sensitivities were handled. Attlee believed in Indian independence and was determined to push it through. Macmillan's skills in dealing with potentially recalcitrant backbenchers and Cabinet colleagues were more manipulative. He knew how to stroke the political vanities of potentially disgruntled Conservative MPs, and was careful to present radical change in what has been described as 'the diction and style of traditional conservatism'. This made it easier for him to neutralise or outflank the limited, but at times potentially damaging, opposition which decolonisation evoked.[62]

The series of retrenchments which began at the turn of the century and culminated with African decolonisation constitute one of the success stories of modern British foreign policy. They illustrate the shrewdness with which power could be handled and a pragmatic capacity for adaptation which was essential if change and decline were not to lead to disaster. But there were also a number of very prominent failures, where the growing gap between ends and means was not successfully bridged. Some of these were post – 1945 phenomena, the more intractable problems thrown up by end of empire, including Palestine, Rhodesia and the Falklands, all of which are considered in later chapters. The most serious difficulties, where policy lacked the necessary unsentimenal realism and sureness of touch, focused on strategic problems. Could Britain afford to defend empire in the face of major rivals? How was it to retain overseas bases, the sinews and symbols of imperial power in the face of nationalist opposition?

The worst disaster of overstretch goes back to the early period of decline, and was a long time in the making. The Singapore strategy has been described as having been 'born out of economy and nurtured on parsimony'.[63] First mooted in 1919 in the impecunious inter-war years when money for military purposes was in very short supply, it took twenty years to open the base and longer to complete it. The underlying problem, however, lay not in the arrangements for its defence or the slow pace of its development, but rather in the related fact that Britain could no longer afford a separate fleet for the Far East and no longer had any allies in the region. The Anglo-Japanese treaty had been terminated under US pressure in 1922, without any compensatory offer of American support. The solution devised was to build a base at Singapore, to which, in the event of emergency or war, the main British Fleet would be sent from European waters. It was a risky strategy. 'In the event of hostilities or strained relations in Europe coinciding with war in the Far East,' a 1924 Admiralty memorandum noted, 'the necessity of ensuring the presence of superior forces in Home Waters will override all other considerations.'[64] The danger of such a coincidence of crises was in fact rather more serious than this suggested, since, as the South African leader, General Jan Smuts, had perceptively remarked a year earlier, Japan was unlikely to create trouble unless it could be assured of some kind of European support.[65] A senior naval commander put it even more bluntly. To plan a two-front naval war without a two-Fleet navy, argued Sir Herbert Richmond, was 'to live in a fool's paradise'.[66]

The 1920s, however, were a period of optimism as well as economy. The German fleet was at the bottom of the North Sea and in the wake of the First World War there was little disposition to think unpleasant and expensive long-term thoughts. The whole of British defence strategy was based on the assumption that there would be no major war for ten years. No less important was the lack of politically acceptable alternatives. To admit that Britain could no longer provide for the defence of the Far East, and thus by implication for the defence of Australia and New Zealand, would be to place the whole imperial system in doubt. It would be an open admission of weakness far more damaging than the acceptance of a naval parity with the American navy in place of the traditional numerical superiority which had been agreed under the terms of the 1922 Washington Naval Treaty. Raymond Callahan's verdict, that the Singapore base was 'the symbol of a great illusion – that Britain's Victorian world power remained intact', is harsh in that in the 1920s Britain still appeared, and certainly still felt itself to be, a power of the first rank.[67] But its international pre-eminence was essentially artificial, since it depended not on its own underlying strength but rather on the temporary weakness or disinterest of other powers. It would have taken immense political courage and determination to premise policy on a decline which was still largely hidden from public sight. Strategic prudence was not a realistic political option.

The consequences of all this could not be indefinitely disguised, however. Japan's forward policy in Manchuria, launched in 1931, was followed by a wholly unexpected naval crisis in the Mediterranean as a result of Mussolini's Abyssinian ambitions. British military planning had not hitherto taken Italy into account as a potential enemy.[68] At the same time, resources were increasingly pre-empted by the more immediate threat posed by German rearmament. By the late 1930s, defence planners found themselves juggling more and more uncomfortably between European and Far Eastern priorities, and the official assumptions about how many, let alone how quickly, ships could be sent to the Far East, were looking increasingly dubious. The best the Admiralty could offer in 1939 in response to the British ambassador in Tokyo's argument that Britain must station a squadron of capital ships in Singapore, or face 'the steady deterioration in our prestige and influence throughout the Far East', was one capital ship by 1942.[69]

Much worse was to follow the fall of France in June 1940, which precipitated Italian entry into the war, and a much more aggressive Japanese policy in South East Asia. The chiefs of staff called for the reinforcement of the Far East. Churchill refused. His strong personal commitment to the Middle East, which he regarded as being, after India, the heartland of Empire, did not extend to the Far East. The loss of Egypt and the Middle East, he argued in April 1941, would be a 'disaster of the first magnitude to Great Britain, second only to successful invasion and final conquest'.[70] He also believed right up to the Japanese attack in December 1941 that the risks were not high. Churchill was by no means the only one, either in Britain or in the USA, to overrate Japanese rationality and underrate Japanese capabilities.[71] As late as September 1941, a conference of senior diplomatic and military commanders in Singapore concluded that it was improbable that Japan was contemplating war in the south Pacific and unlikely to land on the east coast of Malaya, a conclusion which in one military historian's words ran 'counter to all the available evidence'.[72] But the situation by then was sufficiently grave for even the most hard-headed to prefer not to face the facts.

The story of Singapore can be read several ways. It can be argued that the British were unlucky: there was after all nothing inevitable in the chain of events which led from the original decision to defend the Far East from Europe in 1919 to the surrender of Singapore twenty-three years later. If Wall Street had not crashed in 1929, if British policy had been less disoriented in the 1930s, if the USA had been more far-sighted in its Far Eastern policy, the Singapore gamble might have come off. A more convincing line of argument is that this was a disaster waiting to happen. Sooner or later a major challenge to an imperial power unable (to use Campbell-Bannerman's words of 1903, cited at the outset of the chapter,) to provide for 'a fighting empire', was more rather than less likely. In the August 1939 negotiations with the German Foreign Minister, Joachim Ribbentrop, Stalin remarked that Britain was weak and dominated the world through the stupidity of other states who allowed themselves to be bluffed.[73] Once predators began to register this fact, Britain was liable to be in trouble. Singapore was the one case in modern imperial history where Britain did not have, as opposed to be being unwilling to provide, the resources necessary to support her far-reaching imperial ambitions. Her only realistic option, as the joint planners warned, and Churchill himself later publicly admitted, was 'to avoid being weak everywhere'.[74] The most distant part of the empire proved the most dispensable.

Bases were to continue to give problems after the war, but now the problem came, not from rival powers (though the Soviet Union might be regarded as a potential competitor for strategic real estate), but from the same nationalism which was rendering the continuation of formal imperial power untenable. Bases were not uniformly unacceptable. The post-war base which was re-established in Singapore survived until 1971, when it was closed in the face of the strong opposition of the Singaporean government. The withdrawals from Bahrein and Sharjah in the Gulf the same year were similarly the result of British economic weakness rather than nationalist pressure. Nor were officials and ministers unaware of the need to take account of nationalist sentiment, and make concessions accordingly. 'The days are past,' noted Pierson Dixon, Bevin's private secretary in 1946, 'when we could treat Egypt *de haut en bas*, and act as a Great Power using a little Power's territory for our own purposes as and when we judged our interests required it.'[75] 'Better a compromise now in Iraq which has a better chance of lasting, than to hang on a short time longer there on a wicket which will sooner or later become unplayable', another official minuted in 1947. Such arrangements, however, were fragile. The 1948 Treaty of Portsmouth smacked rather too much of window dressing, and was repudiated by the Iraqi government after violent local reaction.[76] Governments placed restrictions on the use of bases precisely when they were most urgently needed. 'In its military aspects a treaty with an Arab country,' the retiring Governor of Aden observed in 1963, 'is like an umbrella which you are not allowed to open when it begins to rain.'[77] And some governments, most notably Egypt, were simply not prepared to allow the continuation of any British military presence.

The Egyptian story is important for what it tells us of the limits of flexibility at the point at which British power was entering the phase of terminal decline. In 1946, the Labour government, much to Churchill's dismay, had been willing to withdraw from the Suez Canal Zone base. But the negotiations foundered over Anglo-Egyptian differences about the future of the Sudan, and with the enforced British withdrawal from Palestine in 1948 and the onset of the Cold War, the British position became much less forthcoming. The Egyptians for their part were equally adamant. A foreign military base was perceived as violation of national dignity and sovereignty and therefore had to go.

By the early 1950s, the issue had become complicated by a new factor which made the last phase of the Egyptian withdrawal so much more difficult than the earlier adjustments in 1920s and 1930s. The Canal Zone was not simply the world's largest base, it was also increasingly a symbol of Britain's ability to retain its status as a Great Power. What now mattered therefore went beyond the question of whether alternative means could be found to protect strategic interests in the region. No less important was that Britain was not seen to be forced out, something which would hurt pride and threaten its whole position in Africa and the Middle East.[78] Pierson Dixon's oddly laboured analysis, written in 1951, is worth quoting at length. The underlying difficulty, he argued, stemmed from the very obvious fact that we lack power. The Egyptians know this, and that accounts for their intransigence. On a strictly realistic view we ought to recognise that our lack of power must limit what we can do, and should lead us to a policy of surrender or near surrender imposed by necessity. But the basic and fundamental aim of British policy is to build up our lost power. Once we despair of doing so, we shall never attain this aim. Power, of course, is not to be measured in terms alone of money and troops: a third ingredient is prestige, or in other words what the rest of the world thinks of us. Here the dilemma arises. We are not physically strong enough to carry out policies needed if we are to retain our position in the world; if we show weakness our position in the world diminishes with repercussions on our world-wide position. The broad position I am driven to is therefore that we ought to make every conceivable effort to avoid a policy of surrender or near surrender.[79]

This view was strongly endorsed by both Churchill, now again Prime Minister, and the Conservative 'Suez Group', who bitterly resented the passing of British greatness.[80] The emotive nature of their position is encapsulated by the frequent references to 'scuttle' – running away or flying from danger or difficulty. The term, which can already be found in discussion of possible withdrawal from Middle Eastern positions in the aftermath of the First World War,[81] gained currency after 1945 with the withdrawal from Burma, India and Palestine, and the failure to take tougher action following the nationalisation of the Anglo-Iranian Oil Company in 1951. Against this background it was fortunate that the military case for retaining the base was diminishing. The entry of Turkey into NATO, appreciation of the implications of the development of thermonuclear weapons, the first tests of which took place in 1954, and the increasingly unfavourable strategic arithmetic forced on the British by the withdrawal of Egyptian labour and the onset of guerrilla action in the Canal Zone, argued in favour of withdrawal. Britain, as ministers and generals were all too aware, was overstretched and overstrained in terms of both money and manpower. Overseas current expenditure, the bulk of which was military, had risen from £160m. in 1950 to an estimated £222m. in 1952. The number of men necessary to defend the base had doubled. Unable to impose their will, the pragmatists argued, Britain had no alternative but to negotiate.[82] 'In the second half of the twentieth century,' Eden warned in a Cabinet memorandum of 1953, entitled 'Egypt : The Alternatives', 'we cannot hope to maintain our position in the Middle East by the methods of the last century. However little we like it, we must face that fact.'[83]

In the end the pragmatists won, the most important battle being fought less perhaps against the Suez Group than the Prime Minister's reactionary instincts. In his memoirs, Macmillan describes the development of Churchill's thinking during the affair as 'fascinating to watch. It illustrated the two sides of his character – the nostalgic memories and pride in our great Imperial system, and the imaginative effort by which even in his great age he could grasp the realities and attune British policy to the conditions of the new era'.[84] One must wonder to what extent the Minister of War, Anthony Head, had the Prime Minister in mind when, in the July 1954 parliamentary debate on the final withdrawal, he expressed his understanding of the reasons 'of pride, and indeed of emotion' prompting opposition to this policy, but warned that this was an occasion 'when emotions come into conflict with common sense'.[85]

Common sense's victory was at best partial. While the pragmatists were undoubtedly right to argue that the British position in Egypt was becoming untenable, the die-hards, including Churchill, may have had a shrewder sense of how far British power was in fact slipping. The British withdrawal – there was a right of return in the event of war under the new seven-year agreement – did not, as Eden had hoped, succeed in putting Anglo-Egyptian relations on a new and more stable basis. On the contrary, relations deteriorated rapidly. A major reason for this was Egypt's opposition to the Baghdad Pact, which Britain was promoting in part as a means of trying to put its bases in Iraq on a more secure footing. When in July 1956, only weeks after the withdrawal of the last troops from the Canal Zone, Egypt nationalised the Suez Canal, the Prime Minister's patience finally snapped.

Nor did the redeployment of British forces in the Middle East end Britain's strategic problems. Land and air forces were redeployed to Jordan and Libya, both of which refused to allow them to be used during the Suez crisis. The headquarters went to Cyprus. The day before the announcement of the British withdrawal from Egypt, there had been a revealing incident in the House of Commons, when Eden declared that 'in the Middle East as elsewhere our defence arrangements must be based on the consent and cooperation of the people concerned. [An Hon. Member, "What about Cyprus?"]'[86]

Cyprus however, unlike Egypt, was sovereign British territory. In the mid-1950s, when the prospects for further large-scale decolonisation still seemed relatively remote, colonies such as Cyprus, Kenya, where independence was not expected until 1975,[87] and Aden, appeared the obvious places to redeploy. (In 1946, Bevin had argued for relocation of the Suez base to Mombassa in Kenya so that 'the whole heart and centre of command shall be on British territory'.[88]) But there were important disadvantages. The lack of port facilities was readily recognised. The political problems likely to be caused by refusing to concede sovereignty only became clear after the outbreak of the Emergency in 1955.[89] For, while sovereignty conferred a legal right, in an anti-imperialist era this was a right which might have to be enforced. And, as the author of a 1957 article entitled 'Imperial Defence and the rise of Nationalism in Colonial Territories' shrewdly noted, it was doubtful whether the British government would feel 'morally sure enough of its position' to continue indefinitely to hold a base against strong local resistance.[90] A Foreign Office paper written two years later spoke of a 'tug-of-war between the conflicting interests of political and military expediency' which had delayed independence in the case of some strategically important territories. 'Unless an alternative strategy can be evolved, the delays are likely to be more frequent in the future, and their political costs greater.'[91]

In the case of Cyprus, Britain found that it had few options. The demand here was not independence but *Enosis*, union with Greece, a demand resolutely opposed by Turkey. As quickly became evident, withdrawal threatened a war between two NATO allies, and Britain had no alternative but to hold its ground. It was only in 1959, when Greece and Turkey finally agreed to reach a solution, that a compromise reflecting the peculiarities of the Cyprus situation was devised. Britain retained control over 'sovereign base areas' in an independent Cyprus, though by now the importance of the bases seems to have had more to do with domestic political rather than strategic considerations.[92] And there was a high long-term cost. Britain became a guarantor power of what rapidly proved to be an unworkable independence settlement. British forces intervened when civil war threatened in 1963, and were again involved during the 1974 crisis following the coup against Makarios and the Turkish military intervention.

While there was no trouble in Kenya, the sudden speeding up of the independence timetable forced withdrawal of base faculties after some £7.5 m. had been spent on them.[93] The real and final problem was Aden, where a major base was built up after Suez to protect British oil interests in the Persian Gulf. Aden, writes the military historian Sir William Jackson, 'had little to commend it other than its geographic location'. But there was nowhere else to put the necessary command and logistic units,[94] and the Arab nationalism so evident in Egypt and the Fertile Crescent had yet to make itself felt in the much more politically backward parts of the Arabian peninsula. The Governor, Sir William Luce, advocated federation between the colony and the protectorates of the tribal hinterland, arguing that the continued use of the base would best be secured by negotiating treaty rights with an independent entity rather than insisting on the indefinite retention of sovereignty. (The local military commander put the case rather more cynically, arguing that, even if the approach did not work, it would be 'a less expensive way of losing a base'.[95]) The chiefs of staff and the Colonial Office, however, were loath to make this concession, and it was only in 1960 that, after extensive controversy in Whitehall, and the idea of sovereign base areas on the lines of Cyprus had been discarded as impractical, federation was accepted.[96]

The establishment of a major base in Aden with its Nasserist trade union movement, turbulent hinterland and hostile Yemeni neighbour was thus a high-risk venture, and the belated attempts to find a political solution got off to a bad start.[97] The inauguration of the South Arabian Federation in 1962 coincided with the republican coup in the Yemen, which Britain refused to recognise, and Egypt quickly intervened in the ensuing civil war. Trouble in Aden soon followed, and in a familiar pattern originally seen in the Suez Canal Zone base area, increasing numbers of troops began to be required to ensure the security of the base. The cost of trying to stay was becoming out of proportion to the strategic gain. Although the Defence Secretary, Denis Healey, declared in March 1965 that it would be 'politically irresponsible and economically wasteful to abandon Aden', the decision to withdraw was announced a year later.[98] British forces were redeployed to Bahrein and Sharjah, and attention also focused on the possibility of building bases on islands in the Indian Ocean, which were assumed to be politically safe. But at the beginning of 1968 the problem of imperial overstretch was finally resolved by the decision to withdraw all British forces East of Suez.

The causes of one of the great disjunctures of modern British foreign policy are not easy to summarise. Although senior ministers were anxious to retain a post-imperial role, there had been growing doubts in the 1960s whether force was still relevant to the defence of economic interests. According to one military observer, by the middle of the decade the view that military protection had become 'outdated and anachronistic' was widespread,[99] a view strengthened by Britain's inability in 1967 to do anything to prevent the Six Day War, with its serious subsequent repercussions for trade and oil supplies. (The Suez Canal was closed and there were significant disruptions of oil production.)[100] At the same time there was also concern about the growing threats to which British forces were being exposed in operations East of Suez. In Julian Amery's crude if apposite words, 'Wogs have Migs.'[101] Christopher Mayhew, the Navy Minister, put it rather more diplomatically following a visit he paid to the Far East in April 1965, where Britain was engaged in a large-scale military 'confrontation' with Indonesia. 'It is not enough for the peacekeeping Power to be able to win its battles, or even to 'give a good account of itself'; it should be dominant enough – as we were in the last century – to make the challenge unthinkable. We are far from this now.'[102] British forces, as Mayhew was acutely aware, were again under-equipped and overstretched. With both the old Indian army reserve and conscription now gone – the army in 1966 was half the size it had been a decade earlier[103] – Britain lacked the troops for the extensive military operations East of Suez in which it found itself engaged. Defence was seen as taking too large a share of resources 'in terms of foreign exchange, scarce types of manpower and load on the most advanced industries'.[104]

Behind these concerns were the pressures generated by the coincidence of growing economic difficulties with the shifts in national priorities resulting from the Labour victory of 1964. Thus when economic push came to shove, as it increasingly did in the middle and latter years of the decade, a Labour government put domestic interests in terms of social welfare before Great Power ambitions. But it did so with considerable reluctance. Between 1964 and 1967, it had sought to continue existing policy, while imposing more stringent limits on the defence budget. This meant a decision in 1966 not to order a new generation of aircraft carriers, critical to any long-term role East of Suez, and the 1967 announcement of a final withdrawal from Singapore and the Far East by the 1970s. The final withdrawal of all forces from East of Suez, including those in the Persian Gulf, which was agreed with the narrowest of Cabinet majorities, came only in response to the devaluation of sterling in November 1967.[105] Devaluation had a traumatic effect on the government, in particular the Prime Minister, Harold Wilson, who had fought hard since he came to office to retain the parity of sterling. According to one minister, Patrick Gordon-Walker, it 'made articulate a decision that had, as it were, subconsciously been reached; but which the Cabinet as a whole and the Prime Minister had flinched from recognising'.[106]

Yet the issue was not simply that means had finally been recognised as inadequate to meet end. There was also a historically new factor – the ends themselves no longer seemed worthwhile. Already in 1963, in the last year of the Conservative government, an American observer had noted 'a phase of doubt, uncertainty, over the shape and meaning "of it all"'.[107] Self-confidence continued to ebb not just because of economic crisis but also because of external reverses: de Gaulle's two vetoes of Britain's application to join the EEC of 1963 and 1967, and Rhodesian UDI of 1965. Playing a Great Power role East of Suez increasingly seemed a pretension beyond Britain's means. Compared with the response to the withdrawal from the Suez Canal Zone base fourteen years earlier, the announcement at the beginning of 1968 that Britain was finally withdrawing from East of Suez provoked remarkably little hostile reaction. As Philip Larkin put it:

> It is hard to say who wanted it to happen
> But now it has been decided nobody minds.[108]

This was not entirely true. The Conservatives were certainly interested in reversing the decision, but found it impossible to do so. 'We had simply lost the will to continue the effort, and Mr Heath was unable to revive it,' Douglas Hurd wrote.[109] But Hurd also describes a dinner given aboard a British warship in Singapore after the signature of the Five Power defence agreement, involving Australia, New Zealand, Britain, Malaysia and Singapore. 'After dinner the Marines beat the retreat on deck in cloudy moonlight. The White Ensign was slowly lowered against the background of the low black hills of Johore and the grey warships anchored alongside. In theory we were celebrating the start of a new venture. In fact the evening was a calm good-humoured elegy for empire.'[110]

The process of decision making was inevitably less elegant. Decisions were announced and reversed with embarrassing speed. The July 1967 Defence White Paper was described as the last of the long series of defence reviews. In November 1967, on the eve of the British withdrawal from Aden, a Foreign Office minister was sent to reassure Gulf rulers that Britain would honour its commitments to them. Two months later, the same minister returned to announce British withdrawal by 1971. 'Governments, Labour and Conservative,' Sir Anthony Parsons, who was closely involved in British Middle East policy, later wrote:

> were like teams embarking on what they believed to be a timeless, at least a five-day Test Match. Suddenly they discovered that the rules had been changed: they were playing a limited-overs game and, at

the beginning of each session, the umpire reduced the number of overs remaining. Long-term strategy and planning, if any, gave way to hasty improvisation, the important lost priority to the urgent, decisions were made for the wrong reasons, or were not made at all, advice from the region was ignored or rejected.[111]

Denis Healey is unsurprisingly more charitable in his verdict. 'By historical standards,' he writes, 'the Wilson government handled the inevitable with reasonable speed and skill.'[112]

Withdrawal is both a painful and difficult process. It requires foresight about what can be very long-term power trends, as well as a hard-headed realism in weighing the risks of withdrawal against those of trying to maintain some form of the status quo. It also requires courage. It is not easy to accept the necessity for contraction and withdrawal, with their larger implications in terms of the country's declining standing in the world, just as it is not easy to sell such a policy to Parliament in the face of the kind of hostility demonstrated by the Suez Group. The temptation in the case of military withdrawal, in contrast to the termination of colonial sovereignty, was to hang on. Precisely because bases represented the last, as well as the most powerful, element of the British imperial presence, there was a greater reluctance to accept the rising power of nationalism than there had been when dealing with purely colonial issues. Short-sightedness was again evident when it came to the economic ability to sustain a British role East of Suez.

These failures were undoubtedly facilitated by the fragmented nature of the decision-making machinery in Whitehall and its incremental approach to problems. To take only one of the weaknesses identified in Philip Darby's study of British defence policy East of Suez, issues were not put squarely to the Cabinet Defence Committee, 'either because departmental perspectives obscured their wider significance or because they were felt to be too open to accident, and departments and ministers preferred to go along as they were. At other times the issues would be too sensitive, too divisive or too disruptive for the collective body to act against its political instinct and settle for a declaratory course.'[113] But the underlying difficulties lay elsewhere. There were obligations, the fact that Britain had commitments in the region which important allies, notably the USA, Australia and New Zealand, wanted her to continue to honour and which it would be damaging to terminate. There was the preoccupation, amounting at times in the 1950s to an obsession, with the vulnerability of oil supplies. Last but by no means least, there was the determination that Britain should remain a Great Power. Right up to the 1967 sterling crisis, therefore, there remained a bias against withdrawal, which because it drew on a powerful mix of pride, tradition and indeed also fear, was often relatively insensitive to the critical political and economic facts which in the final analysis determined the viability of strategy. As elsewhere, policy thus tended to reflect what policy makers wanted, as much as they were still able to achieve.

Ultimately, overstretch shows British policy at its best and worst. For much of the time Britain succeeded in the not inconsiderable feat of living beyond its means. But it is also open to the accusation of irresponsibility and unnecessary risk-taking over the failure to make adequate resources available. While policy makers often showed themselves to be skilful and shrewd, adapting to change in a timely and orderly fashion, they could also be short-sighted, stubborn and unrealistic. Their task was scarcely easy. The conduct of a retreat is never a simple matter, particularly where the nature of the process is for so long obscured or unacknowledged. Some phases, particularly the earlier ones, were easier, not simply to manage, but come to terms with, than others. Much depended on how and where the pressures were exerted, on the prevailing assumptions of how far decline might be expected to go, and on what could still be rescued.

3
The Limits of Pragmatism

The twentieth century proved a period not just of disengagement from imperial commitments, but of increasingly intensive engagement in continental European affairs. British forces were stationed on, or operated on or over, the continent for some seventy-five years. Britain sent expeditionary forces to France in 1914 and 1939, and more British dead are buried in the cemeteries of northern France than in any other country in the world.[1] It joined with the United States in the liberation, first of Italy, and then of western Europe in 1944–5. Two Armies of the Rhine were deployed. The first, which in 1918 initially numbered some 275 000 men, stayed for eleven years. The second, established after the Second World War, remains in place. After the Second World War, Britain became a member of two particularly entangling European alliances, NATO and the EEC, as well as organisations such as the Council of Europe, the Organisation for Economic Cooperation in Europe (OEEC, later the OECD) and more recently the Organisation for Security and Cooperation in Europe (OSCE). This high level of involvement, however, was a matter of necessity rather than choice. While Britain took some important initiatives in the areas of peacemaking and security, commitments, both military and political, were often reluctant and late. The British approach remained throughout the period one of aloofness and wariness verging at times on hostility, with the flexibility which characterised much of the dealings with the problems of imperial overstretch far less in evidence. Europe tends to show up the less pragmatic face of British policy – more ideological, sentimental and resistant to change.

Before trying to explain this paradox, it may be useful to recap briefly Britain's troubled relationship with continental Europe, which in its modern form dates back to the rise of the German battlefleet in the early 1900s. Its architect, Admiral Tirpitz, envisaged the fleet as a means of putting pressure on Britain in support of German *Weltpolitik*. But as the First Lord of the Admiralty, Winston Churchill, put it, Britain 'could never allow another naval power to approach her so nearly as to deflect or restrict her political action by purely naval pressure'.[2] The reaction was thus quick and decisive. The pace of naval building was stepped up, remaining ahead of the German programme for almost the whole of the pre-war period, a new class of battleship, the Dreadnought, was introduced, and warships were redeployed from more distant stations to European waters. When in 1905 Germany challenged the extension of French control in Morocco, the few British ministers immediately involved were sufficiently alarmed to take the unprecedented step of entering into highly secret staff talks with France to consider the help which Britain might provide in the event of a land war. Though insistent that no commitment had been made, an expeditionary force was earmarked, and over the next few years plans for its deployment to France were worked out in detail.

However, the great crisis which broke out in the summer of 1914, following the assassination of the Archduke Ferdinand at Sarajevo, took policy makers by surprise. They did not expect war at this time and few if any of the ministers who took part in the long and difficult Cabinet discussions at the beginning of August realised that Britain was being committed to a four-year-long conflict which would involve the deployment of some sixty divisions on the Western Front, ten times the number in the existing Expeditionary Force, and would make the re-establishment of a stable and lasting peace virtually impossible. While seeking to moderate French territorial and security demands at the Versailles Peace Conference of 1919, Britain made its own contribution to the instability of the settlement through the introduction of the German 'war guilt' clause, designed to justify the unrealistically high levels of economic reparations which it demanded.[3]

The damage, however, could not be undone. Britain had no desire to enforce what was immediately recognised to have been an unjust and unworkable peace settlement. But while the reparations clauses were renegotiated with American help, Britain had neither the power nor the political will to bring about a fundamental revision of the political settlement and create an effective European security system. The nearest it came to the latter were the 1925 Locarno accords, by which Britain guaranteed Germany's western borders. Its commitment was, however, carefully circumscribed. The guarantee of the Rhineland borders was limited to cases where there was a 'flagrant breach' of the treaty and 'unprovoked aggression' by one of the powers, with London left to decide whether these conditions had been met.[4] Though the Cabinet Secretary, Maurice Hankey, recognised that 'some day the cheque might be presented and we should have to honour it', no attempt was made to earmark the necessary forces in what was once again a small volunteer army largely devoted to imperial policing.[5] Nor was there effective British diplomatic follow-up of the accords.

The adjustment to Hitler's accession to power in 1933 proved both materially and psychologically difficult. Continuing public commitment to disarmament, along with economic weakness, meant that the initial rearmament programme was slow. As late as September 1938, Neville Chamberlain's attempt at Munich to reach a settlement with the German leader was greeted by widespread public acclaim. It was only in 1939 that the mood changed. The Prague coup of March, when Hitler occupied the remainder of Czechoslovakia in flagrant breach of the agreements he had signed only six months earlier, finally discredited Appeasement. Under strong public pressure and in what one historian describes as an atmosphere of 'panic, humiliation and moral hysteria', the Chamberlain government took the unprecedented step of providing guarantees to Poland and Rumania.[6] But the lack of effective military back-up, along with Chamberlain's continued reluctance to give up on the prospects of peace, undermined any prospect of deterring Hitler. The declaration of war in September was followed by the despatch of a new Expeditionary Force to France. But it had only been authorised in early Spring, and proved in consequence to be 'inadequately trained and short of every type of equipment, especially guns and tanks'.[7] Michael Howard describes its evacuation at Dunkirk the following May as something of a mercy.[8]

The troops sent over on D Day, by contrast, stayed. From the signature of the Dunkirk treaty with France in 1947 to the creation of the Western European Union, (the WEU,) in 1954, Britain was at the forefront of the highly successful efforts to establish a durable Western security system. Policy makers had learned the lessons of the 1930s. They were much quicker to spot the threat posed by the Soviet Union than that posed by Hitler a decade earlier. And, once established, they found NATO a very congenial forum, in which they exercised considerable influence. Having helped re-establish the European balance of power and embed a rearmed Western Germany within NATO, by the mid-1950s Britain had achieved its immediate security goals in Europe. Some of its continental allies however, who had suffered so much more in terms of physical destruction and the trauma of occupation during the European conflagration, were more ambitious. The result was the establishment of a new set of institutions which radically changed the shape of West European politics. The agenda was broadened from security to a far-reaching series of economic and political changes which from the British point of view were obtrusive and unwelcome

British policy makers now faced a major dilemma, the extent of which was not initially appreciated. The ECSC and EEC represented continental solutions to continental problems which Britain did not share. It could not afford to be seen to be openly thwarting the new initiatives, although a Treasury memorandum of November 1955 argued that Britain should take advantage of the 'various political stresses and strains within the Brussels group' in order to 'encourage the project to die of its own accord'.[9] Nor, however, if a common market were to be established, could it afford to stay out. Britain would then, as the same Treasury memorandum went on to note, be faced 'with a very difficult decision in choosing whether to join it, at the cost of all the disadvantages implicit in any drastic readjustment of our economy (involving perhaps some degree of surrender of sovereignty), or to hold aloof from it, at the cost of losing our competitive commercial position in Europe and possibly facilitating the establishment of a German political hegemony'.[10]

The pragmatic answer would have been to accept the offers of founder membership of both the ECSC and what became the EEC, in order to seek to mould the fledgling institutions into forms more conducive to British interests. How much could have been achieved in this respect can of course only be a matter of guesswork. But Britain was economically the most powerful of the potential members and enjoyed considerable prestige on the continent as a result of its war record. As Russell Bretherton, the British representative to the 1955 Brussels talks, which followed the Messina conference earlier in the year, saw it at the time, 'If we are prepared to take a firm line, that we want to come in and be part of this, we can make this body into whatever we like. But if we don't say that, something will probably happen and we shan't exercise any influence over it.'[11]

This, ministers were unwilling to do. Bretherton, the only national representative at the Brussels talks who was an official at a conference to which all the other participants had sent ministers, was soon withdrawn. Once, however, it became clear that the Six were likely to succeed, Britain came up with a proposal much more congenial to its interests. It took the form of a free trade area of seventeen European countries, restricted to industrial goods, (that is, excluding agriculture), known as 'Plan G'. But this in turn was unacceptable to the Six, particularly France, and in 1959 Britain instead became a founder member of the seven-nation European Free Trade Area. EFTA however was very obviously a second-best solution, and two years later the government finally and reluctantly decided to apply for EEC membership. 'In a changing world,' Macmillan told the House of Commons when making the announcement, 'if we are not to be left behind and to drop out of the main stream of the world's life, we must be prepared to change and adapt our methods. All through history this has been one of the main sources of our strength.'[12]

It was the end of the beginning rather than the beginning of the end. Once the EEC had been formed, the British position had immediately been weakened. Vested interests were created which British membership might threaten; indeed one member, France, went so far as to veto the first two British applications. By the time Britain finally joined in 1973, the overconfidence of the 1950s, which had contributed to the British decision to remain aloof from the European integration projects, had given way to self-doubt. This magnified the fears and uncertainties about the economic costs of entry, along with the sense that the country was being asked to do something which went against the national grain. The remarkable six-day parliamentary debate in October 1971 which formally endorsed the government's policy underscored dislike of the idea of being irrevocably committed to the continent. There was a feeling that Britain had been pushed around for too long, and was now being asked to hand over to 'foreigners everything that we have built up in a thousand years'.[13] Joining Europe was seen as diminution rather than opportunity. The voice of Beckenham, declared its local MP, Philip Goodhardt, who had conducted a mini-referendum in his constituency, was 'uncertain, slightly hesitant, divided and marginally in favour of entry'.[14] The tone and the rhetoric were very different, but there was a sense that, to borrow Leo Amery's famous phrase from the debate of 2 September 1939 on the outbreak of the Second World War, he 'spoke for England'.

Membership of the EEC constitutes one of the great landmarks of modern British foreign policy, and a great deal changed as a result. Contrasting his experience as a foreign diplomat posted to London in the 1970s and again in the 1990s, Raymond Seitz notes the degree to which government had absorbed the business of trying to be European.[15] But a country which had applied late, and jointed reluctantly, was unlikely to make an easy or an enthusiastic member. The problems became worse in the late 1980s and early 1990s, as ministers found themselves grappling with the dilemma of how to respond to the new impetus towards European integration which had followed agreement on the Single European Market and the Maastricht Treaty. The pragmatic reaction, epitomised in the Foreign Secretary, Sir Geoffrey Howe's argument that 'We must play from within with the grain of the European process, with positive proposals likely to attract others',[16] tended to be swamped by the frustration and irritation which prime ministers evinced at constantly finding themselves in a minority position.[17] The result were angry words and obstructive policies which cost Britain the goodwill on which Community influence depended. Domestic opinion also appeared to become increasingly disenchanted. Britain's choice, as one commentator put it in 1998, was seen as being between 'a passive or defiant victim of decisions made in Brussels. Europe is a zero-sum game of winners and losers. And somehow Britain always ends up on the losing side'.[18] Opinion polls in 2000 showed 69 per cent against joining the Euro and 52 per cent who believed that Britain should withdraw from the EU.[19]

The most immediate conclusion to be drawn from this brief and selective account of Britain's involvement in the main currents of continental European affairs is just how mixed the record is. There are on the one hand important successes, most notably in the military and security fields. Britain, as will be argued in more detail in Chapter 7, made a substantial contribution to the long-term, if not always the short-term, maintenance of a European balance of power. At the same time both the number and persistence of mistakes are striking, in particular the difficulties Britain experienced in coming to terms with a dynamic European integration movement. Britain had of course no monopoly of misjudgement of events and policy, especially during the first half of the century. Sir Edward Grey, who had become Foreign Secretary in 1906, was not alone in misjudging the gravity of the European situation, or in misreading German intentions for much of the July crisis. To an outsider, like the American Colonel House who visited Europe in the early summer of 1914, the tensions were palpable. 'It is militarism run stark mad' was the phrase he used when reporting back to Woodrow Wilson.[20] Men who had become used to living with recurrent tensions and arms races saw things less clearly. The assassination of the Archduke was the fifth major international crisis in nine years. The previous four had been successfully weathered. 'It was natural to hope, even expect,' as Grey later wrote in his memoirs, 'that the same methods which had preserved peace hitherto, when it was threatened, would preserve it still.'[21] None of the European chancelleries in July 1914 knew of the 'blank cheque' which Germany had given to Austria after the assassination of Archduke Ferdinand, whereby she effectively guaranteed to support her ally in the event of Russian intervention in an Austrian war with Serbia. No European army was prepared for the kind of warfare they found themselves faced with on the Western Front.

Responsibility for the outcome of the Versailles Treaty is shared with an obsessively insecure France, bent on trying to impose a Carthaginian peace on Germany, and an idealistically naive America intent on promoting the principle of self-determination in Europe regardless of strategic consequences, but in the event unwilling to guarantee the subsequent peace. When it came to Appeasement in the pejorative sense in which the term is generally used with respect to the late 1930s, Britain was very much in the lead. Chamberlain and Halifax were far less realistic in their assessment of the German threat than the French,[22] though not necessarily less so than some Germans ('I think,' Albert Speer remarked long after the war, 'that we saw only what we wanted to see and knew only what we wanted to know'[23]). But the French did not press their views, and there was little in American policy to suggest that, in the event of war, Britain could rely on American support.

As an island power on the periphery of the continent, Britain did, however, have a particular perspective on its disorderly, at times frenzied, affairs. This could be an advantage. British policy tended to avoid the suspicions and misjudgements bred by historic animosities which plagued Franco-German relations in the first half of the century, while remaining sensitive to the fears and insecurities of potential rivals. While Grey saw Germany in the years before 1914 as *a* threat (there were, he remarked in 1912, 'no limits to the ambitions which might be indulged in by Germany'),[24] he did not see it as *the* threat, in the way the Soviet Union was seen as *the* threat during the Cold War. The British Foreign Secretary had a more nuanced view of the complexities of international politics. He remained chary of Russian intentions in Asia, and alive to the dangers of polarising European politics irrevocably between the two great groupings of the day – the Triple Entente and the Dual Alliance. Germany's encirclement psychosis, whether or not in large part self-inflicted, must not be ignored. As Grey remarked in 1909, 'The real isolation of Germany would mean war . . . so would the domination of Germany in Europe. There is a fairly wide course between the two extremes in which European politics should steer.'[25]

On paper at least, the British took a far-sighted, indeed statesman-like view of the German problem after the war. Germany was not a hereditary enemy. 'As regards the Continent of Europe,' a Foreign Office memorandum produced prior to the Versailles conference commented, 'this country has no direct territorial interests or ambitions, nor has it special and peculiar commercial interests; our general objective must be the establishment of stable conditions.'[26] 'You may strip Germany of her colonies,' Lloyd George wrote in his 1919 'Fontainebleau memorandum', 'reduce her armaments to a mere police force and her navy to that of a fifth rate power; all the same in the end if she feels that she has been unjustly treated in the peace of 1919 she will find means of exacting retribution from her conquerors.' The Allies should therefore endeavour to draw up a peaceful settlement as if they were 'impartial arbiters, forgetful of the passions of war.'[27] Austen Chamberlain, who as Foreign Secretary in the mid 1920s modelled his treatment of Germany on Castlereagh's successful treatment of France after 1815 (a precedent which the Foreign Office had carefully studied in its planning for the peace conference), told the German ambassador in 1925 that he wanted a Europe in which Germany 'could take her place as an equal'.[28]

Insular detachment, however, was by no means always an asset, particularly when reinforced by liberal overoptimism. The combination hindered accurate judgement in a period characterised by discontinuities and extremes. Grey, the detached Englishman looking across the Channel at the affairs of the continent (he did not travel there), the decent liberal who shared with his Cabinet colleagues the belief that peace was the natural condition of mankind and could be maintained by rational decisions, saw only part of the picture. He knew that the Kaiser was an unstable character. He had once compared him to 'a great battleship with steam up and the screws going but no rudder and you cannot tell what he will run into or what catastrophe he will cause'.[29] But he did not translate this insight into his interpretation of the events following the Sarajevo assassination. He knew that a European war would be a disaster,[30] and yet, according to Zara Steiner, he also 'cut himself off from forces he did not understand. Grey misjudged situations. He underestimated the new forms of nationalism, the power of revolutionary movements, the role of mass armies, the new technologies and forms of economic competition. In such matters Grey was conservative and insular.'[31]

Similar failings can be found a quarter of a century later in the man described by one of his biographers as a 'sensitive and high-minded product of the Victorian peace'.[32] In the case of Neville Chamberlain, as in so many who misjudged Hitler, the very overtness of the extremes served to distort judgement. It was, to adopt an image used in one of C. P. Snow's novels, as if 'realistic men sometimes got lost when they met the sensational – as though they had seen a giraffe and found that they couldn't believe it'.[33] Policy makers could not credit, would not face the facts which were already beginning to become evident within the first months of the Nazi leader's accession to power. The problem was not one of evidence, as could plausibly be argued in the years before 1914, when Germany, while restless and dissatisfied with the status quo, had as yet no clear strategy for revising it. When in April 1933 the retiring British ambassador, Sir Horace Rumbold, warned of the dangers which the new German leader might pose to the peace of Europe, he drew not only on *Mein Kampf*, written when Hitler was in prison after a failed *putsch* attempt, but on his more recent speeches and, perhaps more important, his character. 'I fear,' Rumbold wrote, 'that it would be misleading to base any hopes on a return to sanity or a serious modification of the views of the Chancellor and his entourage. Hitler's own record goes to show that he is a man of extraordinary obstinacy.'[34] To this would soon be added the evidence of rearmament, the culture of Nazi violence, and first stages of German expansionism, beginning with the 1936 remilitarisation of the Rhineland.

Relatively few Britons, however, saw at first hand what was happening in Germany, and the idea that Hitler was planning to plunge Europe into another war seemed in the later words of one Berlin-based British diplomat, 'inconceivable to anyone living in the sane atmosphere of Britain'.[35] For the vast majority, Hitler was a figure who fell outside their experience and defied their ungruesome imagination, and who was therefore difficult to take at face value. The culture of violence was explained away as temporary exuberances which would soon disappear or that did not represent the government. In occupying the Rhineland the German leader was seen as only occupying his own back yard.[36]

The misjudgement of the momentum behind the European integration movement in the 1950s has at least at first sight very little in common with those of 1914 or the 1930s. There were good reasons, particularly in 1955, for doubting whether the Six would agree to form a Common Market. The supranational European Defence Community, which had originally been proposed by a French minister, had the previous year been rejected by the French National Assembly. France, which was seen as the key to the Common Market's prospects, had a tradition of trade protectionism. The Fourth Republic was weak and appeared to be looking to Britain for a lead. During the summer of 1955, British officials were given to understand that France would only go ahead if the UK 'was also taking part, or in some way closely associated with the operation'.[37] The talks which continued in Brussels after the British pulled out were not easy, indeed according to one of the key figures involved, Paul-Henri Spaak, they were often on the brink of failure.[38]

Nevertheless they did succeed, and the Messina initiative, like the Sarajevo assassination and the accession of Hitler, proved to be one of the radical turning points in European history which British policy makers missed. Writing nearly twenty years later, Lord Gore-Booth, who at the time was a senior Foreign Office official dealing with West European affairs, applied to Europe the famous phrase Macmillan had used about Africa. With hindsight, he believed that most British diplomats had failed to catch 'the wind of change that was blowing through the Community countries at that time'.[39] The few British officials close to the Brussels negotiations were more perceptive,[40] but they were very much in a minority. This was an enterprise which British officials and ministers were not culturally and temperamentally equipped to understand. They were too empirically minded to give credence to the radical, seemingly fanciful, ideas of Jean Monnet. The contrast between the two approaches is underscored by a 1950 telegram outlining the Foreign Office position on the ECSC: 'We believe that it is only through the working out of practical details that a scheme of this kind can hope to operate effectively. To proceed as the French suggest, namely by making advance commitments and hoping that the details will look after themselves is likely to lead to acute disappointment.'[41] The PUS at the Foreign Office, Sir William Strang, was blunter, privately dismissing the ECSC as 'nonsense and a mere French attempt to evade realities'.[42] Similar views prevailed five years later in response to the Messina initiative. A Prime Minister with Eden's pragmatic, essentially tactical, approach to foreign affairs, simply did not believe that a project involving so radical a departure from the past practices of European politics as a Common Market, might succeed.[43] More than thirty years later, Mrs Thatcher was equally sceptical about the initial talk of Europe assuming a new role and recalling its 'great objective' of economic and monetary union. Such rhetoric was written off as 'cloudy and unrealistic aspirations which had no prospect of being implemented'.[44]

The immediate importance of these misjudgements lies in the way in which they help explain policy. Grey would almost certainly not have waited so long before warning Germany of the dangers of a European war, which he did only late in the crisis, had he realised that the Germans were encouraging the Austrians, rather than, as he believed, acting as a source of restraint. Chamberlain would have found it politically impossible to make a deal with Hitler at Czechoslovakia's expense, had he understood Hitler and the nature of his intentions. But misjudgements were also important for a more insidious reason; they helped to rationalise the choices which policy makers, along with the public at large, wanted to make in any case. The Cabinet record of 24 September 1938 contains a fascinating account of Neville Chamberlain, who had just returned from his second meeting with Hitler, seeking to convince his colleagues, and one must also suspect himself, that this was a man one could do business with:

> Herr Hitler had a narrow mind and was violently prejudiced on certain subjects; but he would not deliberately deceive a man whom he respected and with whom he had been seen in negotiation, and he was sure that Herr Hitler now felt some respect for him.... The Prime Minister was sure that Herr Hitler was extremely anxious to secure the friendship of Great Britain. The crucial question was whether Herr Hitler was speaking the truth when he said that he regarded the Sudeten question as a racial question which must be settled, and that the object of his policy was racial unity and not the domination of Europe. Much depends on the answer to this question. The Prime Minister believed that Herr Hitler was speaking the truth.[45]

It was not until Appeasement had been visibly and flagrantly discredited with the German occupation of Prague in March 1939, that such ideas were formally abandoned. The PUS, Sir Alexander Cadogan, privately noted on 20 March, 'I'm afraid we have reached the cross-roads. I always said that, as long as Hitler could *pretend* he was incorporating Germans in the Reich, we could *pretend* that he had a case. If he proceeded to gobble up other nationalities, that would be the time to call "Halt"'[46] (emphasis added). How far the assumption that the Six would fail in 1955 was subconsciously influenced by the desire that they should do so, can only be a matter of conjecture, but it is a plausible one.

Policy on this reading reflected, not so much objective perceptions of the situation, but the preferences and biases of policy makers and their constituents. Across the century, from the Anglo-French staff talks of 1906 to the decision in the 1990s to stay out of the 'Euro', the desire to keep a distance from the troublesome and different mainland remained strong. It did not mean isolation. Britain, as Sir Arthur Nicolson, noted in 1911, was 'not strong enough to stand alone'.[47] 'History and economics,' his son Harold wrote in 1925, 'show that isolation in present conditions spells danger, vulnerability and impotence. Geography and aeronautics show that isolation is not in our case a scientific fact'.[48] What it did mean was that the British were persistently slow to make commitments and tended, as a matter of preference, always to go for the looser option – *entente* rather than alliance before the First World War, 'limited liability' rather than continental commitment in the 1930s, associate membership of the ECSC, free trade area rather than customs union in the late 1950s. The approach had been summarised by Churchill while in Opposition in 1930. 'We are with Europe but not of it. We are linked with her but not comprised.'[49] 'Our attitude towards further economic developments on the Schumann lines' he minuted twenty years later as Prime Minister, 'resembles that which we adopt about the European Army. We help, we dedicate, we play a part, but we are not merged and do not forfeit our *insular and Commonwealth character*'[50] (emphasis added).

The single most important explanation for this determined reserve, or insular aloofness, is the fact that Britain had relatively little ambition in continental affairs. It liked to give a lead, but its primary preoccupation was in ensuring that Europe did not become a source of trouble or danger. Hence the historical concern to maintain a balance of power by throwing the country's weight 'now in this scale and now in that, but ever on the side opposed to the political dictatorship of the strongest single State of group at a given time'.[51] For this it needed a 'free hand'. As Gladstone had put it in 1869,

> [England] should keep entire in her own hands the means of estimating her own obligations upon the various states of facts as they arise; she should not foreclose and narrow her own liberty of choice by declarations made to other Powers, in their real or supposed interests, of which they would claim to be at least joint interpreters.[52]

Despite the change in political and strategic conditions, this policy was only gradually abandoned in the twentieth century. The Anglo-French staff talks were regarded as so politically sensitive that the Cabinet was not initially told,[53] and their implications were carefully glossed over. Formally, as Grey and the Prime Minister, Herbert Asquith, insisted, no obligations or commitments had been entered into. But in the words of one Foreign Office official, Eyre Crowe, 'the honourable expectation has been raised. We cannot repudiate it without exposing our good name to grave criticism'.[54] The one significant post-war commitment prior to 1939, the Locarno treaty, sought to establish Britain in its preferred position of honest broker and balancer, guaranteeing the Rhineland frontiers instead of providing a guarantee to France, as Chamberlain had originally wished to do.[55] As late as 1938, the Foreign Secretary, Lord Halifax, still referred to uncertainty about British intentions as a means of keeping Germany guessing. It was only with the signature of the North Atlantic treaty in 1949 that Britain committed itself to take 'forthwith such military or other action, individually and in concert with the other parties, as may be necessary to restore and assure the security of the North Atlantic area'.[56] Five years later, in order to facilitate the entry of a rearmed (West) Germany into NATO following the collapse of the European Defence Community (EDC), Britain committed itself to maintain four divisions on the continent (though with the proviso that this might be revised in the event of economic or overseas crisis).

The policy makers' desire to retain freedom of diplomatic manoeuvre was reinforced by the public concern to stay out of what were perceived as other people's quarrels. The sentiment was tersely summarised by a remark of a young elector to Gladstone in 1831. 'Damn all foreign countries... What has old England to do with foreign countries?'[57] Quoted in a book published in the late 1930s, entitled *British Foreign Policy – Isolation or Intervention?*, it reflected what in the inter-war years represented a widely held point of view. The last thing the British now wanted to do was to guarantee the independence of the small and relatively weak countries of eastern Europe, established by the Versailles settlement, which were however critical components of the European balance of power. The British people, as Lloyd George had noted in 1924 were unwilling to 'be involved in quarrels which might arise regarding Poland or Danzig of (*sic*) Upper Silesia.... The British people felt that the populations of that quarter of Europe were unstable and excitable; they might start fighting at any time and the rights and wrongs of the dispute might be very hard to disentangle'.[58] Britain was not prepared to guarantee Germany's eastern borders as part of the Locarno settlement, and it showed little or no sympathy for Czechoslovakia in 1938. 'We cannot be expected,' declared an MP in March of that crisis year, 'to guarantee the independence of a country which we can neither get at nor spell.'[59]

French security interests fared little better. The desire to keep out of continental quarrels helped to make ministers extremely cautious about the possibility of establishing another expeditionary force. The prospect was still sufficiently controversial in 1934 for the Prime Minister, Ramsay MacDonald, to ask that no reference to it should appear not only in public but even in CID papers.[60] The next year the Cabinet refused a request by the Foreign Secretary, Sir John Simon, to authorise staff talks with France on the historically inaccurate grounds that such talks had dragged Britain into war in 1914.[61] A request to reaffirm Britain's guarantee of the demilitarised zone in the Rhineland was also overruled, a foretaste of British policy in March 1936.[62] In December 1937, against the opposition of both the chiefs of staff and the head of the Foreign Office, the Cabinet adopted a policy of 'limited liability' which placed the support of Britain's continental allies at the bottom of the list of defence priorities.[63] Ministers placed their hopes of deterrence on the RAF and the unproven capacity of strategic bombing.[64]

The desire to keep a distance from the continent, however, extended beyond the diplomatic and military, into the political and economic sphere. Sovereignty and identity were intensely sensitive issues. An element of nationalism is evident in the insular sense of British identity reflected in the way the writer Eric Newby describes landing as a young soldier in Italy in 1942. 'For the first time in my life I was in Europe.'[65] Its more popular expressions can be found in 'Fairest Isle' from Purcell's opera *King Arthur*, and John of Gaunt's much-quoted dying speech from Shakespeare's *Richard the Second*:

> This fortress built by Nature for herself
> Against infection and the hand of war,
> This happy breed of men, this little world
> This precious stone set in the silver sea,
> Which serves it in the office of a wall,
> Or as a moat defensive to a house,
> Against the envy of less happier lands.[66]

Similar sentiments lay behind much of the opposition to the Channel tunnel, a project first mooted at the beginning of the nineteenth century but only finally built at the end of the twentieth. Although much of the oppositon was couched in strategic terms, the underlying objections were often of a more visceral nature.[67] As Maurice Hankey wrote in an uncirculated memorandum in 1930:

> Great Britain has always been an island. To its insularity it probably owes its peculiar institutions. It has always been able to adopt so much of Continental civilisation as it thought wise and desirable.

In fact, however, it has adapted rather than adopted. The result is something quite unique. British civilisation, as American and Canadian travellers often point out, is more different from Continental civilisation than is one Continental country from another. Thus British characteristics have developed themselves in partial isolation from the rest of the world and have, indeed, made a contribution which is perhaps greater than that of any other country to the civilisation of the world. Probably the strongest opponent of the Channel Tunnel would not claim that peculiar features of British life would disappear if the Tunnel were constructed. The barrier of the Channel would still exist even though communication by land were established. He would say, however, that Great Britain would lose something of that insularity which he prizes so highly, partly owing to increased mixing with natives of Continental countries and partly because the travelling public (which is so large in these islands) would lose that personal contact with the sea which, though brief, makes such an indelible impression on most people's minds.[68]

Such sentiments easily blurred into a compound of superiority – a view of British exceptionalism based on the belief that English institutions were not only different from those of the continent but better – and antipathy. The former, fostered in the earlier part of the century by a widely read group of historians, notably G. M. Trevelyan, H. A. L. Fisher and Arthur Bryant,[69] was reinforced by the experience of the Second World War. 'To put it crudely, in the terms that a forthright colleague of mine used,' Lord Plowden wrote of the ECSC, 'we were being asked to join the Germans, who had started two world wars, the French, who had in 1940 collapsed in the face of German aggression, the Italians, who had changed sides, and the Low Countries, of whom not much was known but who seemed to have put up little resistance to Germany'.[70]

These attitudes did not notably soften with the passage of time. 'The ordinary Englishman's almost innate dislike and suspicion of Europeans' was specifically noted by the 1960 Lee report which marks the shift of official opinion in favour of EEC membership.[71] It was a prejudice shared by some post-war prime ministers. Bernard Donoghue, a senior policy adviser to Wilson, later described him as at root a Little Englander, who did not very much like 'abroad', and recalled the delight with which the Prime Minister cancelled the Channel tunnel project in 1974.[72] Mrs Thatcher, as one of her foreign policy advisers put it, 'did not like Europeans; she did not speak their languages; and she had little time for their traditions'.[73]

One more point, which is again specifically relevant to British aloofness from the European integration movement, should be noted. Over and above any consideration of preference and prejudice, there were very real differences of interest and outlook between Britain and the Six. In 1950, as still in 1955, Britain was, and saw itself as, a Great Power. It had a larger economy, much more powerful armed forces and a world view which, with the exception of France, none of its putative partners shared. Its trading patterns, still very much geared to empire and Commonwealth, were quite different from those of the Six. In 1955, 49.2 per cent of British exports went overseas to countries in the sterling area, compared with 34.2 per cent to Western Europe and the United States.[74] Its agricultural sector was smaller and more efficient. Its way of doing business was different. Once Britain had joined the EEC, ministers and the wider public, if not officials, found it difficult to adjust to a world in which symbols mattered and the pursuit of national interest needed to be subtly camouflaged in *Communautarian* garb.[75] Mrs Thatcher had no time for what she described as 'the un-British combination of high-flown rhetoric and pork-barrel politics which passed for European statesmanship'.[76] John Major complained of the 'pussy-footing' of the European Council and the way in which, when British ministers spoke the more outspoken language of Westminster in Brussels 'it was like spitting in church'.[77] All this contributed to a negative view of EEC membership, as something from which Britain was more likely to lose than to gain.

Against this background it is not difficult to see why Europe tested the limits of British pragmatism far more than the problems of imperial overstretch did. There was less by way of foresight and adaptability. A combination of tradition, interest, fear and prejudice created a persistent bias against the more active engagement in continental affairs which first strategic and later political and economic circumstances required. The consequent tension between the policies Britain wished, and those it needed to pursue, made for a greater degree of wishful thinking than had been seen in coping with nationalism in the African and Asian worlds. John Major's comments to the Conservative Party conference in the wake of the Maastricht treaty go to the core of the matter: 'Debates over our place in Europe have always touched raw nerves – in our party and in our country. I don't find that surprising. There are gut interests at stake . . . For many of you, the heart pulls in one direction and the head in another. There is nothing that can stir the heart like the history of this country.' But, he went on to warn, 'Emotion must not govern policy. At the heart of our policy lies one objective and one only – a cold, clear eyed calculation of the British national interest.'[78]

Emotion, as the previous chapter has underlined, had not been kept completely out of imperial affairs. It had hindered the withdrawal from the Suez Canal Zone base and precipitated the Suez operation. Suez and Messina, the two most serious mistakes in post-war British foreign policy, have more in common than is immediately evident. Both reflected reflex, rather than considered responses, and represented key sticking points in the complex process of adjustment to post-war conditions. Britain was no more willing to accommodate the benign European 'anti-nationalism' of the Six than it was the hostile nationalism represented by Nasser. In both cases the Eden government felt Britain's status as a Great Power was at stake, and believed, wrongly, that it was still powerful enough to get its way. Both reflected a strand of arrogance and condescension. Butler spoke dismissively of the Messina conference as 'archaeological excavations', while in *The Times*' editorial view an international waterway like Suez could 'not be worked by a nation of as low technical and managerial skills as the Egyptians'.[79]

For the most part, however, imperial problems lent themselves more readily to pragmatic solution than European ones did. Change was evolutionary and its impact diffused through a large number of discrete and seemingly separate decisions. The final phase of imperial withdrawal was spread over some twenty-five years, its implications camouflaged by the assumption that Britain would remain a Great Power. Joining Europe, by contrast, involved a heavily publicised and much debated act of accession, for engagement with Europe, military as well as political, was costly in a way that empire never was. While casualties in imperial engagements were politically sensitive, the human costs of fighting overseas paled into insignificance when compared with the numbers killed on the Western Front. Empire had been seen, whether rightly or wrongly is another matter, as a source of economic strength. The economic implications of EEC membership, a matter of endless debate and argument prior to 1973, was often perceived in economically negative terms – a threat to prices and jobs, the bread-and-butter issues on which elections were won and lost. When Britain finally withdrew from East of Suez, nothing dramatic seemed to alter. To quote Philip Larkin again:

> The statues will be standing in the same
> Tree-muffled squares and look nearly the same
> Our children will not know it is a different country.[80]

Joining the EEC, by contrast, had profound implications for the future. In Lord Denning's words, the Treaty of Rome was an 'incoming tide' that flows into the estuaries and up the rivers and 'cannot be held back'.[81]

Issues of national sovereignty were thus brought to the fore in an unprecedented fashion. Britain had accepted derogations of sovereignty in signing the North Atlantic Treaty. But defence was a discreet as well as a discrete business, without direct spillover into other policy areas, and with little impact on the day-to-day power of parliament, let alone the courts. NATO, like the GATT and later the WTO, was not an avowedly supranational organisation. It did not therefore evoke the same visceral response as the ECSC. As one official put it in a radio interview:

> The fundamental novelty of the Monnet concept and the European Community as an international organisation is its basis in Treaty, and Law and legal obligation – something to which we in this country... are exceptionally averse and allergic. Because we do not have a written Constitution. Because the notion that there are certain imperatives which cannot be overridden by Parliament, for instance, is something which we do not have, and are not accustomed to. Therefore the idea that there should be a body with real authority over the decisions of national governments – admittedly in a small and perhaps unimportant field, but *real* authority – was something we felt was grotesque and absurd at that time[82] (emphasis in original).

The supranational EDC evinced a similarly hostile reaction. Churchill referred to the proposed European army as 'sludgy amalgam'.[83] In a speech given in the USA, Eden declared that this was 'something we know in our bones we cannot do'.[84] Or, as Sir Evelyn Shuckburgh the official who drafted the speech later put it, 'we were not the sort of people who could give over control of armed forces, or political decisions, to other people.'[85] (Though it is worth noting, that despite their unwillingness formally to participate in the proposed European army, the government was at one stage prepared to have a British division incorporated within the force.[86]) While supranationalism was not central to the Common Market project, least of all once de Gaulle had come to power, the issue of sovereignty had not gone away. In talks in London in March 1961, the American Under-Secretary of State, George Ball, emphasised that the Treaty of Rome would evolve further institutionally. Frank Lee, the senior official who played a key role in bringing about the British decision to apply for EEC membership, responded that he recognised the movement to federation would continue and that he himself 'did not shrink intellectually from the idea of full political union'.[87] This, however, was very much a minority position, and when the main debate on British membership of the EEC took place in the early 1970s, the question was played down by the government.[88]

While formally therefore Britain accepted the Treaty of Rome's commitment to 'ever closer union', there was no public realisation that this was more than political rhetoric. It was a misunderstanding which had the makings of trouble, for when in the late 1980s the movement for European integration again gathered momentum, culminating in the Maastricht treaty and the single currency, a new gulf opened up between Britain and its partners. This was not the deal which most Britons felt they had originally signed up to. To complicate matters further, the acceleration coincided with, and then reinforced, a new uncertainty about British identity. Consciously or unconsciously, as Linda Colley noted in a highly influential study published in 1992, the British fear assuming a new identity 'in case it obliterates entirely the already insecure identity they currently possess'.[89]

Engagement in Europe was therefore domestically politically contentious in a way that the loosening of imperial ties rarely was. A good deal of the pragmatism which had characterised the British response to overstretch can be explained in terms of the fact that, in the absence of much political or public interest, decisions could be made quietly with a more exclusive eye to the facts of the situation on the ground. Even where policy became controversial, as in the cases of the withdrawal from the Suez Canal Zone base and the arguments over the continuation of the East of Suez policy in the Parliamentary Labour Party in the mid-1960s, the pressures were of a different order of magnitude from those which EEC membership generated within both the main parties. Harold Wilson was only able to maintain party unity in 1974–5 through the unprecedented procedures of first renegotiating the terms of British membership and then holding a referendum in which ministers were free to advocate their personal view. The precedent of Sir Robert Peel, whose repeal of the Corn Laws in 1846 had split the Conservative Party, had already been remarked by Harold Macmillan.[90] Peel's shadow, writes John Major, 'was forever at my side: in all my time in Downing Street he was never to leave it'.[91] Forty years after a Conservative Prime Minister had first decided to join the EEC, 'Europe' came close to splitting what had hitherto seemed the most cohesive and disciplined of the main political parties.

Awareness of the political sensitivity of major European initiatives had in fact long made senior ministers cautious about actions which might lose them votes or undermine party unity, although the distinction between political calculation and personal disinclination is not always clear-cut. While Sir Edward Grey believed in the need for a continental option in the form of the staff talks with France, he was loath to tie his hands to a French alliance. He was no less reluctant to educate public opinion about the possible need to support France in the event of a European war. This can partly be explained in terms of temperament and background. 'Even allowing for the difficulties of a Liberal Imperialist Foreign Secretary in a Liberal–radical government,' Zara Steiner writes, 'Grey was unduly reticent about his choice of alternatives.'[92] But the initial opposition to the prospect of British intervention, when the issue was first put to the Cabinet at the beginning of August 1914, suggests that Grey had good reason to rely on events to argue his case. As a senior official put it to the French ambassador, 'it would not be wise to bring before a Cabinet the question of the course to be pursued in hypothetical cases which had not arisen. A discussion on the subject invariably gives rise to divergences of opinion on questions of principle, whereas in a concrete case unanimity would very likely be secured.'[93] Once, however, aggression was imminent, things would be easier, not only in Cabinet, but also with public opinion, which in Grey's words 'had an instinctive mistrust and dislike of an aggressive and bullying Power'.[94] This policy, which some in the Foreign Office regretted, had the clear disadvantage of limiting the Foreign Secretary's freedom of manoeuvre in the July crisis. Politically, however, it was vindicated by events. In August 1914, the Cabinet endorsed Grey's policy.[95]

The reluctance of ministers to give a stronger lead on Europe becomes more notable in the 1930s. Stanley Baldwin, who was Prime Minister from 1935 to 1937, was acutely conscious of the weight of public opposition to rearmament and the controversy which a new expeditionary force would be likely to arouse. Opinions, wrote Neville Chamberlain, still Chancellor in 1936, 'will no doubt differ as to whether or not this almost instinctive aversion from large scale military preparations corresponds with a sound perception of the principles upon which our foreign policy should be founded. But at least it is a factor which can never be ignored by those responsible for framing our policies'.[96] But Chamberlain had his own economic reasons for opposing the establishment of a new BEF and, as Brian Bond points out, ministers tended to invoke 'public opinion' in support of whatever policy they wished to pursue.[97]

When it came to EEC membership political caution and lack of prime ministerial enthusiasm seem to have gone hand in hand. Macmillan had done little to prepare public opinion for EEC entry, and his 1961 announcement that Britain was not to apply for membership, but enter negotiations to explore the terms on which membership might be obtained, was distinctly low key. The Prime Minister was still a recent convert to the European cause. He had difficulty in persuading his Cabinet colleagues, who had already once rejected the proposal, in 1960.[98] Aware that he was well ahead of public opinion, and anxious to carry along a divided party, his approach was instinctively cautious.[99] Macmillan took the crucial decision; he did not, however, offer a strong national lead.

This had a detrimental impact on the entry negotiations in Brussels. The fact that the public debate on this historic policy change was still taking place made British negotiating concessions more difficult to make, and the negotiations had still not been concluded when, in November 1962, French parliamentary elections gave de Gaulle the domestic political backing he needed to veto the British application.[100] Roy Denman believes that 'Macmillan's attitude could have been bolder. In 1960 and 1961 the influential press was in favour of joining and so was the industrial elite. Although on the part of the general public there was no great enthusiasm, there was a widespread acceptance, as one commentator put it, of the inevitability of "becoming European". A stronger lead would have called forth a stronger response', a view shared by Miriam Camps, who takes a less overtly pro-European line.[101]

While rather more work was done to persuade public opinion of the need for membership under the Heath government, personal disinclination and concern about party unity discouraged his immediate successors, Wilson, Callaghan and Mrs Thatcher from vigorously making the case for the benefits of whole-hearted and active membership.[102] John Major's 1991 attempts to argue that Britain should be at 'the heart of Europe' caused him considerable trouble. 'The myth was created that I was too Euro-friendly, and my speech was used as a distorting mirror in which everyone could see what they wished to see. In the eye of the beholder, differing opinions focused and polarised.'[103] But over and above his very real difficulties with the small but highly influential group of Eurosceptics in a party with a small and declining parliamentary majority, Major also appears to have become increasingly disillusioned with the workings of the EU. Tony Blair was much more instinctively pro-European, declaring in 1999 the 'bold aim – that over the next few years, Britain resolves, once and for all, its ambivalence towards Europe'.[104] But awareness of the unpopularity of the Euro, and the damage which the ERM and EMU had done to the Conservative Party, made him reluctant to press the case for a single currency.[105]

Drafting a balance sheet of the success and failure of British policy towards continental Europe is a difficult and indeed delicate task. Europe remains a deeply contentious issue, and the record is decidedly mixed. Britain achieved its most important objectives. It won its hot wars against Germany and the Cold War against the Soviet Union, albeit with a great deal of allied help, and the importance of this achievement can scarcely be overrated. But it failed to avoid the wars in the first place, which in the 1930s it desperately wanted to do. And it also failed to maintain the more distant relationship with continental Europe which it constantly sought. This proved not just an unrealistic but a misguided objective in so far as it helped substantially to increase the eventual cost of security policy in human as much as material terms, as is all too evident in the underpreparedness which characterised military policy in the early stages of the First, and above all the Second, World War. In the 1950s, it served to lose Britain the opportunity of moulding the European integration movement in the looser, more outward-looking directions conducive to British (if nor necessarily West European) inclinations and interests. The same reluctance later made it difficult to maximise the advantages to be gained from EEC membership, and to prevent European issues becoming a divisive force in domestic politics.

Whether, however, Britain could realistically have been expected to have done significantly better without much more outstanding political leadership is less clear. With the important exception of the 1930s, when economic weakness weighed heavily with Neville Chamberlain, both as Chancellor and later Prime Minister, Britain's problem with continental Europe was not primarily one of resources. The main difficulties lay elsewhere. There was the failure to appreciate the contradiction between objectives – the balance of power vital to the country's security could not be achieved if the maintenance of peace was allowed to become the primary determinant of policy. Similarly, the attempt to maintain a distance from continental Europe was incompatible with the desire to maximise political opportunity and to avoid subjecting the economy to the kind of critical pressures which the two world wars represented. Then there were the misjudgements which derived at least partially from incomplete or ambiguous evidence, as in July 1914 and again in the mid-1950s. And there was the disorienting impact of the trenches, reflected initially in the anger and revanchism which fuelled the demand for reparations at the Versailles peace conference, and then later in the disowning of the treaty and the stubborn attempt to appease an unappeasable German dictator.

Underlying all of this are a set of historical traditions and deeply-ingrained insular instincts which repeatedly made for an inflexibility of policy. Attitudes changed slowly. The basic facts might be quickly acknowledged. Baldwin had already recognised in the 1920s that, with the advent of the aeroplane, Britain's borders were now on the Rhine. Yet thirty years later, when addressing the London conference at which Britain committed itself to maintain forces permanently on the continent, Eden could still say that 'Ours is an island story. We are still an island people in thought and tradition whatever the modern facts may compel.'[106] And it was Eden's government which refused to become involved in the Messina process.

The paradox was that Britain's continental problems, which persisted well after the military lessons had been absorbed, were very much the result of its earlier good fortune. Precisely because it had not shared the full scale of the disasters which had overcome continental Europe in the first half of the century, Britain could not now bring itself to take part in its political successes. It was very difficult for politicians, voters and, to a lesser degree, officials to appreciate the extent to which the political and strategic geography, which had after all held constant over a matter of centuries, had now altered. The nation which had long enjoyed the luxury of keeping apart from the upheavals of the continent remained too emotionally committed to its sense of separateness, and indeed dislike of some of its continental neighbours, to adjust easily to new conditions in which the moat which the Channel had provided was now becoming a barrier. The unsentimental pragmatism which had made it so much easier for Britain than, say, France to cope with decolonisation, did not help when dealing with the new politics of Europe. Speaking in 1955 about the vexed question of Britain's insistence on maintaining sovereignty over Cyprus, the Foreign Secretary Harold Macmillan had said that 'We are a very empirical people. We try to deal with the facts as we see them. Nothing is permanent in the world.'[107] The story of Britain's long struggle to come to terms with the great shifts and disturbances which characterised continental European history in the twentieth century again suggests that the British were less empirical than they cared to think.

4
Kinds of Allies

Few incidents in the history of Britain's relations with continental Europe have more symbolic resonance than Dunkirk. Eight months after sending its second expeditionary force in twenty-five years, Britain was evicted bag and baggage from the continent and found itself on its own. The response seemed one of relief. There was, in Leonard Woolf's words, a sense 'almost of exhilaration – at being left alone, "shut of" all encumbrances, including our allies – "now we can go it alone" in our muddled, make-shift, empirical English way'.[1] Splendid isolation, however, while emotionally satisfying, was bad and unsustainable policy. A declining power living in a turbulent, interdependent world needed alliances, formal or informal. The point had already been registered at the beginning of the century with the Anglo-Japanese treaty of 1902, the *Entente Cordiale* and the Anglo-Russian understanding over Asian rivalries of 1907. With the First World War, the Triple Entente linking Britain, Russia and France turned into a more formal alliance. Although the United States never became a co-belligerent, it did in 1917 enter the war.

Already, however, the cast was beginning to disperse. Russia left the war in the wake of revolution, America returned to isolationism with the Senate's rejection of the Versailles treaty in 1920. The scene was set for a dangerous interlude in which the inadequacy of British resources would be badly exposed. But, once the crises came, the Second World War and Cold Wars once again proved powerful recruiting sergeants, and by the late 1940s alliances had become a permanent and central feature of British foreign policy. The most important was the 'special relationship' with the USA. Closely linked was NATO, which West Germany joined in 1955. In the mid-1950s, Britain was involved in the establishment of two other, albeit secondary, security organisations – the South East

Asian Treaty Organisation (SEATO) and the Baghdad Pact, renamed CENTO after the 1958 Iraqi coup. Close military and intelligence links were also maintained with the original members of the Commonwealth. Empire and Commonwealth had provided substantial numbers of forces in the two world wars, and as late as 1960 the new multiracial Commonwealth was still officially regarded as a 'very important source of political influence'.[2]

The primary importance of alliances was to enable Britain to win its big wars. Germany was a formidable land power which had to be defeated on land. Britain in 1914 was a sea power with, by continental standards, a very small army. Despite the massive expansion of the BEF during the war, Britain did not have the resources, military, or, as became clear in 1917, financial, to defeat Germany on her own. While the bulk of the manpower was provided by France, by tying up some eighty German and Austrian divisions on the Eastern Front, Russia helped to take the pressure off the West. Had Germany been able to deploy even half this number in France, it is doubtful whether the Allied Front there could have held.[3]

The Russian contribution to victory in the Second World War was much more substantial. The Soviet Union bore the brunt of defeating the German army, which was first weakened and then driven back in the East, before the main weight of Allied ground and air forces were brought to bear in the summer of 1944. In February 1943, a senior Foreign Office Official, Oliver Harvey, complained that the Russians 'are very tiresome allies, importunate, graceless, ungrateful, secretive, suspicious, ever asking for more. But they are delivering the goods ... They are winning the war for us'. An estimated 607 Axis divisions were destroyed or disabled by the Soviet Union.[4] Britain's ability to limit its own casualties owed far more than was subsequently acknowledged to this Soviet effort. The key material contribution, however, came from the USA. Overseas finance was Britain's wartime Achilles heel, and American Lendlease covered 54 per cent of Britain's payments deficits during the Second World War.[5] Without the USA, Britain would have been unable to fight on indefinitely, let alone sustain a war on a global scale. After 1945, the USA played a crucial role in deterring and containing Soviet power.

On the imperial front alliances helped first to uphold British ambitions and later make safe the process of withdrawal. The importance of the Anglo-Japanese alliance during the First World War was suggested by the Australian Prime Minister, Billy Hughes, at the 1921 Imperial Conference.

Look at the map and ask yourself what would have happened to that great splash of red down from India to Australia to New Zealand, but for the Anglo-Japanese Treaty. How much of these great rich territories and portions of our Empire would have escaped had Japan been neutral? How much if she had been our enemy?[6]

Although the alliance was in decline by the time it was ended in 1922, its termination left the British position in the Far East dangerously exposed. In the absence of American support in the 1930s, Britain found it could not act in the region. It did not, Eden told an Anglo-French meeting in 1936, 'seem possible to do anything other than await events from day to day, and try to obtain the help of the United States'.[7] The bulk of the task of defeating Japan during the Second World War fell to the USA. After the war, the 'special relationship' with the USA allowed Britain to disengage from the Eastern Mediterranean and the Middle East without leaving dangerous power vacuums which might have been filled by the Soviet Union. British decolonisation, in Anthony Clayton's phrase, took place 'under American protection'.[8]

The American connection was also important after 1945 for another reason. It helped Britain to try to remain a Great Power. This was partly a matter, at least in British minds, of buttressing prestige and self-importance by being, and being seen as, America's Number One ally. Britain gained international influence by being known to have Washington's ear.[9] But the USA also provided more tangible contributions to Britain's Great Power status. The 1946 dollar loan, senior officials and ministers believed, averted a 'financial Dunkirk', which would have resulted in the sudden withdrawal from all overseas responsibilities, 'and our acceptance in the world of the position of a second class power like that of France on the morrow of the German surrender'.[10] The re-establishment of the nuclear link with the USA after the repeal of the MacMahon Act in 1958 significantly eased the burden of Britain's nuclear deterrent on Britain's overstretched defence budgets. After the cancellation of Blue Streak in 1960, Britain was saved the cost of developing strategic missile systems, and Polaris, and later Trident, were acquired on advantageous financial terms.

Finally, and particularly after 1945, alliances helped to determine the balance of gravity of British foreign policy, defining the limits of manoeuvre the country still enjoyed. The 'special relationship' with the USA quickly became the 'sheet-anchor of British foreign policy'.[11] It dominated British thinking on foreign policy and reinforced Britain's instinctive determination to keep its distance from continental groupings (other of course than NATO.) On those few occasions when British prime ministers did contemplate rebalancing alliance links, they found that their options were very limited.

This, however, is to anticipate. In the earlier half of the century, alliances were, as already indicated, easy neither to get nor to keep. Two allies – Russia in 1917 and France in 1940 – collapsed. The Anglo-Japanese alliance was terminated under American pressure. The USA proved elusive. British hopes of retaining close relations with the USA after 1918 were quickly frustrated and, in Lord Beloff's words, America's refusal to underwrite any British security guarantee to the continent 'conditioned the whole of Britain's European policy from 1919 to 1939'.[12] Although Anglo-American military discussions began in 1937, it was only after the outbreak of the war and in particular after the defeat of France that military relations began to gain real substance. By the autumn of 1941, a 'common-law alliance' between the two countries had been established. But Britain had little influence over American policy before Pearl Harbor and America only entered the war when it was itself attacked in December 1941.[13]

The first Anglo-American alliance which now came into being proved in many respects to be highly successful. David Reynolds describes it as 'probably the most remarkable alliance of modern history. No two countries have ever been so completely "mixed up together... for mutual and general advantage".'[14] But it was not that remarkable that it could outlast the conflict. Lendlease was abruptly cancelled without prior negotiation in August 1945, and the terms of the 1946 dollar loan, which turned out to be smaller than the British had hoped for and which was made dependent on the convertibility of sterling, were regarded in London as harsh. During the negotiations with the Americans, Keynes complained that he had been 'speaking poetry to them for the past few days telling of our magnificent feats when we stood alone during the war and thereafter, but they are not interested in poetry, they are only interested in balance sheets'.[15] Nuclear cooperation, which had from the outset been marked by a good deal of conflict, was terminated.[16]

Other tensions had also made themselves felt during the war. Roosevelt, his confidant Harry Hopkins once noted, loves Winston 'as a man for the war, but is horrified by his reactionary attitude for after the war'.[17] The President disliked what he saw as the British propensity to play 'power politics', as well as the imperialism which the Prime Minister so defiantly championed. The latter placed a particular strain on Anglo-American relations, most notably in the Far East where, the two countries were 'allies of a kind'.[18] It was not until the late 1950s, by which time decolonisation was well under way, and the exigencies of the Cold War had come to overlay American sensitivities, that anti-colonialism finally ceased to be an irritant in Anglo-American relations.

The shifting balance of power in favour of the USA provided a further source of tension in what was in effect the second and much more durable Anglo-American alliance, established with the onset of the Cold War. British policy makers would not have been human had they not felt some soreness and resentment that America was taking Britain's place.[19] As Pierson Dixon wrote in 1951 of American policy in the Far East, which seemed relatively impervious to British influence:

> we should accept the disagreeable conclusion, in the end, that we must allow the US to take the lead and follow, or at least not break with them. It is difficult for us, after several centuries of leading others, to resign ourselves to the position of allowing another and greater Power to lead us.[20]

For most of the time the impact of Britain's loss of leadership was cushioned by a combination of pragmatism – the realisation, expressed by Dixon, that there was nothing Britain could do about it – and that sympathy and affinity for their successor already evident at the time of the British withdrawal from the western hemisphere at the turn of the century. A few, however, in the early and mid 1950s, found it more difficult to accept. This was particularly true of the right-wing Conservative 'Suez Group',[21] and more importantly of Anthony Eden, who had what one of his biographers describes as a 'profound strand' of anti-Americanism in his make-up.[22]

On their side the Americans were irritated by the more ill-judged elements of British policy in the Middle East in the years between the nationalisation of the Anglo-Iranian Oil Company and Suez. 'You must learn to live in the world as it is', Acheson is reported to have said after discussions over the AIOC crisis in November 1951.[23] There was irritation too at what was not unreasonably seen as Britain's propensity to dump some of its problems in America's lap[24] and, particularly under the Truman and Eisenhower administrations, to play up the 'special relationship' and 'piggyback' on American power.[25] And there was the tendency of a declining power, in particular one acutely conscious of its vulnerability to thermonuclear attack, to be, from an American viewpoint, overly cautious. They were always, as the Foreign Secretary, Selwyn Lloyd, noted in 1960, trying to hold the Americans back or give them advice 'which seems to end in them not being able to do what they want to do'.[26] When the question of consultation with allies was first raised at the beginning of the Cuban missile crisis, Kennedy remarked that he did not know 'how much use consulting with the British has been. They'll just object'.[27]

These difficulties, however, quickly fall into perspective when compared with the ones which dogged Anglo-Russian and also Anglo-French relations. The former was a matter of pure *realpolitik*, in which the immediate community of strategic interest against Germany was constantly undermined by mutual suspicion and underlying conflicts of longer-term interest. Any prospect of an alliance before the First World War was thwarted by the deep reservoir of Russophobia in Britain, where Russia was seen as the most illiberal and reactionary state in Europe.[28] Comparable sentiments were again at work in the mid and late 1930s when the lack of interest in closer relations with the Soviet Union at a time of growing German power reflected a combination of ideological hostility and 'patrician distaste' for what by any standard was a peculiarly bloody regime. There was also concern about the extent to which the Purges of the 1930s had undermined the army.[29] Neville Chamberlain wrote privately of his 'most profound distrust of Russia. I have no belief whatever in her ability to maintain an effective offensive, even if she wanted to. And I distrust her motives, which seem to me to have little connection with our ideas of liberty, and to be concerned only with getting everyone else by the ears.'[30]

With the extension of the British guarantees to Poland and Rumania in March 1939, however, the question of some kind of alliance with the Soviet Union became pressing. But it had not become any easier to resolve. Even if Chamberlain had been less suspicious, there was now Warsaw's resolute refusal to allow the Soviet Union to send troops into Polish territory. These sensitivities might have been overridden had the Chamberlain government appreciated the imminence of war, or taken more seriously the chiefs of staff's warning of the 'very grave military dangers' inherent in a Soviet pact with Germany.[31] In the event, however, negotiations with Moscow were pursued without any sense of urgency, and the Molotov–Ribbentrop Pact on 23 August was greeted in London with relative indifference. It was a serious misjudgement. In Williamson Murray's view, the Pact 'decisively affected' the course of the Second World War.[32] It helped Germany to defeat Poland and then concentrate against France. German forces had then the advantage of Soviet raw materials, and in May 1940 only felt it necessary to leave seven divisions on the Eastern Front.[33]

After the German attack on the Soviet Union in June 1941, of which Churchill had sought to warn an unreceptive Stalin, the two countries at last became allies. Nevertheless, they fought what were effectively two separate wars. Part of the suspicions, at least on the British side, began to abate as victory neared. Despite strong disagreements over the timing of the opening of a 'second front' against Germany, which Stalin wanted to take some of the pressure off the Red army, Churchill appeared at times to get on well with the Soviet leader. Some policy makers in London, though not the chiefs of staff, believed that, in its potentially weakened post-war state, Britain would need to establish a *modus vivendi* with the Soviet Union and thought that they could do so. Security rather than expansionism was seen as providing the key to post-war Soviet purposes.[34] As late as 1947, Attlee was querying the inevitability of what became the Cold War. But the breach would have been extraordinarily difficult to avoid, given the power vacuum which the war had left in Europe, Stalin's determination to ensure that the Soviet Union was recompensed for its massive, but bitterly expensive victory, and the underlying historical and ideological suspicions between the two countries.[35]

The problems of the Anglo-French relationship – the first formal alliance between the two countries only dates back to the 1947 Treaty of Dunkirk, more than forty years after the original *Entente Cordiale* – were much more complex. Here were two ideologically compatible, neighbouring countries whose modern histories became closely intertwined. On several occasions, in 1940 and perhaps more remarkably in 1956, when Britain and France were planning their joint operation against Nasser, there was talk of Anglo-French union.[36] When the Eden government rejected the latter proposal, the French suggested joining the Commonwealth.[37] Britain did considerable service to France, most notably during the First World War. After the fall of France in 1940, it hosted and initially paid for and equipped the Free French under de Gaulle. It participated in the liberation of France and, in the face of American opposition, helped ensure the re-establishment of France's position as a Great Power, with an occupation zone in Germany. Nevertheless, it was an uneasy and unequal relationship, in which rivalry and tension were never far from the surface.

One of the difficulties lay in the fact that France needed Britain more than Britain needed France, a point dramatically underscored by the British refusal in May 1940 to send additional squadrons of fighter aircraft. When, on 11 June, General Weygand, pleading for all-out British aid, declared that 'Now is the decisive moment', he was met with Churchill's uncompromising rebuttal: 'This is not the decisive point and this is not the decisive moment'.[38] Security had been a source of discord since the end of the First World War. British policy makers had little sympathy for France's seemingly obsessive fears of Germany, evident almost from the moment of the latter's defeat in 1918. The British, who saw security in an open and stable Europe, believed that the hostile policy the French pursued was likely to provoke the very dangers they most feared. Few attempted to see the French dilemma, the smaller French population and lower birth rate, and the fear of German *revanchism* from the French points of view, or accepted the proposition that the French would never, be 'reasonable' until they 'really feel safe in their own homes'.[39] When the British did offer security guarantees, either the associated conditions were not met by the USA, or they proved unacceptable to the French.[40] It was only with the 1925 Locarno pact that the issue was at least temporarily laid to rest.

Once security questions again came to the fore in the 1930s, the British tried to get the best of both worlds. They sought to use the French army as what one official described as a 'shield' behind which to maintain itself in Europe,[41] while doing remarkably little to strengthen this weapon. Although Eden declared that 'Anglo-French cooperation had to be done',[42] the military outcome prior to 1939 was unimpressive. France's alliances in Eastern Europe were treated not as a strategic asset but as potentially dangerous means of getting embroiled in a war. In the aftermath of the German *Anschluss* with Austria in March 1938, London made it clear that the French could not count on British help if they fulfilled their obligations to Czechoslovakia.[43] It was only some months after the Munich agreement that policy makers realised that France's ability to threaten Germany with a two-front war had been totally undermined, and that Britain would have to compensate with a direct offer of military support.

The early post-war years saw a continuation of Britain's condescending approach to France on security matters, though now it was the strength of the Communist Party, allied to serious doubts as to the likely performance of the French army, which made the British wary. French criticism of Britain, by contrast, did not go down well. The suggestion in 1950 that it was not doing enough for Western defence prompted an outburst in Cabinet from Attlee. 'What the hell right [*sic*] have they got to criticise us? ... Tell them to go and clear up their own bloody mess. They haven't got any decent generals. They haven't had a good general since Prince Eugene – and he served their enemies.'[44]

Underlying the tensions generated by differences in strategic need and perceptions, as well as relative strength, was the long history of rivalry and antipathy, dating back to the Hundred Years War in the fourteenth century. Despite the *Entente Cordiale*, the two countries seemed to like one another as little as cat and dog, and were quick to suspect each other's motives. Some indication of the mood on the British side can be gained from the comments. 'The behaviour of the French has been inconceivably atrocious,' Ramsay MacDonald complained *à propos* of French economic policy in 1931.[45] During the Abyssinian crisis of 1935–6, the (pro-French) PUS, Sir Robert Vansittart, referred at various points in his diary to French 'disloyalty', 'treachery' and 'duplicity'. Neville Chamberlain was considerably more unsympathetic.[46] Recriminations were inevitably particularly acute in the aftermath of the French collapse in 1940. Each side felt the other had let it down. Having won the war, the British approach to France was a combination of dismissiveness, most damagingly evident in the negative British attitude to the ECSC, and condescension. There was a feeling, in one historian's words, that France should show 'appropriate gratitude to a British offer of friendship and respond by following Britain's lead'.[47]

The one point, however, at which rivalry did serious damage to British interests was in the 1960s, when France prevented Britain from joining the EEC. Already in 1958, shortly after de Gaulle had returned to power, France had exercised an effective veto on discussion of the larger European free trade area which the British had been promoting once it became clear that the Six were determined to go ahead and establish a Common Market. When in 1961 the British government decided to apply for EEC membership, Macmillan was acutely aware of the potential stumbling block which de Gaulle represented. As the Prime Minister noted in his diary, he and his old wartime companion whom he had helped in Algiers in 1943, agreed on a great deal:

> We like the political Europe (*union des patries* . . .) that de Gaulle likes. We are anti-federalists; so is he. We are pragmatists in our economic planning; so is he . . . We agree; but his pride, his inherited hatred of England (since Joan of Arc) . . . above all, his intense 'vanity' for France – she must dominate – make him half welcome, half repel us with a strange 'love–hate' complex. Sometimes when I am with him, I feel I have overcome it. But he goes back to his distrust and dislike, like a dog to his vomit.[48]

Macmillan was undoubtedly right in his diagnosis of what one of the President's biographers describes as the French leader's 'excessive attachment to a past in which Hastings, Agincourt, Waterloo and Fashoda loomed large'.[49] The very public nature of the first veto, the seemingly deliberate attempt to wound and humiliate, suggests a conscious turning of the tables against Britain, a settling of scores. (The leaking of the story that de Gaulle had told his Cabinet that when Macmillan, who was a very emotional man, had come close to tears at their last meeting at Rambouillet, the French President had wanted to respond to his visitor with Piaf's *'Ne pleurez pas, milord'*, is particularly striking in this context.)[50] But the more important point was that de Gaulle saw British entry as a threat to the kind of Common Market he wanted to see develop.[51] British membership, and Macmillan had ill-defined ambitions to take a lead, threatened among other things de Gaulle's hopes of transforming the Six into a unified political grouping able, under French leadership, to play a role on the world stage increasingly autonomous of the USA.[52] The 'special relationship' counted heavily against Britain in de Gaulle's eyes, as also did the Commonwealth.[53] In the weakened state which both the government and the country's foreign policy found itself in by 1963, de Gaulle's veto inflicted real damage. Britain, as Macmillan well knew, had no alternative or fall-back position. The Prime Minister's diary entry of 28 January 1963, 'all our policies at home and abroad are in ruins',[54] was not simply hyperbole. More than the crisis of 1940, which was, quite literally, the product of *force majeure*, 1963 represents the nadir of the *Entente Cordiale*.

Another, although much less dramatic, veto quickly followed Wilson's membership bid in 1967.[55] In 1969, when de Gaulle suggested that the EEC might be transformed into a looser organisation in which Britain and other EFTA applicants could find a place, with France, Britain, Italy and Germany assuming a leading role and coordinating their positions on military and political affairs (the so-called 'Soames affair'), the Foreign Office suspected a trap and leaked the talks to the Germans.[56] De Gaulle's successor, Georges Pompidou, did not entertain the same kind of grand designs as the general. He was also much less antagonistically inclined towards Britain and rather more worried about German power. But Pompidou was not interested in Heath's suggestions for nuclear cooperation and the warmth of the relationship which the two men established did not outlast them. Valéry Giscard d'Estaing was by nature more inclined to view London as rival than partner, and believed that the smaller London's role, the greater the scope for Paris.[57]

It was only in the 1990s, with the end of the Cold War and the unification of Germany, that Anglo-French relations again began to take on more substantive dimensions, starting with the close cooperation between their two armies in Bosnia. Later in the decade there was a scaling down of what the French Foreign Minister, Hubert Védrine, described as the 'pointless' Anglo-French competition in Africa,[58] and the emergence of a common interest in the development of a European defence capability. Over and above the joint conventional defence projects which went back to the 1960s, the two countries came to realise that they had a good deal in common. They were the only EU members with nuclear weapons, global foreign policies and permanent seats in the UN Security Council, where they cooperated closely.[59] As Tony Blair told the French National Assembly in 1998, 'We are both nations that are used to power. We are not frightened of it or ashamed of it.'[60]

The history of Anglo-Soviet and Anglo-French relations suggests that, contrary to Palmerston's oft-quoted assertion that Britain had no permanent friends or enemies, only interests, sentiment clearly did influence Britain's alliance relationships. This view is reinforced by consideration of two other key post-war alliances. While the hostile image of Germany prevalent during the First World War had receded after the Versailles treaty and the publication of Keynes' *Economic Consequences of the Peace*, the Second World War left a much more lasting legacy of British hostility. British public opinion was among the most anti-German of all the NATO allies.[61] These sentiments were strongly shared by at least two post-war prime ministers, Harold Macmillan, who had fought in the trenches, and Margaret Thatcher. They help explain Macmillan's handling of the Berlin crisis of the late 1950s, and early 1960s, during which the Prime Minister evinced little sympathy for the West German position, and seemed more interested in pursuing the possibilities of negotiation with the Soviet Union. When the Berlin wall eventually came down in 1989, Margaret Thatcher made no attempt to hide her anti-German feelings. Like many other European leaders, she feared a united Germany, predicting that it would be 'the Japan of Europe, but worse than Japan. Japan is an off-shore power with an enormous trade surplus. Germany is in the heart of a continent of countries, most of which she has attacked and occupied'.[62] The German Chancellor, Helmut Kohl may however have put his finger on another reason for the Prime Minister's hostility when he remarked to President Bush, 'Margaret Thatcher: I can't do anything about her. I can't understand her. The Empire declined [while] fighting Germany – she thinks the UK paid this enormous price, and here comes Germany again.'[63] It was a classic example of prime ministerial heart overriding, at least temporarily, the pragmatic heads of her Foreign Secretary and officials.[64]

How much damage either of these incidents did, beyond giving offence, is less easy to judge. Macmillan's approach to the Berlin crisis, in particular his 1959 visit to Moscow, seriously annoyed Adenauer.[65] But it does not necessarily explain the latter's refusal to give greater support to British membership of the EEC in the face of de Gaulle's opposition. Adenauer had tried and failed in the early 1950s to bring Britain into the net of European institutions. De Gaulle had taken his opportunity. By the early 1960s, the West German Chancellor had become both unambiguously anti-British – the American Under Secretary of State, George Ball recalls him as saying 'with a scorn verging on bitterness' that Macmillan was not ready for Europe – and strongly pro-French. Europe, he believed, could only be built around the basis of Franco-German understanding, which British membership of the EEC would disrupt.[66] Anti-German sentiment certainly complicated Britain's EEC membership problems in the early 1960s. It did not cause them however. And it did not prevent close cooperation between the two countries' armed forces, which, according to one observer in 1988, was 'infinitely more intense than the much-publicised Franco-German military relationship'.[67]

If sentiment hampered some alliances, the converse is also true. It reinforced Britain's interests in promoting Anglo-American relations. Friendly cooperation with the USA, declared Lloyd George in 1921, was for Britain 'a cardinal principal, dictated by what seems to us the proper nature of things, dictated by instinct quite as much as by reason and common sense'.[68] 'No Englishman,' wrote Austen Chamberlain, 'would speak of an American as a foreigner'.[69] This affinity of two countries who both figuratively and literally spoke the same language made for an ease and frankness of contact lacking in Britain's relations with most other countries. There was far less by way of recrimination when things went wrong than in the case of Anglo-French relations. As a 1961 State Department briefing paper noted, 'While important differences arise between us from time to time, one of the strengths of our association is that we can agree to disagree'.[70] Sentiment thus reinforced what after the fall of France became an instinctive disposition to look across the Atlantic rather than the Channel.

But it was not of course the primary consideration. The most important of Britain's alliances was underwritten by a strong community of Anglo-American purpose, which in the Cold War years was much broader than that with continental European countries. The underlying facts of power were self-evident. The Americans had the material power, technological resources and political will which continental European states either individually or collectively did not have, or could not match. 'Only the Americans,' Macmillan noted in his diary during a

Middle East crisis in 1957, 'can bring the power to bear (a) to stop Arabs, etc., from falling, (b) to risk the consequences – i.e. Russian threats to Turkey, Iraq, etc. (c) to stop this degenerating into global war'.[71] Similar considerations had applied to Europe in the immediate aftermath of the Second World War; they still applied at the end of the century when the Americans provided the large bulk of the forces which expelled Iraq from Kuwait in 1990, and of the airpower which helped induce the Serbian withdrawal from Kosovo in 1999.

Yet while the British, who still thought primarily in global and strategic terms, had good reason to focus their attention across the Atlantic, their lack of interest in seeking any kind of balance to the American connection is nevertheless striking. Surprisingly little seems to have been done to ward off the risk, increased by the decline of British power, of becoming a satellite. A very large number of British eggs were placed in the American basket, a point brought dramatically home by the American decision in November 1962 to cancel the Skybolt missile. As the Defence Minister, Anthony Thorneycroft, bluntly told his American opposite number, 'We have cancelled our projects, we have made ourselves absolutely dependent upon you.'[72]

In the event, Britain was fortunate. In broad strategic terms, the USA proved a reliable and steady ally. None of the fears which the Europeans harboured materialised. The USA did not revert to isolationism. Despite occasional rhetoric, it did not behave intemperately and irresponsibly. Britain was never dragged into war against its better judgement, as it sometimes feared it might be in the 1950s, at the time of the various Far Eastern crises over Korea and the Chinese offshore islands of Quemoy and Matsu. With the momentary exception of the extraordinary 1986 Reykjavik summit, the USA did not make bargains with the Soviet Union above Europe's head. Had things been otherwise, had for example the Soviet Union proved a less prudent adversary, Britain was relatively better placed than other NATO countries to protect its interests by virtue of the reinsurance offered by its own nuclear forces. But it would be unwise to make too much of this argument. The use to which a small and very vulnerable island might have been able to put its deterrent in the event of a first-degree crisis is a highly speculative proposition.

When it came to its day-to-day dealings with its much more powerful ally, Britain enjoyed a certain degree of political protection against undue pressure. Weakness could be put to advantage; indeed, according to an American report on the Skybolt affair, using weakness as 'a weapon to assure our acquiescence was S[tandard] O[perating] P[rocedure]' for

Macmillan, 'the classic technique of the weaker ally'.[73] More generally as leader of a worldwide alliance network, the USA could not afford to quarrel too openly or put too much pressure on Britain. 'If we were to appear to be "double-crossing" our oldest and closest ally – and it might well appear this way', the State Department had noted at the time of the Skybolt affair, 'it would be a serious blow to our whole alliance system'.[74] The initiative for the rapid and, in the event, far-reaching Anglo-American *rapprochement* after Suez had come from Washington.

The British thus could and did resist American pressure to do things they did not want to do. They gained exemption from American plans for European integration in the late 1940s. They refused to become militarily involved in Indochina in 1954 or in Vietnam in the 1960s. After the devaluation of sterling in November 1967, they resisted strong American pressure to maintain a military presence East of Suez. They did not allow the USA to use British bases during the 1973 Yom Kippur war. These actions were not cost free. British non-participation in the Vietnam war put 'tremendous strains' on the alliance, and differences over the Yom Kippur war reached the point where the Americans briefly cut the flow of intelligence.[75] More generally, as Lord Renwick, a former British ambassador to Washington, points out, 'the price of consultation always has been presence and participation'.[76] There were also of course times, such as granting the USA use of Holy Loch in Scotland as a Polaris missile base, permission for the USA to use Christmas Island for resumed nuclear testing in 1961,[77] or the American air raid on Libya in 1985, mounted from bases in Britain, when London did consent to actions about which it was unhappy. And there were things which Britain would have liked to have done – Suez, the sharing of nuclear information with France – which the USA would not allow her to do. There was also after 1956 an important element of self-restraint, in the sense that British governments were determined never again to get so badly out of step with Washington. But on key issues Britain could, and did, say no.

The more serious danger of Britain's avowedly pro-American policy, which had so little by way of European counterweight, was perhaps more insidious. A combination of the growing scale of dependence – for support in crucial areas such as the Middle East, for intelligence, advanced military technology, including, after 1960, nuclear delivery systems, along with the increasing material inequality of the relationship was bound to take its toll. America might not necessarily become more demanding of a weakened Britain. But British behaviour could scarcely remain immune to this shifting balance of power. John Nott, who was Defence Secretary at the time of the Falklands campaign, is reported as saying that the Royal Navy 'cannot think independently of the United States because no steps can be taken without them'.[78] Robin Edmonds, a former Foreign Office official who had close dealings with the USA, notes that, from the late 1940s onwards, officials tended to react to problems by minuting a file in the first instances with the words 'Consult Washington'. There thus evolved 'a way of thinking, or rather not thinking a problem through', which made it difficult to consider alternatives which might conflict with conventional Anglo-Saxon wisdom.[79] Another former senior official, Sir James Cable, decries reliance on the USA as 'habit-forming' and claims that the ability to retain American goodwill became a condition of promotion.[80] The extent of such attitudes is difficult to document. But there certainly was a risk that, by getting too close to Washington, Britain could find itself being taken for granted by its senior ally, while being dismissed by others as a client.[81]

A further argument against the Atlantic bias in Britain's post-war alliance relationships is the way it was allowed to retard Britain's adjustment to the emergence of the EEC. At first sight this seems paradoxical since, from the late 1940s onwards, the Americans had gone out of their way to support European integration, and express their hope that the UK would take an active and indeed leading role in it. But until the late 1950s the British insisted that closer links with Europe were incompatible with its 'special relationship' with the USA. This may have had something to do with British post-war determination to be acknowledged by Washington as a 'cut above' the continental Europeans. The UK, the Americans were told during Anglo-American official discussions in April 1950, 'must be regarded as a power with world interests and not merely a potential unit of a Federated Europe'.[82] Britain was anxious not to be eased out of its privileged association with Washington in favour of European links which offered potentially far less in terms of supporting British power and influence. But one must also suspect that the American connection provided an excuse and rationalisation for avoiding the move towards Europe which the British did not want to make.

That said, it must also be noted that, when British prime ministers did seek greater balance in their alliance relationships, they ran into trouble. As de Gaulle remarked to Macmillan in 1962, 'It was difficult ... to be both with the Americans and Europe.'[83] Although Macmillan had gone out of his way to rebuild the 'special relationship' with Washington after Suez, even before the decision to seek membership of the EEC, he was trying to 'restore our old relations with the French without disloyalty to the Americans'.[84] His attempt to woo de Gaulle by backing his Great Power ambitions focused initially on support for de Gaulle's attempts to establish a form of tripartite directorate within NATO, a highly sensitive issue given inevitable West German and Italian objections.[85] But while the Americans were willing to make concessions, they did not go far enough for de Gaulle.[86] More striking is Macmillan's willingness to consider providing France with various possible forms of technical help for the development of its nuclear deterrent (the first French nuclear test only took place in 1960) and even the establishment of a European nuclear deterrent based on jointly controlled Anglo-French nuclear forces. While this did not mean that the 'special relationship' with Washington would disappear, the ideas Macmillan put forward to de Gaulle in the summer of 1962, when he talked about a 'double-headed' alliance, implied that they would be complemented by an equally close rapport between London and Paris.[87]

Macmillan, however, found himself stymied on both the American and the French fronts. He could not share nuclear secrets, most of which had come originally from the USA, without American approval and this the Americans, increasingly opposed to the idea of other European allies possessing nuclear weapons, would not give. Britain, as Kennedy's National Security Adviser, McGeorge Bundy put it, 'would be appeasing the French with our secrets and no good would come of it for Europe or for us'.[88] For his part, de Gaulle did want technical information from Britain. But he was insistent on the need to ensure the independence of the French force, and does not appear to have found the proposals outlined by Macmillan to have been either credible or attractive.[89] Even though at times he seems to have been close to pressing loyalty to the Anglo-American relationship to its limits, Macmillan never had enough strategically to offer to tempt the general to overcome his objections to British membership of the EEC.

When Britain did eventually join the EEC in 1973 there was a crisis in Anglo-American relations. Heath was the one British Prime Minister whose instincts were Euro rather than Atlantic-centric. There are, he once remarked, 'some people who always want to nestle on the shoulders of an American president. That's no future for Britain.'[90] The Prime Minister was well aware of the growing disparity between British and American power, and of Washington's increasing preoccupation with the new relationship it was forging with the Soviet Union as part of the *détente* of the early 1970s.[91] As British negotiator for EEC membership a decade earlier, he had seen the difficulties which the 'special relationship' created with France. He was thus very conscious of the need, once

Britain became a member of the EEC, to prove the country's European credentials, by seeking to align policy with new European partners, rather than had traditionally been the case, with the USA. Dr Kissinger's unexpected and unwelcome 1973 'Year of Europe' initiative provided an opportunity to demonstrate a shift in the centre of gravity of British foreign policy from the Atlantic to the continent. In July, Heath told Nixon that in future the members of the EEC would share all information 'which they obtain in the framework of bilateral exchanges with the US', which, as Kissinger noted, meant the ending of confidential bilateral exchanges.[92] The strain on Anglo-American relations soon showed.[93]

The change of government the next year brought a rapid shift back to a more Atlanticist orientation. Not only did bilateral diplomatic exchanges continue but Britain, despite opposition from the Foreign Secretary, David Owen, continued to provide the USA with intelligence about its European allies.[94] This was largely as a matter of instinct, but there was also the fact that foreign policy was, and remained, one of the weakest areas of cooperation within the EEC. America too was ambivalent. The official message, constantly reiterated, was that long-term influence in Washington depended on Britain's influence in Brussels. At the same time, the Americans wanted Britain to continue to act militarily with Washington, without waiting for her slow European partners. And while the USA liked the idea of closer European cooperation, it often seemed much less easy with the reality, which implied greater European leverage at the expense of the USA, and reduced American influence.[95]

Given these various pitfalls, the question arises whether the Atlantic connection paid a dividend commensurate with the high British investment in it. Despite the wealth of material available, it is not easy to reach a comprehensive, or fully nuanced, answer. While the major issues and crises, Korea, Suez, the Skybolt affair, the Cuban missile crisis, the Falklands and Gulf wars are well documented, the constant day-to-day exchanges between the two capitals, including some of the highly sensitive interchanges on security and intelligence issues, are inevitably much less well documented. One paradox is immediately evident, however, The alliance clearly did not come up to the high hopes invested in it in the post-war years. Anglo-American relations, from Churchill onwards, were often the subject of a good deal of British wishful thinking.[96]

British leverage in Washington was inherently limited. Over and above the growing disparity of power, the USA both needed and wanted to take the sensitivities of other major allies into account. An overtly privileged relationship with London created jealousy in Paris, if no-where else. Hence the failure in the early post-war years of the attempts, most notably by Churchill, to re-establish the relations of near-equality enjoyed during the early wartime years. Although Macmillan went some way towards reviving the old intimacies, he was aware of the uncertainty of American policy 'towards us – treated now as just another country, now as an ally in a special and unique category'.[97] In a number of areas, including the Middle and Far East, the two countries' interests and perspectives did not coincide. America distrusted British judgement in the Middle East in the early and mid-1950s; Britain could not persuade the Americans to see Far Eastern developments from a less rigidly anti-Communist, and anti-Chinese, perspective.

Nuclear relations created a different kind of difficulty. Congress had put an end to the wartime cooperation with the MacMahon Act. During the Korean war, in 1950, Attlee tried to get a commitment from President Truman not to use atomic weapons without consulting Britain. The President was warned by his Secretary of State that he could not do so under American law.[98] When the real crisis came in Cuba, the British did better than any of their allies. While they were not consulted about the initial decision to impose a blockade, they were secretly informed of what was happening early on in the crisis.[99] There were close contacts between Kennedy and the British ambassador, David Ormsby-Gore, in Washington and direct phone contacts between Prime Minister and President after the crisis had been publicly announced. According to the editors of White House tapes of the crisis, Macmillan and David Ormsby-Gore became 'de facto members' of Kennedy's advisory committee, Excomm.[100] If things had got worse, Macmillan would have had the access to make his views clear. 'I'll talk to you on the phone before we do anything of a drastic nature,' Kennedy told him at the height of the crisis on 26 October.[101] But this was an American crisis, handled first and foremost by the Americans. The British were informed more than they were consulted.[102]

Anglo-American relationship, in other words, did not depart fundamentally from alliance norms. Where interests differed, Washington saw no reason why the views of its junior partner should prevail. The instructions given to a senior State Department official by Kissinger during the 1974 Cyprus crisis are worth noting: 'Be co-operative and helpful to Callaghan but on those things that affect our interests, we must make the decisions ourselves.'[103]

There were, however, exceptions and, from a British point of view, they were important. After the repeal of the MacMahon Act in 1958, the

Americans were generous in their provision of nuclear know-how and, later, hardware. Despite a 1961 National Security Council Policy Directive that 'over the long run it would be desirable if the British decided to phase out of the nuclear deterrent business',[104] the opportunity to do this provided by the cancellation (on cost and technical reasons) of Skybolt was not taken. The agreement to sell Trident in the early 1980s is reported to have gone through 'on the nod'.[105] During the Falklands campaign the Americans provided Britain with what one former British ambassador to Washington sees as the sort of help it would not have given to any other state.[106] Mrs Thatcher was influential in modifying Reagan's views on his Strategic Defence Initiative, as well as the anti-nuclear stance he had expressed at the Reykavik summit with Gorbachev.

Britain was perhaps best able to influence Washington to do things it would rather not have done when, most notably over the Skybolt and Falkland crises, the stakes for Britain were substantially higher than they were for the USA.[107] In these two cases there was also what might be described as an element of bad American conscience, for the breaking of nuclear cooperation in the immediate aftermath of the Second World War and, in the case of Falklands, for the way Britain had been pressurised over Suez.[108] Influence could also be exerted where there were divisions within the administration, and London was frequently lobbied by bureaucratic interest groups in Washington, and in particular where British views coincided with presidential predispositions. Macmillan's advice against US intervention in Laos in 1961 appears to have reinforced Kennedy's own scepticism as to the wisdom of intervention.[109]

Where, as was more often the case, interests coincided, the British found the Atlantic connection invaluable. This was especially true in the military sphere. According to a senior British naval officer, areas where the relations were particularly close included the development of nuclear weapons, intelligence collection and evaluation, the research and development of missile guidance systems, anti-submarine warfare and the operation of nuclear submarines. There were, he went on to note, 'very few fields within the whole spectrum of military activity that have not been the subjects of bilateral Anglo-American agreements for the exchange of information and techniques'.[110] James Woolsey, who was CIA director in the Clinton administration, remarks that, 'although no one is a complete friend in the intelligence world, with Britain and America it is as close as it gets'.[111]

The potential for political influence is indicated by the privileged access to American officials and decision making which British diplomats enjoyed. Acheson took the unusual initiative of proposing regular talks to the new British ambassador, Sir Oliver Franks,

> in complete personal confidence, about any international problems we saw arising. Neither would report or quote the other unless, thinking that it would be useful in promoting action, he got the other's consent and agreement on the terms of a reporting memorandum or cable. The dangers and difficulties of such a relationship were obvious, but its usefulness proved to be so great that we continued it for four years.[112]

David Ormsby-Gore had a uniquely close relationship with Kennedy, who was said to trust him as he would one of his Cabinet, and would consult him on domestic matters.[113] Kissinger frequently consulted John Freeman, who became ambassador in the late 1960s, 'on matters outside his official purview'.[114]

This is perhaps a classic example of Britain 'punching above her weight' and the explanation is worth pausing over, for what it tells us both about British skills in alliance management and more widely about British foreign policy in the second half of the twentieth century. Britain had originally brought considerable material assets to the alliance. The Britain of the late 1940s, when Sir Oliver Franks arrived in Washington, was still very much a Great Power. It had substantial conventional military forces, and an incipient nuclear programme; it had an empire and a Commonwealth and a worldwide system of bases. It was the world's second-largest economy and the hub of its second-largest international trading system, the Sterling area.[115] These assets would decline appreciably over the coming years, as the Americans were keenly aware. Eden's visit to Washington in early 1956 was preceded by a telegram from the American embassy in London, which noted that the Prime Minister would be hampered by limitations on resources and balance of payment difficulties. 'Hence, however willing UK's spirit maybe, its flesh is unavoidably weak.'[116] A joint chiefs of staff assessment of 1958 noted that Britain was reducing its forces to the point where 'they could no longer be considered a major reliance with problems around the world'.[117] But the decline was at least partially offset from the mid and late 1950s by increasing nuclear cooperation.[118] Nuclear sharing, in Andrew Pierre's words, 'created an environment in which the American trust in the British government deepened so that American officials discussed a wider range of military and political topics more frankly with their British counterparts than with officials of other friendly nations'.[119]

What is perhaps less obvious is that, even after the withdrawal from East of Suez, Britain still had what from the US point of view were significant strategic assets. In Europe there was the British Army of the Rhine and the Royal Navy's role in the defence of the Channel and the East Atlantic.[120] While the big overseas bases had by now gone, there remained an important string of overseas garrisons and intelligence listening points – Belize, Oman, Cyprus, Diego Garcia, Ascension Island and Hong Kong – to make Britain, in the words of one senior, albeit notably Anglophile, American diplomat, 'an important player in the global competition'.[121] Meanwhile the British maintained their seat at the UN Security Council and were 'almost always able to find a seat at the global table'.[122]

To this must be added a more intangible set of British assets. Kissinger spoke of the Foreign Office's 'judgement, expertise and that rare, intangible quality of *Fingerspitzengefuehl*' (finger-tip feel).[123] 'What Americans can get from clever Britons', wrote two American commentators, 'is an informed, but objective view, presented in a language that makes conversation easy'.[124] All this made it possible for the British to establish a pattern of regular and continuous consultations which, according to Kissinger, made it 'psychologically impossible to ignore British views'. British influence was great 'precisely because the British never insisted on it'.[125] A well-staffed embassy in Washington understood the complex ways in which the American capital worked, keeping closely in touch with all levels of bureaucracy, as well as Capitol Hill.[126] They knew where and when to intervene. They were mostly strongly supported by prime ministers who were overtly pro-American and tried hard to cultivate the incumbent in the White House. Criticism was largely contained to the private exchanges and frustrations were usually contained. This did not, however, preclude hard bargaining or even, at times (the Skybolt crisis which revealed British nuclear nakedness is perhaps the most obvious example) an element of emotional blackmail.[127]

A more typical example of the British approach is the way in which they managed to make clear that, while they needed US help, the Americans in turn needed the British. As Macmillan put in his 1957 discussions with Eisenhower at Bermuda in the wake of the Suez crisis, 'Powerful as you are I don't believe that you can do it alone.'[128] These arguments were given weight by the fact that, in contrast to the French, the British were loyal, and in contrast to the West Germans and the Japanese, they were active allies. This mattered to a country which, while a superpower, had achieved its position of Western leadership out of necessity rather than choice. America needed allies for political and psychological, as well as strategic, reasons. British participation strengthened the administration in its attempts to gain Congressional support for military action.[129] It helped legitimise American actions internationally. 'Without allies and associates,' Eisenhower once remarked 'the leader is just an adventurer like Genghis Khan'.[130] A letter written by President Ford at the time of the 1974 Defence Review expressed the hope that Britain would retain a capacity to act East of Suez since 'for obvious reasons the United States should not be the only Western Power which is capable of intervening on a world-wide scale'.[131] What the Americans wanted however was not simply cover, but also 'company' in a confusing and unfriendly world.[132] The British contingents – in Korea in the early 1950s or Operation 'Desert Fox' in Iraq in 1998 – might be small, but they helped the Americans to feel less lonely. As Dean Rusk is reported to have remarked at the time of the Skybolt crisis, 'We must have someone to talk to in the World – the British are the only people we can be *sure* of talking to in the World' (emphasis in original).[133]

Alliance policy was very much the prerogative of the professionals. While public opinion may occasionally have served to limit freedom of diplomatic manoeuvre, particularly in the case of relations with Russia prior to the First World War, and was of course a major constraint on any continental commitment, alliance relationships were rarely complicated by domestic political pressures. This was perhaps just as well. Alliances are inherently difficult relationships to handle. The community of interest which they reflect is often temporary, rarely all-encompassing. Few alliances are those between equals; few do not bear some historical or sentimental freightage, or are uninfluenced by personal rivalries. Making alliances, however, can be even more difficult than keeping them in good repair, and it is here, particularly in the crucial period of the 1930s, that the British record is most open to criticism. That the British could have gained much more from the USA, still deeply immersed in isolationism in this period, seems unlikely. They could certainly, however, have done more to support France and ensure that the Soviet Union, Hitler's main target as he had already made clear in *Mein Kampf*, was friendly. That they did not do so reflects their misreading of German intentions and unwillingness before 1939 to accept the need for a new continental commitment. A more supportive policy for France might not have made a difference in

the crucial crisis of May and June 1940: France's internal political problems, and the weaknesses of the French army were too deep-rooted for
the country to be rescued by outsiders, and in May 1940 Britain only
had ten divisions in France. But it would certainly have been consistent
with British strategy which, prior to 1940, saw France, not the USA, as
Britain's main ally against Germany. And Britain can be seen as having
directly harmed the French through its pressure on Czechoslovakia in
1938 and failure, in which the French themselves were also implicated,
to pre-empt the Molotov–Ribbentrop pact.

Once alliances were formed, the British record in minimising friction
and maximising advantage was uneven. In the Soviet case there was
probably not much more which could have been done. Stalin was a
particularly suspicious and difficult ally. The French case is much more
open to debate. Alliance with France had far fewer champions than that
with the USA. This is unsurprising. The French were often difficult; more
important, they were, for a forty-year period after the First World War,
weak. The USA proved a much more reliable and powerful bet. But
British prejudices were also too evidently on display, and often resulted
in high-handed treatment. From this we should perhaps exclude the
exceptional circumstances of the shelling of the French fleet in 1940 at
Mers el Kebir, which continued, at least in French naval circles, to rankle
some forty years later.[134] Britain at the time faced a seemingly desperate
situation and could not take the risk that the French fleet might fall into
German hands. But there are a range of other incidents where the
French had reason to feel aggrieved. They include the 1935 Anglo-
German naval treaty, entered into secretly despite prior Anglo-French
agreement to negotiate jointly with Germany on armaments questions,
and the exclusion of de Gaulle from the Yalta and Potsdam summits in
1945. France (in contrast to America) was given no notice of the devaluation of sterling in 1949. The French felt excluded from Anglo-American
policy discussions on the Middle East in the early and mid-1950s (and
again in 1958, when American forces were sent into Lebanon and British
troops to Jordan). As one British official noted in February 1956, 'A good
deal of the present unsatisfactory French attitude can be traced to our
inability [*sic*] to consult them, in the fullest sense, on one occasion or
another'.[135] The Suez operation, which was under British command,
was unilaterally ended without any attempt to consult France.

The Americans too had some reason to deplore British arrogance and
high-handedness. There was, particularly in the earlier years of the
post-war alliance, an element of superiority and condescension in the
British approach, famously summarised by Macmillan's notion of Britain

playing Greeks in America's Roman empire. 'These Americans represent the new Roman Empire and we Britons, like the Greeks of old, must teach them how to make it go.'[136] 'You supply the muscle and we will furnish the brains,' Kissinger reports Callaghan as telling him at the beginning of the 1974 Cyprus crisis.[137] British policy in the Middle East in the 1950s, in particular the reoccupation in 1955 of the Buraimi oasis where Oman and Saudi Arabia, with whom Washington's links were very close, were in dispute, and above all Suez, where Eisenhower felt himself to have been personally deceived by Britain, deeply angered Washington.[138]

Such behaviour goes some way to explaining the odd fact that two of the worst humiliations suffered by Britain in the post-war years – Suez and de Gaulle's vetoes – came at the hands of allies rather than enemies. These were, however, very much self-inflicted wounds. Given the long-term problems of reoccupying parts of Egypt, and the failure to devise and 'exit strategy', Suez would have been a political failure, whatever the Americans had done.[139] De Gaulle would not have had the chance to veto British membership of the EEC if Britain had accepted the offer of founder membership in the mid-1950s.

But it is the vital 'special relationship' with Washington by which British alliance management skills must primarily be judged, if only because it was here that such an extensive effort to minimise friction and maximise advantage was made. That the relationship showed such a marked propensity to both repair and survive – at the time of the Kosovo war, White House officials were describing the alliance as the strongest it had been since the Second World War, in marked contrast to the situation a few years earlier over Bosnia, when Anglo-American relations had come under considerable strain – is at least in part a tribute to British diplomacy.[140] The real question is whether in fact the British did too well out of the American connection, whether the privileged access they enjoyed to the policy-making machinery, as to American intelligence and military technology, did not exact a higher price than London was willing to admit. By emphasising the 'special' nature of the relationship, London risked overdependence, the limiting of European options and the tendency to place on it a weight which, as one former British ambassador to Washington put it, the connection 'will not bear'.[141] While the American link helped Britain to stave off the impact of decline, the price may have been the damaging tendency to hang on too long to the unsustainable notion that Britain remained a Great Power.

That said, the alternatives were much easier to define than to implement. A host of factors – habit, sentiment, the strong strand of anti-

Americanism which de Gaulle brought to the fore in French policy, and the hard facts of military power – made the balance of alliance relationships established after the Second World War very difficult to readjust. The ideal was spelled out by Macmillan in April 1961, when he said that the historic role Britain could play was 'as the bridge between Europe and North America', a phrase being used publicly by Tony Blair more than three decades later.[142] The reality, for reasons which were only partly within British control, proved much more elusive.

5
The Strategic Dimension

Foreign policy was defined in Chapter 1 as 'the exercise of power (including imperial power) and influence in the international arena in the promotion of British interests and purposes'. Power, particularly in as unstable and violent a period as the twentieth century, implies the capacity to threaten and use force, and this broadens the scope of our enquiry. Over and above the quality of decision making at the strategic level, we are also concerned with military competence and national will. Force exposes some of the contradictions in the British approach to foreign policy. Those between ambition and parsimony, which here takes the form of underpreparedness, and between professionalism and efficiency on the one hand and improvisation and muddle on the other, are already familiar. That between Britain's martial tradition and its liberal, at times pacific, instincts is less so. How these were or were not resolved was a key factor determining the success and failure of the use of force in support of British foreign policy.

To make sense of the succession of military operations from the Boer war at the beginning of the century to Kosovo at the end of it, it is useful to divide the exercise of force – the term will be used to cover both threat and actual use – into three main categories: the big 'balance of power wars' and their associated conflicts, imperial and post-imperial deployments, and 'internationalist' actions. Britain was engaged in large-scale warfare for ten years, from 1914 to 1918 and again from 1939 to 1945. Military expenditure at the height of the two world wars amounted to just over 50 per cent of GNP, compared with 3.5 per cent of net product in 1905 and 2.8 per cent of GNP in 1998.[1] The containment of Soviet power, which began almost immediately after the defeat of Germany in 1945, involved little by way of direct fighting – the Korean war being very much the exception. But it did require what was by historic peacetime standards a quite unprecedented degree of military effort in terms of spending, precommitment and forward deployment on the continental mainland. Most striking of all, the Cold War lasted some forty years.

These big wars spawned, and were heralded by, smaller conflicts. The First World War in particular sparked a raft of deployments and actions: intervention in the Russian civil war following the Revolution of 1917, a variety of operations in the Middle East, trouble in India and insurgency in Ireland. A decade later, naval deployments in the Mediterranean in the mid- and late 1930s in response to Mussolini's move against Abyssinia and the Spanish civil war heralded the next big conflict, which in turn left its own legacy of instability. In addition to the war sparked by the division of Korea, there was civil war in Greece and Palestine.

The aftermath of the balance of power wars also increased the incidence of what statistically constitutes the bulk of the British military deployment: the imperial and post-imperial. Some of them involved colonies, others protectorates, League of Nation mandated territories in the Middle East, and the enforcement of treaty rights, notably in China, which was still in the 1930s the Royal Navy's third largest sea command.[2] Most such operations were on a small scale, a matter of maintaining law and order, defending borders against raids or incursions, and of putting down minor revolts. Others, Iraq in 1920 and again in 1941 (the Ali Rashid revolt), the Arab Revolt in Palestine of 1936–9, some of the fighting along India's North West Frontier and the insurgencies of the late 1940s and 1950s, were not. The Malayan emergency which began in 1948 continued for twelve years, and at its height involved some 35 000 troops. The four-year long Cyprus emergency was to have lasting repercussions for the stability of NATO's eastern flank.

Imperial operations did not, however, end with empire. By the late 1950 the pattern was subtly changing. Force was used with more caution and discretion. It also began to be used for different purposes – to buttress newly independent governments in the face of mutiny or threatened coup as in Jordan in 1958 and East Africa in 1965, and to protect newly independent states such as Kuwait or Malaysia, menaced by aggressive neighbours. The language too changes; the talk is of maintaining 'stability' or 'international peacekeeping'. This did not mean that British national interests were no longer a consideration. On the contrary, policy makers remained highly conscious, not just of the economic stakes in the Gulf, the centre of Middle Eastern oil production, but also of the contribution which these tasks made towards sustaining the 'special relationship' with the United States, and Britain's claim to a world role.

The scene, however, was increasingly set for a new 'internationalist' category of deployments, which came to the fore with the end of the Cold War. The concept, which is still in the stage of evolution, embraces actions in support of what the UN Charter categorises as 'international peace and security', as well as the humanitarian interventions which became one of the most striking international innovations of the 1990s. British involvement in international peacekeeping operations, which had begun with the establishment of UNFICYP in Cyprus in 1964, now expanded, with nearly 4 000 British personnel taking part in some six operations in 1993.[3] The RAF patrolled two 'no-fly' zones designed to protect Shia Arabs in southern Iraq and Kurds in northern Iraq. Britain participated prominently in the two main peacekeeping forces in Bosnia and Kosovo, as well as in the force sent in 1999 to East Timor immediately after the referendum which voted for independence from Indonesia. The country gravitated naturally to this evolving category of 'internationalist' action, a reflection of a combination of the liberal tradition going back to Gladstone, a long-standing interest in the rule of international law, and the activist instincts of what Tony Blair described as a 'pivotal' country, still willing and eager to play a prominent part on the world stage.

Even at the end of the century, therefore, when Britain no longer claimed to be a Great Power, force remained a prominent instrument of its foreign policy. Yet, while it had a strong military tradition and took pride in the success and competence of its armed forces, Britain was in no sense a militarist state. It tried hard, at times, as in the 1930s, too hard, to keep the peace. It was suspicious of standing armies. It did not, in contrast to the French or the Soviet Union, have annual military parades. Grey's remark on the eve of the First World War, 'I hate war', reflected a widely-held Liberal sentiment. The British, A.J.P.Taylor noted, 'were the only people who went through both world wars from beginning to end. Yet they remained a peaceful and civilised people, tolerant, patient and generous.'[4] At the same time they were by no means squeamish. The events of the 1990s indicated that they were more willing to accept casualties than were many of their allies, especially the USA. Where necessary, they could be ruthless. The French experienced this on a minor scale when, in July 1940, the Royal Navy bombarded the French fleet at Mers el Kebir. Much more dramatic evidence came in the form of the strategic bombing of German cities, in which the houses of industrial workers were specific targets, culminating in the massive raid on Dresden in 1945.

The two world wars illustrate a number of other points about the British use of force. When necessary the country could fight and fight hard, if not always imaginatively. Britain proved the most resilient of the major protagonists in the First World War. There were no serious army mutinies, as there were in France in 1917, let alone revolution, as in Russia. Unlike the German army in 1918, the British did not break. There was of course the damaging subsequent reaction. 'Trench phobia' was a form of delayed national shellshock, which lasted some twenty years and was only exorcised when Hitler tore up the Munich agreement which he had signed with Chamberlain and took over Prague in March 1939. Nevertheless, a year later the British again stood solidly in the face of a situation far more dangerous than anything they had experienced during the First World War.

Britain proved effective at mobilising resources. At its peak the first British Expeditionary Force numbered some two million men, and proved the greatest single enterprise mounted by Britain in the whole century.[5] At the peak of British mobilisation during the Second World War, twenty-two-and-three-quarter million men and women out of a population of thirty-three million between the ages of fourteen and sixty-four were either serving in the Armed Forces or Civil Defence or employed in industry, a level of mobilisation never achieved in Germany.[6] The war also underscored the country's capacity to put technological and scientific ability to good military effect, as reflected for example in the successes of code breaking, the effectiveness of the British air defence system in 1940, as well as the initial work done on the atomic bomb. At the decision-making level, Churchill used the committee system originally developed during the First World War, to facilitate the effective utilisation and allocation of resources and ensure thorough examination of strategic options.[7]

One other factor should, however, be taken into account where the crucial balance of power conflicts were concerned. The British were lucky, most importantly in their geography. As late as 1940, the Channel remained a formidable barrier to invasion. The German problem was not simply the heavy naval losses sustained during the Norwegian campaign in April 1940. The German forces, as many of their commanders recognised, were simply not equipped for such an ambitious amphibious undertaking. They had neither the force structure, training nor doctrine. According to Jehuda Wallach, Hitler never seriously intended to carry out Operation Sealion, for the invasion of England.[8] Britain was lucky too in the mistakes its enemies made. The shift of *Luftwaffe* attacks from RAF bases to cities in August 1940 relieved pressure on the badly stretched air defence forces. The following year, the Germans and Japanese overreached themselves, the former bringing the Soviet Union, the latter the USA, into the war. Britain could not have won the war alone. Thanks to its enemies' ambitions, it did not need to do so.

The small and medium-size operations mounted at the imperial and internationalist level illustrate a different set of skills. Policy makers were quick to recognise the potential of the combination of the lorry, armoured car, wireless and, most dramatically, the aeroplane for imperial policing after the First World War. These offered the prospects of significant economies in imperial garrisons, a particularly important consideration in the early 1920s when budgets were under intense pressure. Military expenditure in Iraq was running at a politically unacceptable level of £32 m in 1920–21, and without recourse to airpower, withdrawal might well have been necessary.[9] Airpower also had other advantages. Aircraft could arrive much more quickly on the scene of a revolt, making incidents easier to contain and preventing the trouble from spreading. Casualties and damage were more readily concealed from critics of empire.[10] The counter-insurgency campaigns of the post-1945 period were facilitated by a combination of radar surveillance and signals interception, the advent of troop-carrying aircraft, commando carriers and the use of helicopters. The latter were of particular value for rapid reaction transport and logistic support, though not, in marked contrast to American use, as gunships.[11]

Britain's eschewal of this latter role underlines the key point about its imperial operations, sensitivity to political constraint and context. Political shrewdness rather than weaponry mattered in this kind of conflict. By the end of the Boer war in 1902, what Anthony Clayton describes as the 'pioneering, ruthlessly free-booting early days of empire' were over.[12] Rules now mattered, partly because Parliament was likely to cause trouble if they were broken, but also because it was becoming counterproductive locally to break them. The admonition of the Hunter Commission which had been set up to enquire into the Amritsar massacre of 1919, that the 'employment of excessive measures is as likely as not to produce the opposite results to that desired', was taken to heart.[13] Drawing from their experience of imperial policing in the 1920s and 1930s, the army developed highly effective counter-insurgency techniques. First used in Malaya, and later in 'Confrontation' with Indonesia in the mid-1960s and in the early 1970s in the Dhofar province of

Oman, they focused on the need to win 'hearts and minds', which meant placing a premium on respect for law, as well as the minimum use of force.[14] As General Sir William Walker later remarked of the Malaysian campaign, 'It was indelibly inscribed on our minds that one civilian killed by us would do more harm than ten killed by the enemy.'[15] This was in marked contrast to French tactics in Indochina and American tactics in Vietnam, both of which made indiscriminate use of firepower.[16]

Restraint was also observed in other post-war operations, Suez being the exception which ultimately reinforced the rule. The controversy in Britain which Suez provoked, along with the speed with which the Cabinet ended the operation, confirmed the view of a pre-war German commentator, which had been quoted in a pamphlet published by the Central Office of Information in 1954. British power, the author had argued, could not be used arbitrarily in operations that were

> condemned as unethical by the British people and by world opinion. The British government would have the choice of abandoning such unethical undertakings altogether or of seeking to give them a moral cloak by means of propaganda. However the effect of such propaganda will always be limited by the decency of the overwhelming majority of the British people, by the mistrust and by the special interests of the Dominions and by the critical judgement of the rest of the world.[17]

Less than three weeks after the nationalisation of the Suez Canal, the Cabinet Secretary Sir Norman Brook was warning the Prime Minister that the idea of using force was becoming increasingly unpopular. 'How do you do it in this age? Call together Parliament, send in the troops and get a positive vote of perhaps forty-six in Parliament and a vote against you in the UN? It just isn't on'.[18] When it was all over, the commander of the operation, General Sir Charles Keightley, reported that the overriding lesson of Suez was that 'world opinion is now an absolute principle of war... However successful the purely military operations may be, they will fail... unless national, Commonwealth and Western world opinion is sufficiently on our side.'[19] This realisation made for discretion particularly in the use of airpower against civilian populations, and in cross-border raids.[20] Incursions into Indonesian territory during the Malaysian 'Confrontation' were subject to rigorous political control from London and kept secret.[21] Decision makers were highly sensitive to the need for timely action – to get the troops in before the coup (as in Jordan in 1958) or the threatened invasion (as in Kuwait in 1961) – and, in marked contrast to the Suez affair, to the need to devise an early means of getting the forces out again.

The converse, or corollary, of this was a sense of where force could not be expected to work. In 1951, Attlee had faced a situation analogous to the nationalisation of the Suez Canal. The nationalisation of the Anglo-Iranian Oil Company was serious both as an economic reverse,[22] and in its impact on British prestige, and generated a great deal of anger. Senior ministers, like the Foreign Secretary, Herbert Morrison, argued that a military response 'might be expected to produce a salutary effect throughout the Middle East and elsewhere, as evidence that the UK interests could not be recklessly molested with impunity. Indeed failure to exhibit firmness in this matter may prejudice our interests through-out the Middle East'.[23] Egypt, he warned, might be emboldened to breach the 1936 treaty or even nationalise the Suez Canal. Attlee reso-lutely opposed these arguments, recognising the impracticality of mili-tary action, which he believed might serve to strengthen rather than topple the Iranian Prime Minister, Mohammed Mossadegh, the likely absence of support at the UN, as well the international legal compli-cations. Most important of all, he was acutely sensitive to the clearly-expressed American opposition. 'We could not,' he told the Cabinet, 'afford to break with the United States on an issue of this kind.'[24] In the event the problem was eventually resolved not by military action but by an Anglo-American coup against Mossadegh.

Several other instances of post-war British realism over the limitations of military action should be noted. In 1954, the Cabinet resisted Ameri-can pressure to become involved in what it regarded as an ill-conceived military action in support of France in Indochina.[25] Another impractical plan, this time advocated by the Prime Minister, Harold Wilson, in the run-up to the 1967 Six Day War to maintain freedom of navigation in the Straits of Tiran at the mouth of the Red Sea, was also rejected by the Cabinet.[26] In the early aftermath of the Cold War, when international peacekeeping mushroomed, British policy makers were chary of oper-ations which lacked clear political objectives or where a military solu-tion was manifestly impossible. They had nearly had their hands badly burned by the experience in the early 1980s of the multinational force in Lebanon, in which Britain had participated with a small contingent at American request, and in which the Americans and French sustained heavy casualties. Britain, the Defence Secretary, Malcolm Rifkind argued in 1993, should not be 'coy' about pointing out publicly when proposed operations seemed 'unwise or ill-conceived'.[27]

Force, then, as this brief survey indicates, effectively underwrote the key objectives of British foreign policy. It ensured the country's security and independence. It kept Britain its empire, at least until the fall of Singapore in 1942. It subsequently helped to ensure that the process of decolonisation could proceed in an orderly fashion, with power usually transferred to friendly, non-Communist successor governments. As General Sir William Jackson puts it in his survey of the Mau Mau emergency in Kenya, the British army 'prevented the simi replacing the ballot box as the arbiter of Kenya's affairs'.[28] It also served to bolster confidence. This is particularly true of the Second World War, but also of the Falklands, a war fought against the odds after a period of low national morale. Mrs Thatcher's subsequent declaration that 'We have ceased to be a nation in retreat'[29] was more than a triumphalist boast.

This picture of strategic proficiency has, to be qualified however, by a relatively small but damaging number of instances of political misman-agement and military incompetence. These involve some of the most serious crises of the period and left their own list of political casualties. The resignation of at least four prime ministers – Asquith in 1916, Lloyd George following the Chanak affair, Chamberlain in the wake of the 1940 Norwegian campaign failure, and Eden after Suez – are all linked with some form of military mismanagement. The major problem lay as much with those occasions where strategic policy proved 'inefficient' in containing the costs and upheavals of conflict, as with the outright failures where force failed to achieve the objectives policy makers sought.

Instances of the latter focus first upon the First World War, and then after 1945 on the Middle East. Strictly speaking, Gallipoli is a failed campaign, analogous to the Norwegian campaign of 1940 and Greek expedition of 1941, and therefore lies outside this survey. But it does provide a case study in the laxity of thinking which sometimes charac-terised strategic policy making, as well as the first indicator of the way in which the stalemate of the Western Front threw policy makers off balance. Once the trenches were dug along the Western Front in the autumn of 1914 and a breakthrough began to appear impossible, the politicians began to look for more rewarding theatres of operations, particularly one which, by forcing the Dardanelles and taking Constan-tinople, would help a hard-pressed Russian ally. 'Think what Constan-tinople is to the East,' wrote Churchill, First Lord of the Admiralty in April 1915. 'It is more than London, Paris and Berlin all rolled in one are to the West. Think how it dominated the East. Think how it will affect Bulgaria, Greece, Roumania and Italy.'[30] Far less thought was given by the politicians to the military difficulties of an opposed amphibious operation, although these had been underscored by a General Staff survey of 1906 which was recirculated in February 1915.[31] In the event, the operation came close to success in the opening stages, but the advantage was not pressed down and the Allies had eventually to withdraw. Churchill, who resigned over the affair, had never conducted a thorough examination of the complex problems involved. The initiation of the campaign was marked by what Robert Rhodes-James describes as a 'series of decisions, half-decisions and evasions', with the government drifting into a vast commitment of men and resources, which ultimately culminated in failure.[32]

Wishful thinking and a reluctance to think a difficult situation through is even more evident in the case of British intervention in the civil war which broke out in the wake of the Russian revolution. Its original aim was to prevent Germany gaining control over Russian economic resources. But the proposed means simply did not match the highly ambitious ends. As one historian puts it, 'What was envisaged was in effect an attempt to reconstitute Russian national resistance to the German forces by means of landings of relatively small Allied contingents at three points separated by several thousand miles of exceptionally difficult terrain. As a scheme, it bordered on the fantastic.'[33] 'Five months of discussion and the absence of any alternative plan had left ministers so wedded to the scheme that by June 1918 they were prepared to close their eyes to its inherent impracticability and abandon all reserve.'[34] British forces were finally withdrawn the following year.

Outright military failure in the Middle East after the Second World War reflects the growing weakness of British policy in the region, and the difficulties policy makers experienced in coming to terms with it. The abandonment of the League of Nations mandate for Palestine, and the withdrawal of British forces in 1948, constitute a rare act of abdication on the part of a country which normally prided itself on its ability to withdraw in an orderly fashion.[35] To understand why this happened we have to go back thirty years to the First World War when hopes of mobilising world Jewry in support of the allied cause, allied to imperial ambition – the hope of establishing a reliable client population in an area of strategic importance – led to the issue in November 1917 of the Balfour declaration.[36] His Majesty's Government, Balfour wrote to Lord Rothschild, 'view with favour the establishment in Palestine of a national home for the Jewish people and will use their best endeavours to facilitate the achievement of this object'. Although Balfour's letter went on to make the qualification that 'the civil and religious rights of existing non-Jewish communities in Palestine' should not be prejudiced, the potential contradiction between the two positions was not appreciated. Ministers did not expect serious opposition from their Arab allies in the region, and they assumed that a natural harmony of interests between Arabs and Jews, who at the time constituted less than 10 per cent of the local population, would prevail.[37]

If this was at best optimistic, and there was soon concern on the part of officials once the policy began to be implemented, nobody could foresee the anti-Semitic convulsions which in the 1930s would result in a major influx of Jews into Palestine precisely at the time when British power was weakening. The consequence was the 1936 Arab revolt. The end of the Second World War found Britain in an impossible position. Humanitarian considerations in favour of increased Jewish immigration in the wake of the Holocaust were reinforced by American political pressure and local Jewish insurgency. On the other side of the equation were hard material interests in the form of British relations with the Arab world, Middle East oil, bases and the risk of Soviet expansion in the region. By 1947, Britain had no political solution to offer, and had neither the will nor the manpower to hold the ring. Force could not rescue failed policy.

The origins of the Suez débâcle were very different. Twenty years earlier, in the mid-1930s, policy makers had lost their nerve and appeased Hitler and Mussolini. Now they panicked as they tried to break out of the tightening set of constraints on Britain's freedom of action imposed by Arab nationalism, dependence on the USA and inadequate resources. Suez is one of the landmarks of post-war foreign policy whose significance extends well beyond the confines of the Middle East. This was a crisis which had been building up for some time, as a succession of reverses, Palestine, the nationalisation of the Anglo-Iranian Oil Company and the withdrawal from the Canal Zone base, created a pent-up reservoir of frustration and anger. An early indication can be seen in Cyprus, with the appointment as Governor in 1955 of a senior military figure, Field Marshal Sir John Harding, and Macmillan's private comment that 'we cannot afford to give any impression that we are on the run in Cyprus' lest it weaken the British position elsewhere in the Middle East.[38]

If not 'on the run', the British were clearly on the defensive. Evidence of Soviet penetration prompted a Foreign Office brief of December 1955 to speak of 'a general feeling of frustration' and a lack of direct and definite answers to the major problems of the region.[39] The incipient mood of panic is suggested by an entry in Evelyn Shuckburgh' s diary of 15 March 1956 (Shuckburgh was the senior Foreign Office official responsible for Middle East affairs) following the dismissal of the British commander of the Arab Legion in Jordan, Glubb Pasha, and rioting in Bahrein:

> We have now got to a state where each telegram that comes in causes Ministers to meet, telephone one another, draft replies and curse everybody. Not only does each of our telegrams contradict the one before, but each paragraph in each telegram contradicts the paragraph before.[40]

A few weeks later Shuckburgh asked to be relieved of his post, unable to continue lying awake at night 'worrying about the headlong descent of our fortunes' (in the region).[41] Eden, also in ill-health, and under political pressure from those who had opposed his policy of withdrawing from the Canal Zone base, reacted very differently from the way in which Attlee had responded to the Iranian crisis five years earlier. Anthony Nutting, who was Minister of State at the Foreign Office, quotes the Prime Minister as saying that he wanted Nasser 'murdered'.[42] The nationalisation of the Canal, only weeks after the withdrawal of the last British troops from Egypt, provided him with an apparently more promising opportunity to try to remove the Egyptian leader.

Suez was a peculiarly inflammable mix: oil, the Russians, Nasser who was the first Third World leader to challenge Britain's imperial position on a regional scale, and the memories of Appeasement of the 1930s. The language tells its own story. The PUS, Sir Ivone Kirkpatrick, warned that, if Britain were denied Middle East oil for one to two years, the gold reserves would go and the sterling area disintegrate. Britain then could not afford 'the bare minimum necessary for our defence. And a country that cannot provide for its defence is finished'.[43] We must, Eden told the Cabinet in August 1956, 'secure the defeat of Nasser by one method or another. If not, we would rot away'.[44] Lord Salisbury, Colonial Secretary and one of the grandees of the Tory Party, spoke of the risk of 'progressive decline' if Britain did not make a stand.[45] In private at least, Dulles agreed.[46]

Policy in consequence lost its sense of proportion, with the British, as Eisenhower complained, 'making Nasser a much more important figure than he is',[47] and a fundamentally misconceived military operation ensued. When in mid October Nasser was asked how he intended to defend himself he replied, with a percipience which his adversaries were quite unable to appreciate, 'But I do not intend to fight them. I intend to stand back and wait for world opinion to save me.'[48] The fear and anger which propelled this attempt to put the imperial clock back prevented ministers answering, or in some cases asking, the obvious questions. They knew they faced American opposition, but managed to convince themselves that it would not become a serious problem.[49] They knew military action would be in breach of international law. How, as the Minister of Defence, Sir Walter Monckton, who was a lawyer, asked, 'do you actually start this war?'[50] But they settled for the clumsy and implausible device of pretending to intervene to separate Egyptian and Israeli combatants. Macmillan later remarked of the final military plan, 'I can't honestly say I liked it, *but I agreed to it – as I was all for going in.*' It was, he told his biographer, 'a muddle – rather like Gallipoli'. He should have taken a stronger position 'in insisting on knowing just exactly how they were going to bring it about; and what were the chances of success and what were the dangers'[51] (emphasis added). The question of what would happen once the Canal was taken, and how British troops would extricate themselves from Egypt, was never satisfactorily addressed.[52]

The operation intended to stem the decline of British power served by its inevitable and dramatic failure to accelerate the process. This did not mean immediate collapse, indeed some of the initial assessments of the impact of Suez were exaggerated. But Suez did indirect and long-term damage to British interests which is difficult to document. Suez tilted the balance in the Arab world against pro-Western regimes and helped precipitate the 1958 coup in Iraq, described by Macmillan in his memoirs as 'devastating news, destroying at a blow a whole system of security which successive British Governments had built up'.[53] In Europe it hastened the collapse of the French Fourth Republic. De Gaulle's return to power revived Anglo-French rivalry and led to the early termination of the French colonial presence in West Africa, which in turn undermined Britain's ability to retain its colonial presence in Africa.[54] Despite the rapid and successful revival of relations with Washington, Suez left its mark on the 'special relationship'. Prior to 1956, the British, while clearly junior partners, were, as Sean Greenwood puts it,

frequently innovators. Many of what were to become the received idioms of the early Cold War – globalism, domino theory, nuclear deterrence, containment, *détente* and summitry – could claim to be British conceptions, though they may have failed to register the copyright to the precise terminology. Borrowing a cliché from the world of postwar technology, Britain was capable of remarkable invention, but others outpaced them in their application. Suez provided a further lurch in this general direction. Washington continued to place great importance on British support, but something had been lost and politico/strategic creativity tended to become the domain of the Americans.[55]

Last but by no means least is the way in which the operation undermined self-confidence. 'We have,' wrote Sir Charles Johnson in 1961, when he was Governor of Aden, 'lost confidence in our ability to deal with situations... it is something which has happened inside ourselves and bears no particular relation to the facts as observed in the field.'[56] This did not mean that Macmillan's ambitions to bring about a new order in the Middle East had been quenched. In the immediate aftermath of the 1958 Iraqi coup, the Prime Minister was urging on Eisenhower a major Anglo-American operation throughout the region.[57] When the Americans proved unwilling, the British sent forces to Jordan, not simply to strengthen King Hussein, but to underline to Nasser their determination to thwart what were seen as his intrigues, and bolster British prestige in the region.[58] Ministers were prepared to do this despite the risks of an operation described by Macmillan in his diary as 'without a [line of communications]; with a supply by air only if the Israelis agree to overflying; no sea base; no real purpose or future – since we cannot attempt to invade Iraq – and even if we wanted to do so, it would not be through Amman'.[59] Risks were again taken in Kuwait in 1961 in the face of a potential Iraqi threat immediately following the termination of the 1899 treaty.

Yet the sense of anxiety surrounding what were by previous standards relatively small operations was often palpable. This was particularly evident during a minor operation to suppress a rebellion in Oman, undertaken less than a year after Suez, in the summer of 1957. Ministers were intensely nervous about international reaction and the risk of failure.[60] The shadow of Suez could still be discerned at the time of Rhodesia's unilateral declaration of independence and the 1974 Cyprus crisis, when the Foreign Secretary, Jim Callaghan, was unwilling to use force to contain the Turkish invasion without American support. A subsequent failure, he later wrote, 'would have resembled a second Suez'.[61] According to the Cabinet Secretary of the time, Lord Armstrong, it was not until the Falklands war that Britain was at least partially able to restore 'faith in itself as a power which was able to exercise influence outside its immediate surroundings'.[62]

The last of the Middle Eastern cases where force failed to rescue policy was Aden. Here, as has already been discussed in Chapter 2, the problem resulted from the way in which Aden's future had been determined by strategic considerations, with the establishment of the South Arabian Federation in 1962. Once the decision to withdraw had been announced in 1966, Britain effectively lost control over the situation, as the two main rival factions, FLOSY and the NLF, which had previously opposed the British presence, fought out a war of succession. The actual military withdrawal in 1967 was skilfully conducted, but Britain left behind the only People's Democratic Republic in the Middle East, which provided the Soviet Union with access to the old Aden base.

Yet less damage was done by these defeats than by the military victories of the two world wars. Victory in the first of these conflicts undermined the national will to maintain a future balance of power in Europe. The strategy of 'attrition' which the army adopted proved horrendously expensive in lives. But over and above the immediate human and social tragedy, which still cast a shadow at the end of the century, the failure of the blood-letting of the trenches to achieve apparent tangible gain in terms of clear-cut military victory or ground gained created an impression of futility and waste. This was the image which the public carried into the 1930s, rather than any appreciation of the way in which the Somme and Passchendaele had undermined the German army, thereby facilitating its eventual collapse in 1918, or indeed of the victories of the last 'Hundred Days' of the conflict, when mobile warfare had been restored.

The Second World War had the paradoxical impact of demoting Britain from the rank of a first class power, while also making it much more difficult for her to adjust to her reduced position in the world. Pride at having stood alone in 1940 and won the war against such heavy odds obscured the cost of victory. Something of the consequent unrealism which pervaded policy over the next two decades is suggested by Jim Callaghan's comments at a dinner given in Bonn in 1976, that 'The mistake we made was to think we won the war.' The Germans and British, one of those present recalls, agreed 'that this was a comment which went to the heart of the matter'.[63] Jean Monnet made much the same point when, discussing the British failure to join the European integration movement, he spoke of 'the price of victory – the illusion that you could maintain what you had, without change'.[64]

The scale of these costs is partly to be explained by the magnitude of the conflicts. These were total wars fought against formidable adversaries, with ample resources and considerable military aptitude.[65] But that is at most part of the story. It does not explain the nature of the tactics and strategy which Britain adopted in the First World War, and takes no account of the question of whether the costs of the Second World War could have been reduced by prompter military preparation and action. Here we move beyond the confines of strategic decision making to focus more on the culture and competence of the armed forces, and the broader technological and political environment in which they had to operate.

The problems of assimilating technological change were particularly acute in the earlier part of the century and, while they certainly affected the Royal Navy, proved most damaging in the case of the army. All the major European armies, including the highly professional German forces, experienced great difficulties in adapting to the conditions of the Western Front. No general staff had the technology or the technical know-how to suppress, overrun and penetrate 'a well-sited defence system some four miles deep, the front edge of which was only a short distance from one's own, protected by massive wire entanglements and covered by the flanking fire of machine guns and a wall of artillery and mortars of all calibres sited in depth'.[66] Pre-war armies had shown a uniform reluctance to recognise and acknowledge the impact of the great changes in land warfare, of which the revolution in firepower, which came to be symbolised by the machine gun, was the most dramatic instance, which had been taking place since the late nineteenth century.[67] When in 1899 Ivan Bloch published his six-volume work, *The Future of War*, which accurately predicted the stalemate on the Western Front, the military reception was highly critical. 'Granted,' wrote the anonymous reviewer in the *Journal of the Royal United Services Institute*,

> that if the slaughter of war really depended on the mechanical perfection of the arms in use, M. Bloch has proved his case up to the hilt; but all military history proves in the most conclusive manner that the perfection of the weapon being duly adapted to the fighting spirit of the contending forces, it is the man behind the weapon which conditions the result, and practically nothing else.[68]

There were dissenting voices, sometimes at very senior levels.[69] But the prevailing assumption remained that the next war would be a short sharp conflict in which the advantage would lie with the offensive. Certainly, this was the war which the British prepared for. Nobody therefore knew how to resolve the 'riddle of the trenches',[70] and Kitchener's lament, 'I don't know what is to be done ... this isn't war',[71] could have been spoken by commanders on both sides.

But the British were at a particular set of disadvantages. Historically their main military investment had been in seapower, the army having concentrated its attention since the Crimean war in the 1850s on relatively small-scale imperial wars. This had begun to change in response to the rise of Germany. Hence the Anglo-French staff talks and the earmarking of the first BEF. Training , armaments and organisation of the army increasingly took account of the potential European commitment.[72] The claim by a government spokesman in 1912 that the ability to mobilise a force of 150 000 men with all their arms and equipment for a three-month campaign within a few days marked 'the most extraordinary advance in the whole military history of this country'[73] was justified.

It was not, however, enough. The size of the BEF reflected the number of troops readily available, rather than any realistic assessment of what an expeditionary force of a mere six divisions could achieve on a continent in which the size of the major armies was numbered in millions.[74] This had something to do with the lack of knowledge or interest on the part of the politicians, who assumed that, as in the past, Britain could rely primarily on seapower, leaving the bulk of the fighting to its continental allies.[75] More important was the reluctance to raise the highly contentious issue of peacetime conscription. No party, declared Lloyd George in 1910, dare touch it 'because of the violent prejudice which would be excited even if it were suspected that a Government contemplated the possibility of establishing anything of the kind'.[76] Conscription, Asquith claimed after the war, 'would have split the Cabinet, split the House of Commons, split both political parties and split the nation'.[77] In a world in which war was regarded as a possibility rather than a probability, the pre-war army was allowed to remain dangerously small.

The outbreak of war in August 1914 solved the immediate issue of manpower. Nearly 479 000 volunteers joined the colours between 4 August and 12 September.[78] Raw recruits, however, could not be rapidly turned into effective soldiers. There was neither the equipment, nor the trained officers and NCOs. It took time to build up an army capable of making a real difference on the Western Front, time which the exigencies of Coalition warfare did not allow. Insufficient training provides part of the explanation for the horrendous casualty lists produced by the Somme offensive of July 1916. Senior officers feared that their new recruits would be unable to emulate the French forces, who advanced by rushing in small groups from one piece of dead ground to another, without disintegrating into uncoordinated groups, or taking cover and staying there. Instead they were made to advance slowly in waves, as if on an Aldershot parade ground, straight into machine gun fire.[79]

Lack of training, however, were only part of the army's difficulties. British generals did not have experience in fighting much more professional continental armies or handling very large bodies of troops.[80] The British Commander-in-Chief, Sir Douglas Haig, brought to the Western Front ideas learned some twenty years earlier at Staff College. These in turn went back to the Napoleonic wars a century earlier, and in Haig's case were supplemented only by experience of colonial campaigns in the Sudan and South Africa.[81] This might have mattered less given greater flexibility of mind and imagination, or a less hierarchical approach to warfare. It is difficult to envisage Haig ever contemplating emulating the German commander, Erich von Ludendorff, who, when preparing for his initially highly successful 1918 Spring offensive, brought together the best tactical thinkers in the German army regardless of rank, to devise new tactics for a breakthrough of Allied lines.[82]

By the end of the war the British army had in fact become a highly effective force. But in the wake of the anti-militarist reaction which set in immediately after victory, lessons were not properly drawn, and the lead which Britain had established in the area of mechanised warfare was soon lost. Despite producing two of the century's foremost military thinkers, Major General J.F.C. Fuller and Captain Basil Liddell Hart, the army did not keep abreast of contemporary technical developments. In marked contrast to the German army, which remained much more willing to tolerate outspoken officers with new ideas of warfare,[83] it appeared to revert to its more reactionary pre-war mentality. A training memorandum of 1927 warned that, 'We must not allow the threat of action by a mechanised enemy to upset all our preconceived notions of war.'[84] Two years before the outbreak of the Second World War, Lord Gort, Chief of the Imperial General Staff, told Liddell Hart that 'We mustn't upset the people in the clubs by moving too fast.'[85] At the outset of the Second World War therefore not only the equipment but the 'tactical doctrines and habits of mind of the British Army – particularly in the field of armoured and anti-armoured capability and philosophy – made them largely unfit for modern war'.[86] This in turn is reflected in the army's poor performance in the earlier years of the conflict.[87]

The other and more obvious factor underlying the army's weakness was underfunding. The protection historically provided by the Channel created a bias towards underinsurance, which meant a reluctance on the part of politicians and the electorate to pay for large peacetime forces. Increased defence budgets were a politically sensitive issue for a Liberal government bent on social reform in the years before the First World War. Military spending was even more unpopular after 1918. The 'Ten Year Rule', under which planning was premised on the absence of major war for a decade, was initially adopted in 1919 in what Brian Bond describes as 'confused circumstances without the full participation of Service Ministers or their professional advisers and at a time when the international situation was still in a state of flux'.[88] It could of course be argued, as Churchill did in 1921, that 'before a great war can come there must be a period where the antagonisms of the principal nations will be revealed, and then as a precautionary measure', Britain could strengthen its services.[89] German forces had been substantially disarmed under the terms of the Versailles treaty, the army having been reduced to 100 000 men. In the event it took six years before Hitler was in a position to launch a major military operation in Europe. But Churchill underestimated the difficulties of rapid rearmament under modern conditions.

Some of these were technical. The further defence industries were run down, the longer it took to rebuild factories and assembly lines. But much of course also depended here on the resources made available, and here the quite unprecedented scale of simultaneous threats from Hitler in central Europe, Mussolini in the Mediterranean and the increasingly assertive policy pursued by Japan in the Far East, helped to throw policy makers off balance. Britain did not have the resources to fight this line-up. Its population was some 47 million, compared with Germany's 67 million (prior to the *Anschluss* with Austria and the absorption of the Sudetenland). Steel production in 1937 of 13 million tonnes compared with Germany's 20 million. Germany produced twice as many machine tools as Britain, while capital goods production exceeded that of Britain and France combined. A further particular concern for the Treasury was Britain's ability to finance purchases from abroad. In July 1939, it was warning that financial weakness would make victory impossible.[90]

The other handicaps which Churchill had failed to foresee were political and psychological. The government was reluctant to court electoral unpopularity by moving far ahead of public opinion. The Prime Minister, Stanley Baldwin, had been badly scarred by the result of the 1934

East Fulham by-election, in which the Conservative candidate, who had advocated rearmament, was defeated. Ahead of the November 1935 general election, when he tried to assure voters that there would be no return to great armaments, political considerations came first.[91] But if one of Britain's most serious defence deficiences, as the first Defence Requirement's Committee Report (which had been set up to review the state of defences in 1933) noted, was the 'moral disarmament' of the population,[92] the underlying difficulty handicapping the British ability to respond with the rapidity and ruthlessness which the Nazi threat required, as well as the confusion which characterised British policy in the 1930s, was demoralisation. Governments of the period succumbed to a mood of national fatalism, which made it next to impossible to see beyond the immediate dangers and crises.[93] The situation as it would actually unfold, with Britain standing defiantly alone in 1940 and the USA driven to its support as a matter of basic American self-interest, was beyond ministerial imagination. This was a world still living in the shadow of the trenches, in which the very idea of war struck horror.

To Baldwin war was the 'most fearful terror and prostitution of man's knowledge that ever was known'.[94] In Parliament in 1935, he spoke of being 'almost physically sick', while studying air raid precautions to think that nearly two thousand years after the Crucifixion we should be spending time thinking 'how we can get the mangled bodies of children to the hospital and how we can keep the poison gas from going down the throats of the people'.[95] Another war would mean the final breakdown of civilisation.

It was a world too which, in the aftermath of the Depression, conspicuously lacked the resolution which subsequently infused the war effort. The mood is epitomised by Baldwin's blunt assertion in 1933 that 'the bomber would always get through'. There was, as Churchill remarked in response, 'the same kind of helplessness and hopelessness about dealing with this air problem, as there is about dealing with the unemployment problem, or the question of the economy. Why,' he continued – and this was in fact only two years before the discovery of radar – 'should we fear the air? We have as good technical knowledge as any country.'[96] Delay did not cost Britain the war. The substantial progress made in air defence in the late 1930s ensured that Britain managed, if by a narrow margin, to win its most important battle in 1940. But British policy conceded Hitler strategically valuable assets in the form of the Rhineland and the Czech arms industry, and, perhaps more important, time. Hitler was given six years to build up his forces, as well as the opportunity to test them during the *Anschluss* with Austria in 1938 and the campaign against Poland in 1939. By 1941, the Wehrmacht was proficient and strong enough to overrun most of the continent.

Whether earlier attempts to confront him would have resulted in a more limited war, most obviously at the time of the reoccupation of the Rhineland which Hitler undertook with a minimum of reserves, and whether this in turn would have allowed Britain to retain its status as a Great Power, is a natural but ultimately unprofitable question.[97] The political option never existed. Churchill would certainly have moved more quickly and decisively against Hitler. He was much more conscious of the German leader's aggressive nature than Chamberlain, much less sensitive to the burden of British economic weakness. But until 1939, the critics of Chamberlain's policy were very much in the minority. It was Chamberlain who was in tune with public opinion, and it was not until war finally broke out that Churchill was able to return to government. The causes of the underpreparedness of the 1930s, the most serious and comprehensive failure of policy of the century, were deep-rooted, going well beyond the responsibility of Chamberlain, Halifax and the supporters of Appeasement in the Foreign Office. As Ernest Bevin remarked in 1941, 'If anyone asks me who was responsible for the British policy leading up to the war, I will, as a Labour man myself make a confession and say, "All of us." We refused absolutely to face the facts.'[98] 'Somehow,' writes the historian Williamson Murray, 'British society in the widest sense failed to meet the challenges of the 1930s.'[99]

Before concluding this assessment of the strategic record, we need to look at two other military problems which arose during the process of decolonisation. From the military, and to some extent a political, point of view the Falklands campaign was a considerable success. British prestige, as indeed national morale, rose as a result of a difficult operation. But this was an avoidable war,[100] which left Britain with an unwelcome long-term military commitment in the South Atlantic. Successive British governments would have preferred to negotiate a compromise with Argentina over these remote and underpopulated territories. But they found their path blocked by determined opposition from a small but powerful parliamentary lobby, who managed to turn the islands into the equivalent of what one official later described as 'a village in Kent'.[101] Their gut resistance was reinforced by a feeling again recognisable from the time of Suez, of not being prepared to be 'pushed around'.[102] Principle too was very much at stake in the form of the right of the islanders to determine their own future.[103]

Ministers were thus left with a politically difficult, though by no means impossible position. The problem was that they were willing neither to step up the defence of the Falklands at a time when the overall defence budget was under pressure, nor to expend domestic political capital to resolve an issue which was not recognised as being urgent.[104] As one senior official later put it, 'the only time when one would really get a British Cabinet to *focus* on the issue was at a time when it was manifestly going to cause real difficulty if they did not'[105] (emphasis in original). Policy was thus allowed to drift. In this state of 'general Micawberism',[106] warning signs of increasing Argentinean restiveness were missed. When British territory was suddenly seized, a major political crisis broke in Britain. A task force was immediately sent to the South Atlantic by an angry Prime Minister, supported by an angry nation, despite the advice of the Ministry of Defence that, once seized, the islands could not be retaken, and before the full scale of the problems of the operation had been realised.[107] The analogy with Suez, however, cannot be taken any further. This time Britain had international law, and the Americans, on its side. This time it won. The Falklands provides an unusual combination of political weakness and military strength.

The case of Rhodesia, by contrast, only reflects weakness. Rhodesia was one of Britain's few settler colonies, and could draw on a good deal of public sympathy in Britain, not least in the British armed forces. Its unilateral declaration of independence in 1965 came at a time when military manpower was in short supply – conscription had now ended – and when the new Labour government which had come to power a year earlier had a wafer-thin majority. Military action would have been difficult and divisive. Michael Stewart, Foreign Secretary at the time, suggests that the Boer war might have provided a potential and unhappy analogy.[108] What is more surprising is that no attempt was made to put any military pressure on the Rhodesian armed forces, who owed their loyalty to the Crown, to bolster Britain's unsuccessful efforts to negotiate a settlement.[109] Wilson explicitly ruled out the possible use of force and UDI dragged on for fourteen years, creating friction within the Commonwealth and undermining British prestige and self-confidence.

The foreign policy of a Great Power, or any power claiming a prominent place in the international system, depends ultimately on the extent to which it can be backed up by force. What was striking in the British case was not simply the range of military activities undertaken, from the great battles of the two world wars to counterinsurgency and peacekeeping, but the continuity of military activity. The operations at the end of the century were different from those earlier in the period. They were undertaken in cooperation with allies or the UN, and were 'internationalist' rather than imperial. Most of them were on a relatively limited scale, though some 46 000 troops were deployed during the 1991 Gulf war, and Britain would have been prepared to provide 54 000 for a ground invasion of Kosovo had that proved necessary.[110] But the fact remains that military activity did not appear to reduce visibly as a result of the withdrawal of the bases or international decline.

Striking too are the contrasts: defeat at Dunkirk followed immediately afterwards by victory in the Battle of Britain, the crudity of British strategy on the Western Front contrasted with the sophistication of many small-scale imperial, post-imperial and 'internationalist' actions. The problems were most serious in the first part of the century, and were by no means confined to Whitehall. The army was unimaginative and slow to adapt to change. But it was handicapped by public reluctance to support the necessary levels of military preparedness, which in turn raises the problem familiar from previous chapters, of the failure of ministers to provide the necessary lead to public opinion. Ministers can also be faulted for not thinking military problems through: Gallipoli, the intervention in the Russian civil war and Suez, being the prime examples. No less important was the failure to provide adequate supervision of military planning. On only one occasion before the outbreak of war in 1914 did the Committee for Imperial Defence discuss matters of grand strategy, and little or no attempt seems to have been made to probe the assumptions which underpinned the planning for the establishment of the first British Expeditionary Force.[111]

Over the years lessons were learned. The army learned how to keep down its losses in the Second World War[112] and adapted to new technology after 1945; it learned much about peacekeeping as a result of Ulster. By the 1990s, Britain possessed what President Chirac once called 'the best small army in the world'.[113] Military preparedness in the postwar years was much more satisfactory than it had been in the first half of the century. But the margins often remained thin. Overstretch remained a constant problem. Confrontation with Malaysia in the 1960s 'a miracle of improvisation.'[114] Three decades later the Kosovo war revealed serious defects in equipment. In the final analysis the main weakness of British military policy throughout the period remained the overreliance on that celebrated capacity for improvisation and muddling through.

This provided an essential safety net against the consequences of political failure and underpreparedness. But it also ensured that the ultimate costs of protecting British interests would be significantly higher than they might have been. It is impossible to compute the cumulative costs incurred as a result of the various forms of underpreparedness which characterised British policy prior to the two world wars. What is clear is that certainly in the two major conflicts in which Britain was engaged, high cost made for ambiguous victories in which military success was heavily qualified by long-term political failure.

6
The Sound Barrier

Of all the problems facing British policy makers during the twentieth century, none was more painful and disagreeable than what a 1962 State Department brief described as the 'shift from major to lesser power status'.[1] The attempt to retain Britain's status as a Great Power continued for approximately a quarter of a century – from the defeat of Germany and Japan in 1945 to the final withdrawal from East of Suez in 1971. Even then the loss was not finally conceded. Although Edward Heath spoke of Britain as a 'medium Power of the first rank', he saw EEC membership as a way back to Great Power status.[2] The reversal of British decline and restoration of its international status was a central theme of Mrs Thatcher's premiership.[3] While Tony Blair spoke a different language, specifically eschewing reference to Britain as a Great Power, the underlying spirit of his comments often seemed remarkably similar to that of his predecessor's.[4]

This drawn-out crisis of status had been precipitated by the Second World War, which finally mobilised the military potential of the two powers in the world with substantially larger economic and population bases. By 1945, it was clear that Britain was no longer in the same league as the United States and the Soviet Union. Britain was never a superpower (though William Fox, who first coined the term the year before the explosion of the first atomic bomb, did class Britain as one).[5] The facts in terms of economic strength, and numbers of divisions, were too obvious to ignore. In 1938, the British armed forces had been slightly larger than those of the Americans. In 1945, Britain had 4.68 million men under arms compared with the Americans' 12.13 million. In 1939, the USAAF had 2177 aircraft against the RAF's 1911. In 1945, the relative figures were 63715 American to 8752 British.[6] Small wonder if Churchill spoke of a small British lion accompanying a large American eagle and

Russian bear, or if senior Foreign Office officials saw Britain occupying Lepidus's role in the triumvirate with Mark Anthony and Augustus Caesar.[7]

The long-term implications were rather more controversial. For some, very much a minority, the writing was clearly on the wall. Thus the 1949 Harwood committee, set up to examine how defence spending could be kept to £700 m., concluded that, while there was no insuperable difficulty in designing a balanced modern force within this budgetary limit, 'its size may well be deemed insufficient to support in peace the position in the world which we desire to occupy and provide in war a contribution to the Allied effort commensurate with that position'.[8] The same year, Sir Henry Tizard argued that Britain should give up production of nuclear weapons. 'We are not a Great Power and never will be again. We are a great nation. But if we continue to behave like a Great Power we shall soon cease to be a great nation.'[9] The Prime Minister too had been prepared to toy with some radical measures. 'In the changed circumstances of the world, and in the modern conditions of three dimensional warfare,' Attlee wrote in 1946:

> it is, I think, necessary to view with an open mind strategic conceptions which have held for many years. In the present era we must consider very carefully how to make the most of our limited resources. We must not, for sentimental reasons, give hostages to fortune. It may be we shall have to consider the British Isles as an easterly extension of a strategic area the centre of which is the American continent than [*sic*] as a Power looking eastwards through the Mediterranean and the East.[10]

His proposal for withdrawal from large parts of the Middle East, however, was blocked by the determined opposition of Bevin and the chiefs of staff. By the early 1950s, the immediate economic crisis created by the war had eased. But the imbalance between resources and commitments of a country spending nearly 12 per cent of its gross national product on defence – the figure had shot up dramatically as a result of the Korean war – remained a constant source of concern. Rigorous maintenance of present commitments, Eden warned in 1952, placed a burden on the economy 'which is beyond the resources of the country'.[11] While defence spending declined, the theme was to be reiterated over the next sixteen years.

No Foreign Secretary or Prime Minister, however, was ultimately willing to accept the logical conclusions of British weakness. If Britain was no longer a power of the first rank, it was and remained until the late 1950s and early 1960s the world's Number Three Power, and it was determined to stay that way. Exactly what was meant by being a Great Power, the term normally used, was in typically English fashion, not spelled out. 'I do not think I need discuss the exact definition of a Great Power,' Lord Franks had remarked in the 1954 BBC Reith Lecture:

> We all have a good idea. A nation which is a Great Power has a certain range of choice and manoeuvre in world affairs and can take an effective part in the great decisions which affect the course of history. The action of a Great Power can decisively shape the fate of other Great Powers.[12]

But from Bevin, who in May 1947 declared 'that His Majesty's Government do not accept the view...that we have ceased to be a great Power',[13] to Wilson, who in his first speech as Prime Minister in 1964 declared that 'whatever we do in the fields of cost effectiveness, value for money and stringent view of expenditure, we cannot afford to relinquish our world role',[14] the message was the same. It was not altered by Suez even though Britain's treatment at the hands of the USA was clearly not that of a Great Power.[15] Indeed, it was only in the late 1960s, when economic crisis became critical, that government and country reluctantly came to realise that, in the words of the Duncan Report set up in the wake of the decision to withdraw from East of Suez, Britain was now only 'a major Power of the second order'.[16]

This was wholly unsurprising. All Britain's reflexes were those of a country used to greatness. To quote Lord Franks again, it was not 'a belief arrived at after reflection by a conscious decision. It is part of the habit and furniture of our minds; a principle so much one with our outlook and character that it determines the way we act without emerging itself into clear consciousness'.[17] Sean Greenwood puts it somewhat differently, describing British policy makers as the product 'of a society with a fixation for rank. In much the same way that they would disdain identification as a third-(or even second-) class brain, British leaders deplored the possibility that their country might become what was so often so dismissively termed a "minor" Power.'[18] To men of Churchill's and Eden's generation it was inconceivable that Britain, which had just been part of the coalition which directed and won the Second World War, should not have an independent and probably dominant voice on every major international issue.[19] British leaders did not quite echo de Gaulle's claim that 'France cannot be France without greatness', though they sometimes seemed close to doing so.[20] Being a Great Power was part of their self-image and an important source of national self-esteem. It conferred on the country as a whole, and on its elite and its Prime Minister in particular, a considerable sense of importance. The buzz of being at the centre of world events was – and indeed still is – much appreciated, not least in No.10 Downing Street.

The converse of this proposition was at least as important. Great Powers resign their status as reluctantly as great prime ministers resign their office. Writing to Eisenhower a few months after his reluctant retirement in 1955, Churchill referred to 'a strange and formidable experience laying down responsibility and letting the trappings of power fall in a heap to the ground'.[21] 'The status barrier is as difficult to break through as the sound barrier,' Richard Crossman noted immediately after the final decisions on East of Suez withdrawal had been made. 'It splits your ears and it's terribly painful when it happens.'[22] But it was not only that pride was hurt. There was also the fear of those who harked back to Kipling's 'What do they know of England who only England know?'[23] that Britain was losing an essential part of itself. The British were a great people primarily because of the things they had done outside their own island. To move back within these insular confines would condemn them to become a 'another Netherlands', 'a sort of poor man's Sweden'. This might not be a widely held view, but it was held by some of the men involved in the decisions of the time.[24]

The desire to believe that Britain was still a Great Power, one of the most persistent examples of wishful thinking in British foreign policy, and a clear case of heart triumphing over head, is by no means the only explanation for residual power being overestimated for a twenty-year period. But it is one of the most compelling, not least because it helped to tilt the balance in favour of a more optimistic reading of Britain's prospects. *Pace* Tizard and the Harwood committee, the optimists could make a case. The Second World War was not read at the time as the 'ambivalent' victory it was later proved to be. Winning against the odds had led Britain to regain much of the self-confidence lost in the 1930s, and this in turn made it easier to write off immediate economic weakness as a temporary phenomenon. As Lord Plowden later wrote:

> We had come to believe that our industry had proved itself in wartime to be more efficient than German industry. We could see that much of the industry of continental Europe had been severely damaged. This country was the largest industrial producer in Western Europe in the years immediately following the war and, although

we knew that our productivity was only about a third of that of the United States, we could still believe that we were economically a world power. Because our wartime management had been successful we thought we knew better than most how a country and an economy should be run.[25]

Britain retained an important place in the international financial system; in 1956, sterling financed half the world's trade and payments.[26] It was still an Imperial Power, with all the economic advantages this was believed to confer. 'If only we pushed on and developed Africa,' Bevin remarked to the Chancellor of the Exchequer, Hugh Dalton, 'we could have US dependent on us, and eating out of our hand, in four or five years.'[27]

A decade later, Britain's power base had clearly weakened. The talk now was increasingly of influence rather than power. But, as the 1960 'Future Policy Study' underscored, Britain still retained substantial connections and assets:

> Our leadership of the Commonwealth, the progressive fulfilment of our Colonial responsibilities, our special relationship with the United States, our European associations, the legacy of our Imperial past, the maturity of our experience outside Europe, our national quality of rising to an emergency and our reliability in the defence of freedom and justice: all these can continue to justify for the United Kingdom a leading position among the Powers and a higher place in their counsels than our material assets alone would strictly warrant.[28]

Yet if this, in the light of hindsight seems obviously overstated, the fact also remain that decline seems more inevitable in retrospect than it did at the time. The simple and much used word hides a complex, incremental process in which the dramatic failure symbolised by Suez was the exception rather than the rule. Economic growth rates in the post-war years were higher than they had been for much of the earlier part of the century.[29] The economy was judged in 1960 to have recovered well since the Second World War. Industrial and technological resources were better attuned to world demand 'than for a very long time'.[30] It was only gradually that the relative weakness of performance *vis-à-vis* Britain's main competitors, became evident. In 1952, Britain's gross national product outstripped that of France, West Germany and Japan. Ten years later, West Germany had overtaken Britain. By 1972, the British figure of 128 billion dollars lagged well behind France ($224 billion), West Germany ($229 billion) and Japan ($317 billion).[31] The problem was no longer of course that these were rivals who would translate economic wealth into military muscle. But in an age in which growth rates were increasingly competing with military power as symbols of international success, the growing discrepancy began to sap self-confidence and morale. And there were also more direct economic consequences. Relatively poor performance accentuated the vulnerability of sterling, whose weakness in turn reduced the country's ability to maintain defence spending.

This mattered because it was becoming more expensive to stay in the top military league. The rapid pace of technological advance was substantially raising the costs of weaponry, and the research and development which produced it. Britain could afford the first generation nuclear delivery system based on bomber aircraft. By 1960, however, it was evident that it no longer felt itself in a position to stay in the forefront of the nuclear arms race. Blue Streak, a land-based, liquid-fuelled missile, threatened to be obsolescent before it was deployed, and with nuclear cooperation with the USA restored after the repeal of the MacMahon Act, the government opted for an American-made alternative (Skybolt).[32] It was a decision of historic significance. For the first time, as one MP pointed out in the subsequent parliamentary debate, Britain was dropping out of a major military development.[33] To make matters worse, the British deterrent was becoming very visibly overshadowed in an age of nuclear and thermonuclear overkill. The Americans, the former Defence Minister, Anthony Head noted in the same debate, 'spend £4,350 million. We spend, perhaps 3 or 4 per cent of that figure. We spend three counters to their hundred. After five years, we would have spent fifteen counters to their 500. We have too small a stake at this vast poker game to think that we will influence policy as an atomic Power.'[34]

This rapid undermining of Britain's new-found nuclear power (the first nuclear test had only taken place in 1952) was only one part of a larger and more disturbing picture. Britain was not only falling militarily and technically behind the superpowers. As the political aftershocks of the Second World War continued to make themselves felt well into the 1950s, it was also losing ground *vis-à-vis* two other groupings. One was Afro-Asian nationalism. The optimistic assumptions about Britain's long-term future of the late 1940s had been partly based on the belief that Indian independence had not established an early precedent for the rest of the Empire and that military bases could be retained. But Ghanaian independence in 1957 began the process of the unravelling of empire in Africa, while the problem of bases proved much more intractable than had been anticipated. Meanwhile in Europe the pace of economic recovery, and the anti-nationalist reaction to the two world wars, were taking their toll on Britain's standing. The successful formation of the EEC, the re-emergence of de Gaulle in 1958 and the Franco-German reconciliation he promoted, combined with the undeftness of British policy, seriously undermined Britain's standing. The leading position it had occupied in the late 1940s, and even the early 1950s, was permanently lost.

Individually, all of these factors were recognised. The problem was pulling the strands together, a task for which, as noted in Chapter 1,Whitehall was neither organisationally nor culturally well equipped. Its preference for dealing with issues on a case-by-case basis made it difficult to take the necessary overview. The cumulative impact of the precedent set by the granting of independence to a colony here, the loss of a base there, and the cancellation of a weapon system, were not immediately recognised. Officials and ministers concentrated on the immediate issue, not just as a matter of pragmatic temperament but because the sheer pressure of events did not give them time to do otherwise. As Sir Frederick Hoyar-Millar, one of several PUSes of the period to make the point, later told an interviewer:

> One was always being distracted by the day-to-day horrors – having worries about what the Russians were going to do, trying to align one's attitudes with the Americans *and* the French, all sorts of horrors in the Middle East, in Cyprus, in the Far East too. Purely administrative problems take a hell of a long time.

> You may have had a short Cabinet committee meeting perhaps, and they would get side-tracked into deciding whether to send troops into Jordan or something like that. That's the whole trouble. All these things that ought to have been looked at from the long-term point of view, carefully weighing out where our interests lay – then you always get side-tracked by some immediate decision on oil or something. There probably should have been some clearly preconceived plan, but I don't believe there was.[35]

In fact the problem appears to have been less the lack of planning, than the failure of the planners to foresee the pace of change or come up with radical alternatives. The mid- and late 1950s were a period of almost constant review. The most radical, in terms of impact, were those in the defence field, where the lead-time for decisions were long, and the pressure of resources was acute. The strategic implications of the H bomb and the belief expressed in a joint memorandum of March 1956 by the Foreign Secretary, Harold Macmillan and the Defence Minister, Sir Walter Monckton, that 'at present we are spending a great deal of money to provide defences that are not effective, and in some important respects are little more than a facade', led to the 1957 Sandys Defence Review, which abolished conscription and put heavy emphasis on nuclear deterrence.[36] Macmillan's 'Audit of Empire' of the same year helped prepare the groundwork for the later withdrawal from Africa.[37]

On the broader foreign policy front rather less was achieved. A 1958 review that was commissioned to consider the 'extent of the authority' Britain hoped to continue to exert in world affairs, and the means at its disposal for doing so, proved disappointing.[38] A year later a new and much more far-reaching ten-year review was commissioned by Macmillan and the Cabinet Secretary, Sir Norman Brook, which sought to try and transcend the normal limitations of Whitehall thinking. The members of its Working Group were specifically exhorted to be bold and imaginative and get outside 'the range of ordinary Departmental doctrine'.[39] This, as Sir John Coles notes, was strategic and long-term planning at the highest level.[40] But while the very detailed studies which emerged did point to a decline in Britain's relative position in the world by 1970, the overall conclusion was not unduly discouraging. Britain's 'status need not necessarily decline correspondingly'. Influence 'need not shrink in proportion to our material strength'.[41]

Given such relatively optimistic prognoses, the reaction to decline was one of adjustment rather than radical change of direction. There were cut-backs and rationalisations, a growing emphasis on the role of allies and the shift from quantity in the sense of power, to quality in the sense of influence and superior statecraft. But there was little new thinking about the kind of role which Britain could realistically hope to play in the future. 'Role' was not in fact a term British policy makers usually used. It was brought into general currency by Dean Acheson's famous and much resented jibe of 1962, that Britain had lost an empire but failed to find a role. This, however, simply articulated a problem which policy makers had long sensed. A variety of ideas had been floated since the Second World War. Bevin had toyed with the idea of Britain as the leader of a 'Third Force', a union 'including not only the countries of western Europe but also their Colonial possessions in Africa and the East; this would form a *bloc* which, both in population and productive capacity, could stand on an equality with the western hemisphere and the Soviet *blocs*'.[42] But it was quickly evident that this was little more than a pipe-dream.

A more lasting concept, and the nearest approximation to a big idea to emerge in the post-war years, came not from a government minister, but from the leader of the Opposition. 'As I look out upon the future of our country in the changing scene of human destiny,' Churchill declared in 1948,

> I feel the existence of three great circles among the free nations and democracies...The first circle for us is naturally the British Commonwealth and Empire, with all that comprises. Then there is also the English-speaking world in which we, Canada and the other British Dominions, and the United States play so important a part. And finally there is United Europe. These three majestic circles are co-existent and if they are linked together there is no force or combination which could overthrow them or even challenge them. Now if you think of the three interlinked circles you will see that we are the only country which has a great part in every one of them. We stand in fact at the very point of junction and here is the island at the very centre of the seaways and perhaps of the airways too; we have the opportunity of joining them all together.[43]

Such thinking made sense in 1948, when Britain was still basking in the afterglow of military victory. Britain *was* uniquely well-connected. The Commonwealth had just proved its potential military significance, having made a substantial contribution to the war effort. Britain's prestige in Europe was high and cooperation was still safely (from the British point of view) confined to the intergovernmental level. At the same time Britain was reviving much of its wartime intimacy with the USA. The Atlantic connection, so conspicuously absent before the Second World War, was a major new asset. The sheer diversity of its connections seemed an obvious source of strength for Britain to capitalise on.

But how was policy to do this? These were unequal circles to which Britain attached unequal weight. Instinctively, Britain leaned towards the two Anglo-Saxon circles. Yet, while the power of the Americans was self-evident, that of the Commonwealth was not. Officially, the Commonwealth remained for most of the 1950s as an essential prop of British world power, and in 1955 when officials examined the case for British membership of a European Common Market, Commonwealth considerations were a major factor in their opposition to the idea.[44] Given lesser British antipathy to the idea of engagement with continental Europe, as well as a clearer appreciation of the declining economic and political importance of the Commonwealth, more might have been made of the range of opportunities which Churchill had identified. As it was, Britain failed to solve the problem of how rhetoric might be translated into reality.

By the late 1950s, as more and more countries in the Indian Ocean region gained independence, a more narrowly based alternative emerged. 'The legacy of sites, influence and interests all around the world from the old days of the Pax Britannica,' remarked *The Observer* in 1958, 'makes our potential contribution, both political and material, uniquely apt and great. Instead of either seeking to become a super-power ourselves, or retreating into being merely a corner of Europe, Britain's proper role is as a world influence in the capacity of landlord turned bailiff.'[45] This was a classic example of the British approach of the period – evolutionary change in its old stamping ground – the term 'East of Suez' came from Kipling. Britain would maintain 'stability', a much-used if ill-defined term, in the Gulf and Indian Ocean, to protect its economic interests, as a specifically British contribution to containing communist influence and, under the Labour government, as an exercise in international peacekeeping. It was a role, in other words, which lent itself to a variety of interpretations, both realistic and idealistic.

Both were appealing, but the rhetoric, reflecting perhaps the overly self-conscious attempt to find a rationale for a role which did not long escape critical scrutiny, was sometimes overblown, Wilson's reference in the wake of the 1962 Chinese attack on India to Britain's frontiers being on the Himalayas, being the most obvious example. More important, the role never seems to have been properly costed, while the foreign policy goals which the East of Suez presence was intended to serve were not clearly defined.[46] For all the formal rationalisations advanced, the underlying motives had as much to do with the preoccupation with status, along with the atavistic appeal which the despatch of military expeditionary forces to 'far-way, often seemingly-exotic places' seemed to exercise, as with the protection of British interests.[47] In a more affluent era this would not have been a problem. Against the economic problems of the mid- and late 1960s, such sentimental motives were no longer sufficient.

Other ideas of role which were advanced were more inchoate. They focused upon attempts to capitalise on a combination of prestige, experience and connections. The most famous, if arrogant, formulation was Macmillan's notion of Britain playing the role of the civilising

'Greeks' in uncouth America's 'Roman' empire. On a more general level, there was the attempt to play what one commentator referred to as the role of 'a kind of international *éminence grise*'.[48] Britain in the nuclear age could establish, to quote Macmillan again, 'a position of authority as the chief source of moral inspiration in the world'. It would be a peace-maker and mediator – not just between East and West, but between America and Europe, and between the Afro-Asian and older-established countries.[49] Twenty years later, James Callaghan, outlined a similar scenario:

> We have country by country connections throughout the world. We have the experience. In my opinion *we have the policy* which can enable Britain to make a contribution out of all proportion to our individual size and power to the problems facing the world. In these circumstances we may have found the role – for Britain which ... Dean Acheson asserted we had lost with our empire. We are the bridge builders [original emphasis].[50]

At the end of the century, Tony Blair was to make much the same point. Britain was 'the bridge between the United States and Europe', a 'pivotal' power.[51]

The implications of these failures to evaluate the pace of decline more accurately, and identify a realistic new role, were disturbing. For some twenty-five years, British foreign policy was based on overestimation of British power and an overambitious set of goals. This goes a long way to explaining why the mid-1950s witnessed some of the most serious mistakes of the post-war period. Suez, Messina, the build-up of the Cyprus and Aden bases, were all premised on the belief that Britain was and could remain a Great Power. The mood and assumptions varied. The withdrawal from the Brussels talks in November 1955 reflected an unreflective complacency about Britain's international prospects. Suez, by contrast, has an element of desperation about it, a sudden raging against the dying of the imperial light. But like the decisions about the future of strategic bases, they were the choices of men who believed that, to use Churchill's words, Britain should not be content to be 'relegated to a tame and minor role in the world'.[52]

Another area where Britain tended to overplay its hand was the succession of attempts by Churchill, Eden and Macmillan to resurrect the medium of summit diplomacy. This would clearly establish Britain's claim to a seat at the 'top table', particularly if, as Macmillan hoped, the summits were established as annual affairs, analogous to the nineteenth-century Congress system.[53] The danger with this policy was that it exaggerated the prospects for substantive progress at a stage of the Cold War when neither of the main protagonists was yet ready to do serious business with the other, and created, certainly in Britain, unrealistic expectations. Occasionally prime ministers would admit to the temptation of wishful thinking. Evelyn Shuckburgh recounts a revealing exchange with Eden, by then Prime Minister, after the 1955 Geneva Summit:

> He said that his own private view was that the Russians were looking ahead, and saw in ten or twenty years a very strong China to the east of them and a perhaps very strong Germany to the west, and were looking out for someone to hold their hands a little. They could not expect anything from America, and they saw that the French were no use, so they were looking to us. I said this was a gratifying thought – just the sort of role we should like to play – to which he replied that perhaps it was only wishful thinking.[54]

This, however, was an unusual moment of candour. The Cabinet minutes on Macmillan's return from his 1959 Moscow visit record the dubious verdict that 'Effectively, the leadership of the Western world now rested with the United Kingdom government.'[55] The view did not survive the collapse of the 1960 Paris summit following revelations of the American U2 reconnaissance flights over the Soviet Union, which highlighted the underlying British weakness which Macmillan's summit diplomacy was trying to disguise. Rather than being seen as indispensable to an East–West settlement – playing the role of international *éminence grise* – it was clear, not least to Macmillan himself, that Britain did not have the power to bring the two sides together. As his influential private secretary, Philip de Zulueta, later put, it, 'this was the moment he suddenly realised that Britain counted for nothing; he couldn't move Ike to make a gesture towards Khrushchev, and de Gaulle was simply not interested'.[56]

Preoccupation with status is also evident in a number of projects justified as much in terms of prestige as of their security or other value. The maintenance of the Sterling Area comes into this category, as does the determination, only gradually abandoned in the late 1950s and early 1960s, that Britain should develop and produce its own military equipment, rather than taking the cheaper option of buying from abroad.[57] Above all, there was the question of nuclear weapons. The decision to develop first, nuclear, and then, in 1954, thermonuclear weapons, was very much a Great Power reflex. These were the latest and most powerful weapons. Britain would acquire them as a matter of course.[58] By the mid-1950s, however, the arguments for nuclear weapons were increasingly beginning to reflect weakness rather than strength. Nuclear weapons compensated for decline. As a report from the British embassy in Washington, written shortly after Suez, noted, 'Our acceptance as a Great Power now, rests to a large extent on our having a military nuclear programme . . . it would be difficult to overestimate at this juncture the importance of our having megaton as well as kiloton weapons.'[59] A rather cruder version of this thesis came from Randolph Churchill, who claimed that Britain's ability to 'knock down' twelve cities in the region of Stalingrad and Moscow made her 'a major power again'.[60] Such sentiments made life easier for the Conservative leadership, providing a smokescreen behind which to make adjustments, such as withdrawal from Africa, which might otherwise have met with greater opposition within the party.[61] By the same token, they served to reinforce an unrealistic view of Britain's place in the world.

The suggestion therefore that Britain might lose its nuclear capability, brought suddenly to the fore by the cancellation of the American Skybolt missile in 1962, precipitated a major crisis in Anglo-American relations. The American account of one session during the sometimes fraught Nassau summit, during which Britain was in fact offered Polaris, tells its own story:

> 'Actually,' said the Prime Minister, 'the whole thing is ridiculous.' What do seven or eight UK units add to the existing nuclear strength, which is enough to blow up the world? So why does the UK want it? It's partly a question of keeping up with the Joneses, which is human. We have not yet reached the point of a melting pot of nations. So countries which have played a great role in history must retain their dignity. This area is not merely a question of difference of degree, but of order. The UK does not want to be just a clown, or a satellite.[62]

The deal reached at Nassau was ambiguous on this score. While Britain gained the much more effective Polaris missile, its dependence on the USA was very publicly reinforced.

The critical subtext of the Skybolt crisis was Britain's economic ability to continue its Great Power role. While ministers were broadly aware of operating very close to the margins of what the country could still afford, they were by no means fully aware of all the costs. This was particularly true of attempts to maintain the reserve role of sterling, which Susan Strange ascribes to what she calls 'top currency syndrome.'[63] The damaging economic effects of high levels of defence expenditure, which in 1959 were still running at 8.4 per cent of GDP, were by contrast much more widely recognised.[64] Status was not of course the only consideration here. Britain was engaged in a long-term confrontation with the Soviet Union, in which the ability to sustain high levels of defence spending would, as the events of the late 1980s proved, eventually be crucial. But it is notable that Britain, with its wider international commitments and claims to world status, spent a higher proportion of GNP. on defence than most of its NATO allies.

The exact repercussions of this are open to debate. Peter Hennessy has argued that the consequences of the large rearmament programme sparked by the Korean war 'were enduringly damaging to a British economy still fragile but definitely on-the-turn towards greater vitality and robustness'.[65] Korea on this reading – and the scale of British rearmament was influenced by the desire to strengthen British credentials with the Americans as well as the perceived need to contain a globally expansionist communist threat – helped lose Britain the best opportunity of the post-war years for a sustained export boom. 'With luck,' he writes, this might 'have put the British economy on to a higher and sustainable trajectory before Germany, in particular, recovered to the point where our export markets were once more highly vulnerable.'[66] The argument, however, does not stop with Korea. By pre-empting a disproportionately large amount of research and development and high technology inputs which might otherwise have contributed to economic modernisation and exports, and absorbing large amounts of foreign exchange, defence expenditure served to undermine growth rates over the long term.[67] While obviously too much should not be made of one of a complex of factors contributing to Britain's relative economic underperformance, the larger economic price of Great Power status was greater than Britain could afford.

One final cost of Britain's overambitious foreign policy of the post-war years should be noted. Precisely because Britain had tried so long to hang on to Great Power status and failed to do so, the subsequent reaction in the late 1960s and the 1970s may have been that much greater. The point is difficult to prove. Dramatic failure abroad – de Gaulle's two vetoes, Rhodesia's successful UDI – and the devaluation of sterling coincided with a loss of confidence at home. Traditional values, social as much as imperial ones, were already being challenged at the end of Macmillan's premiership. The subsequent worsening of British economic performance, inflation, growing concern over the power of the trade unions in the late 1960s and early 1970s, and talk about Britain becoming ungovernable only served to reinforce a mood of national self-doubt, in which the notion that Britain could claim to be a Great Power suddenly seemed pretentious and anachronistic.

But it is difficult not also to see an element of overreaction to the ambition of the earlier years, in the new hesitancy in foreign policy which followed the East of Suez withdrawals. The realisation that Britain had lost its long battle to retain Great Power status in which so much by way of material resources and emotional energy had been invested, and become a second-class power inevitably took its toll. There was now a tendency to set ambitions unduly low, with an emphasis on little more than damage limitation.[68] Two American observers catch something of the mood. Raymond Seitz, stationed in the American embassy in London, writes how, in the mid-1970s, the British

> seemed unsure what they really were. But they were pretty sure what they were not. They were not a superpower. Nor were they just a regional power. They were not wholly American in orientation but neither were they entirely European. They were not what they used to be but they weren't what they would yet become.[69]

Henry Kissinger is somewhat harsher in his verdict. British leaders, he writes, while still possessing the experience and intellectual resources of a Great Power, with every passing year 'acted less as if their decisions mattered. They offered advice, usually sage; they rarely sought to embody it in a policy of their own. British statesmen were content to act as honoured consultants to our deliberations'.[70] It was only in the 1980s, with the recovery of the economy and the success of the Falklands campaign, that an activist Prime Minister was able to restore some of the old self-confidence.

Judged against Britain's own objectives, the failure of an important strand of post-war foreign policy is evident. Prestige and resources were wasted in pursuit of the preservation of a Great Power status, which the British economy could not in the event sustain. Policy makers insisted on trying 'to fit new pictures into old frames', thereby restricting their flexibility and losing opportunities to move into fundamentally new directions.[71] Unwilling to face unpalatable facts, they paid an accordingly high price. These were not of course disasters on the scale of the failure to foresee and then adapt more quickly to the revolution in land warfare during the early years of the century, or the policies of the 1930s. While national pride was hurt, no vital interests were endangered. The damage to the economy was one of degree. Despite the high levels of spending on defence and foreign policy, the post-war years saw an unparalleled increase in living standards, with total personal income at constant prices, and after taxation doubling in the years between 1951 and 1975.[72]

The case against policy makers of the quarter century which followed the Second World War needs therefore to be kept in perspective. While they can certainly be faulted for not setting more realistic goals, the damage done was not critical. Criticism also needs to be tempered by a sense of what was politically and, no less important, psychologically possible. How quickly can a proud and still in many respects powerful state adjust to decline? Could any post-war prime minister have abjured Great Power status, thereby effectively ending a two century-long period of British history, before the absence of alternatives became unambiguously clear in the 1960s?

The problems facing officials and ministers from 1945 onwards were a combinaton of recognising the extent of decline, and coming to terms with the fact. They knew that the pursuit of Great Power status was making demands which the economy could barely meet. They were aware that British residual power was ebbing, and that in future Britain would have to rely increasingly on influence and on allies. In an address to British diplomats in 1958, Macmillan drew an analogy between the position of Britain and 'a great land-owner who, faced with high taxation and heavy death duties, declined to give up the old house even though he had to close some of the wings and cut down some of the trees'.[73] Sometimes they did ask the really hard questions of exactly how much power was still left, and how long it would be expected to last. But they did not appear to have the time to consider the answers when these were given, and were in any case undisposed to accept starkly negative prognoses, which could be too readily dismissed as defeatist. Their tenacious assumption that Britain was, and could remain, a Great Power was a matter not just of habit, as Lord Franks put it in 1954, but also an act of faith. The alternative was too unpalatable and, in the words of another senior official, Sir Roger Makins, too 'intolerable' to contemplate.[74] Accepting what was in effect second class citizenship in the international system, breaking Crossman's 'sound barrier', was very difficult.

One way of coping was to deal with decline on a piecemeal and incremental basis. Components of the problem, such as the need for decolonisation and nationalist opposition to a particular military base, were manageable both because pragmatic temperament and training helped to impose sensible solutions, and because a piecemeal approach seemed to be limited in its import. The bigger steps – the withdrawal from East of Suez, the reorientation towards Europe – took longer to come to terms with. They also sometimes took new men. Lord Carver quotes the retiring Chief of the Imperial General Staff, Field Marshal Lord Templer, as saying to him in 1958, 'Young man, I know you think most of my ideas are out date. You are probably right and lots of things should be changed; but I was damned if they were going to be changed in my time.'[75] The decision to apply for EEC membership was preceded by a Cabinet reshuffle. The shift from a lack of interest bordering on hostility in the early 1950s to a clear enthusiasm for membership in the Foreign Office twenty years later was accompanied by a generational change among officials.[76]

To these constraints must be added the handicaps imposed by the culture and organisation of the Whitehall machine, whose departmental warriors tended to resolve their battles through the unradical but very British instrument of compromise. And then there were domestic politics. Adjustment was hampered by a paradoxical mixture of a largely tacit support for the Great Power status quo and lack of interest. There was little by way of public debate about where Britain was going prior to the 1961 government decision to try to join the EEC and the growing controversy in the mid- and late 1960s about Britain's role of East of Suez. This, however, meant that policy was not subject to the rigours and stimulus of external critique, rather than that policy makers had a free hand. It was only in the late 1960s, when British weakness had become self-evident and the idea of claiming Great Power status was coming to seem outdated, that politicians were prepared to take the political risk of rewriting national purpose in line with the country's reduced circumstances. This would have been impossible in the immediate aftermath of the war when large-scale withdrawal would have been seen as throwing away the fruits of victory and betraying 'those who fought in the common cause'.[77] Evidence of decline in the 1950s, and the very public reverse Britain suffered at Suez, made the prospect of withdrawal even more difficult.[78] Wilson's championing of Britain's role East of Suez, as also his retention of nuclear weapons, can both be at least partially explained by the fact that they were electorally popular.[79]

At the same time ministers, prime ministers in particular, did relatively little to educate the public to the implications of decline.[80] Churchill had no inclination to do so; Eden, of whom the same is probably true, had not the time.[81] Attlee, like Macmillan, while relatively more realistic, had quite enough difficulty with his immediate colleagues and supporters. But they had all also, as a matter of both necessity and inclination, nailed their colours too firmly to the Great Power mast. An angry entry in Macmillan's diary of July 1959, reacting to Eisenhower's invitation to Khrushchev to visit America, which seemed to cut out Britain's self-appointed intermediary role, underlines the scale of this problem:

> My own position here will be greatly weakened. Everyone will assume that the two Great Powers . . . are going to fix up a deal over our heads and behind our backs. My whole policy – pursued for many years and especially during my Premiership – of close alliance and co-operation with America will be undermined. People will ask, 'Why should U.K. try to stay in the big game? Why should she be a nuclear power? You told us that this would give you power and authority in the world. But you and we have been made fools of. This shows that Gaitskell and Crossman and Co. are right. U.K. had better give up the struggle and accept, as gracefully as possible, the position of a second-rate power.'[82]

The result, to quote Anthony Head again, speaking in the 1960 parliamentary debate on the cancellation of the Blue Streak missile, was that the public did not realise Britain's 'true position in world affairs today. It is unpleasant for the political world to have to explain it, and explain it in the blunt way of taking action that patently demonstrates it.'[83]

Prime ministers from Attlee to Wilson faced a further problem when it came to leading public opinion. Unlike de Gaulle, they had no alternative vision to offer.[84] But the French had two advantages over the British. France looked not to a large and heterogeneous Commonwealth for its post-imperial global status, but to Francophone Africa, where power and resources were concentrated to greater political effect. If a somewhat narrow base, it was more substantive than the broad-brush image of Britain at the centre of three intersecting circles, or the image of a Britain living off its influence and wits, as it had done in the age of Elizabeth I and the Duke of Marlborough, which Macmillan sometimes

promoted. Secondly, of course, the EEC offered France a new and potentially very rewarding set of opportunities. On occasions British policy
makers did talk of taking the lead in Europe, but there is little evidence
that they had any clear idea of what they wanted to do with such a
leadership, other than to bolster Britain's wider claims to Great Power
status.[85] Given this lack of European vocation, it is questionable
whether there was a post-war role which Britain failed to find. It had
values, virtues and connections which gave it a high international
profile. But the phrases 'international *éminence grise*', 'bridge-builders',
the 'pivotal power' did not translate into an identifiable 'role'.

In the final analysis, therefore, it is easier to see *where* Britain could
have been done better, what should and should not have done, rather
than *how*. In an ideal world policy makers would indeed have been more
realistic and far-sighted. As F. S. Northedge observes at the end of *The
Troubled Giant*, his study of British policy in the interwar years:

> If there is any general conclusion to be derived from this record
> perhaps it is that men at all times, and especially when their country's
> power is declining relative to that of others, have a special respons-
> ibility to examine and re-examine the things they take for granted
> about the political world they inhabit. The failure of British policy
> between the two wars was indeed a failure of resources; but it was
> more truly a failure of ideas, or rather a failure to adjust ideas born in
> one age to the requirements of another.[86]

The same could be said of much of the post-war period, characterised as
it often is by unrealistic ambitions and the avoidance of choice.[87] Ministers and officials, as Butler admitted with regard to the EEC, *should*
have been more far-sighted.[88] Yet, valid as these criticisms are, they tend
to overlook the psychology of the period and the disorientation which
the threatened loss of Great Power status engendered. The very circumstances which necessitated the re-examination of assumptions also
served to make it particularly difficult. Decline has its own inertia and
evasions. States, like the individuals who conduct their foreign policy,
need time to discard ideas and policies which they only gradually realise
have become obsolete. This may mean continuing to do things which
others find ridiculous, exposing the country to setbacks and humiliations, and straining the economy. But Britain, unlike France with its
colonial campaigns in Indochina and Algeria, and the spectacular but
overambitious diplomacy pursued by de Gaulle in the mid- and late
1960s, was saved from the most dangerous excesses by its underlying

pragmatism. The jury must still be out on what is still a relatively recent period, the repercussions of which, as will be argued in Chapter 8, have still not fully worked themselves out. Meanwhile, Kenneth Waltz's verdict of the late 1960s seems to stand the test of time:

> Gracefully withdrawing from Empire, phasing out one base while jumping to another, muddling toward Europe, climbing summits in pursuit of a world influence for which the material basis is lacking, substituting the myth of Commonwealth for the reality of Empire: most of these are not inspiring ways of adjusting to decline in a country's international status, but they are benign. Quicker response and bolder movement have often produced worse results.[89]

7
International Impact

Great Powers have, by definition, a disproportionate impact on the international system. In Britain's case, that impact was potentially unusually benign. It was a status quo power with a strong interest in the maintenance of the balance of power, as of international law and order. In one of the classic documents of British foreign policy, written in 1907, a senior Foreign Office official set out the case for the principle of enlightened self-interest which informed, even if it did not always determine, foreign policy. As a maritime power, Eyre Crowe argued, England was 'in the literal sense of the word, the neighbour of every country accessible by sea'. Since its naval supremacy was bound to inspire 'universal jealousy and fear', Britain must harmonise its policies 'with the general desires and ideals common to all mankind,' and identity itself 'with the primary and vital interests of a majority, or as many as possible, of the other nations'. England thus had 'a direct and positive interest' in maintaining the independence of all nations, and must therefore be 'the natural enemy of any country threatening the independence of others and the natural protector of the weaker communities'.[1] Britain's task, remarked the Foreign Secretary, Lord Curzon fourteen years later, was 'to reconcile, not defy; to pacify, not to conquer'.[2]

It was also to try to keep the peace. This, as the Foreign Office memorandum of 1926 cited at the outset of Chapter 1, candidly remarked, was not simply a matter of altruism:

His Majesty's Government cannot lay this unction to their souls. The fact is that war and rumours of war, quarrels and friction, in any corner of the world spell loss and harm to British commercial and financial interests. It is for the sake of these interests that we

endeavour to pour oil on troubled waters. So manifold and ubiqui-
tous are British trade and British finance that, whatever else may be
the outcome of a disturbance of the peace, we shall be losers.[3]

Self-interest however was only part of the story. From 1918 onwards, it
was reinforced by a combination of fear and revulsion of war. 'There is in
the United Kingdom to-day,' a 1938 Chatham House report noted:

> a profound love of peace for its own sake. The British know the
> futility of war as well as any people, and they have no cause since
> 1918 to foster illusions as to its glory. There is a deep moral convic-
> tion, however ill-informed and crudely expressed, behind the great
> volume of popular support for official acts like the signature of the
> Briand–Kellogg Pact for the Renunciation of War, and for unofficial
> organisations that seek to promote international peace and good-
> will.[4]

While this strain becomes more muted after 1945, realisation of Britain's
vulnerability to nuclear and, above all, thermonuclear weapons was
reflected both in the rise of the Campaign for Nuclear Disarmament
(CND) in the mid- and late 1950s and in the policy of the Prime Minister. The American record of a 1959 Anglo-American discussion on the
prospects for an East–West summit records how at one point Macmillan
became

> exceedingly emotional. He said we were dealing with a matter which
> in his judgement affected the whole future of mankind . . . he could
> not take his people into war without trying the Summit first. If war
> was to result there was much that he must do. They had no civil
> defence worthy of the name and this must be rectified. They must
> mobilise and disperse a substantial part of their people to Australia
> and Canada. Eight bombs, the Prime Minister said, would mean 20 or
> 30 million Englishmen dead. Throughout the discussion he kept
> repeating this reference to eight bombs.[5]

To interest and fear must be added ideology and instinct. As a liberal
power, the British had clear ideas about the nature of civilised behaviour
and the ways in which international society should be organised. These
ideas were not always realistic. Liberal thinking on foreign affairs relied
too heavily on the power of goodwill and reason in what was for the
most part an unreasonable world,[6] and in the 1920s and above all the

1930s, this encouraged a dangerous degree of wishful thinking. On the other hand, liberalism softened the impact of British power. It made for restraint in the exercise of force, and helped to ease the way for decolonisation.

Finally, and most ambiguously, there is the element of altruism bred not just from idealism but also ambition, the instinctive British tendency, still evident at the end of the century, to take a lead. There is a sense of international *noblesse oblige* about British foreign policy. As a great and a civilised power, one which believed in tolerance, fair play and the rule of law, the British believed that they had a unique responsibility for the maintenance of international order. 'The British people,' the French embassy reported on 1 September 1939,

> is united...in its determination to oppose any German attempt at domination and to safeguard the essential principles of international morality. It knows it is engaging in an ordeal which will undoubtedly be long and which will require the heaviest sacrifices but it is determined to carry out to the end what it considers to be at once a duty and a mission, not only to its own country but to all civilised nations.[7]

The point recurs. 'It comes naturally to people in Britain,' wrote the historian, Lord Beloff in 1969, 'to feel that if there is something wrong in the world there is some kind of obligation upon Britain to put it right.'[8] Decent people, Douglas Hurd argued in the aftermath of the Cold War, should have a 'sound instinct' to 'make some contribution to working for a more decent world'.[9] The Blair government spoke of Britain as 'a force for good' in the world.[10] But while genuinely felt, such comments need to be read in the context of what Henry Kissinger described as 'ethical egoism', the belief that what was good for Britain, 'was best for the rest'.[11]

So much for potential. To assess the reality of the influence of a declining Power, whose policy was by no means always enlightened and far-sighted, this chapter will look at four key elements of the British record. First and foremost is the British contribution to the maintenance of an international balance of power in the face of the German and Soviet hegemonial challenges. Related, though at times uneasily with this, is Britain's peace diplomacy. Third is the British contribution to the development of the norms and institutions of an emerging international society in the place of predatory *realpolitik* which characterised international relations during the first of the century. Finally there is

Britain's impact, deriving from its status as the premier imperial power, on the stability of the post-colonial order.

Although the main weaknesses of British diplomatic stance *vis a vis* Germany have already been discussed, two additional elements need to be explored. The question of whether Britain could have deterred Germany in July 1914 was much debated in the wake of the First World War. Indeed as late as 1962 Macmillan was arguing to de Gaulle that if Germany 'had known for certain that Britain would fight with France the First World War might not have occurred'.[12] The evidence for the proposition is however suggestive rather than conclusive. The crisis which followed the Sarajevo assassination reflected the new willingness of the German government to take risk, rather than a clear-cut decision to pursue a major European war. An early and clear statement of Britain's intention to intervene, might therefore have swayed opinion in Berlin in favour of restraint, but this was not made and the Chancellor in 1914, Bethmann-Hollweg, failed to appreciate that Britain was bound as a matter of tradition and self-interest to act to maintain the balance of power in Europe. This failure may help explain the German willingness to provide Austria with the 'blank cheque' against potential Russian intervention against Serbia.[13] It was only as the prospect of a European war suddenly loomed at the end of the month that both Chancellor and Kaiser showed signs of wanting to draw back.

How far these arguments can be pressed is a matter of conjecture. In discounting British intervention, Bethmann-Hollweg may have believed what he wanted to believe. The credibility of British intervention would also have been undermined by the small size of the British army. It had certainly not affected Germany's chief military planner, Count Alfred von Schlieffen, who in contrast to Bethmann-Hollweg, had expected German violation of Belgian neutrality to result in British intervention. What is clear is that by not making its position unambiguously clear until late in July, Britain failed to bring its full weight to bear in the crisis culminating in what George Kennan has called 'the seminal catastrophe' of twentieth century history.[14] To that extent it must bear its own responsibility for what ensued, if not necessarily a decisive responsibility.

Britain was again damaging slow in making its position clear in the 1930s.[15] The lead in resisting this new phase of German expansionism had fallen to Britain by default, as a result of American isolationism and French weakness. Only in March 1939 was Britain finally prepared to draw a 'red line' along the Polish border, transgression of which would trigger war. This did not constitute, and arguably could not have constituted, an effective deterrent. Britain had no military means of supporting the guarantees which it was now offering in Central Europe, and the British track record in the wake of its long-standing attempts to appease was too weak to carry credibility with Hitler, who was in any case too determined to pursue his programme of expansionism. What the British action did do was to help precipitate the crisis which was to begin the slow and desperately painful process by which Hitler would eventually be defeated and destroyed. When Poland was attacked six months later, Britain finally took the lead in declaring war, dragging a reluctant France with her.

The main British contribution to the maintenance of the European balance of power during the first half of the century was therefore military rather than diplomatic. Small as it was, the British Expeditionary Force sent in August 1914 helped stave off French defeat in September at the first battle of Ypres.[16] Two years later, Britain was taking on much of the military burden of wearing down the German army. According to Ludendorff, by the end of 1916, the year of Verdun and the Somme, the German army 'had been fought to a standstill and was utterly worn out'.[17] In all the British Empire mobilised some 9.5 million men out of an allied total of 40.7 million, while the British contribution to an overall war expenditure of 57.7 billion dollars came to 23 billion.[18] Britain made a relatively smaller contribution during the Second World War, a point underscored by the economic statistics. Armaments production in 1943 was valued at 11.1 billion dollars, compared with 13.9 billion for the Soviet Union and 37.5 billion for the United States.[19] In absolute terms, however, these were very substantial figures. British resistance in 1940 prevented total German victory in Europe.[20] Four years later, Britain provided the vital forward base, as well as many of the forces, for the American-led liberation of western Europe. The impact of strategic bombing in which the RAF was heavily involved is more controversial. But, according to Richard Overy, 'the combined effects of direct destruction and the diversion of resources denied German forces approximately half their battlefront weapons and equipment in 1944'.[21] British forces were prominent in other theatres of the war, playing a major role in the defeat of Italy, as well as in North Africa and the Middle East.[22] The use of the Enigma code-breaking machine in Britain is credited with shortening the war by as much as two years.[23]

Britain's post-war role in the creation of a predictable and responsible West Germany which by 1990 could lead the process of unification without destabilising the rest of the continent is overshadowed by others. America was clearly by now the lead player. France, which had after the First World War sought security against Germany, now pursued the far more imaginative course of partnership with her, thereby considerably strengthening the architecture of the post-war European order. But as one of the occupying powers with responsibility for the industrial heartland of the Ruhr, Britain was instrumental in the establishment of a federal, democratic, pro-Western German state.[24]

After 1951, when West Germany gained its independence, Britain's primary contribution was in the field of security. British diplomacy was central to finding an acceptable institutional framework within which the unpopular prospect of West German rearmament could be accommodated. The French had tried and failed with the idea of a supranational European Defence Community. The British alternative was more conventional. Germany was brought into the 1948 Brussels Pact, which now became the Western European Union (the WEU), before its admission into NATO. Eden, as Sean Greenwood puts it, had done more than manoeuvre the West out of a major crisis. 'He had enlarged that system and by paving the way for West Germany's entry into NATO, he had banished immediate fears of German neutralism and given the West's most formidable Cold War structure its final shape before the collapse of the USSR.'[25]

Thereafter the British role was more low key. It maintained the British Army of the Rhine, albeit in reduced numbers. As one of the occupying powers it was heavily involved in the Berlin crisis of the late 1950s and early 1960s, though disinclined to take the unyieldingly tough line supported by Adenauer and de Gaulle. It was a party to the 1971 Quadripartite agreement on Berlin and the 'Two plus Four' talks which handled much of the formal business of reunification in 1990. But British policy under Mrs Thatcher was overtly opposed to the direction of events, and can take little credit for the relative ease with which this last and momentous chapter of the twentieth-century German problem was eventually closed.

Britain's other contributions to helping contain Soviet power follow a similar pattern, with the main impact made in the early Cold War years, most notably the late 1940s, when it helped marshall the Western alliance. This was a particularly effective period of British foreign policy. While no longer in the first league, Britain was still obviously a Great Power, able to provide a firm lead. In Ernest Bevin it had a strong Foreign Secretary capable of formulating clear long-term aims and with the capacity to combine pragmatism and vision.[26] He had responded immediately to Marshall's Harvard speech of 5 June 1947, in part it should be said to head off any French attempt to lead what became the European Recovery Programme, (the Marshall Plan.) He was quick to recognise the need to stand up to Soviet pressure, whether in the Middle East or Berlin. Bevin believed that the abandonment of Berlin would have 'serious, if not disastrous consequences in Western Germany and throughout Western Europe', and acted accordingly. Much of the inspiration and initiative for the 1948 airlift, the highly imaginative means by which the Allies overcame Soviet interference with the surface communications to the divided German capital, came from the British.[27] As one historian puts it, 'Between 1945 and 1948 all the Russians had to do was push at weak spots around the territorial core which they controlled and see whether they would be stopped. A good deal of the credit for the failure of these tactical explorations must go to the British decision to stand firm.'[28]

At the same time Bevin was at the forefront of the efforts to establish an Atlantic security system. His initial efforts were at the European level, resulting in the Brussels treaty linking Britain, France and the Benelux countries. More important, Bevin initiated the negotiations which led to the establishment of NATO. This represented a major change in American foreign policy, and one of Bevin's most important contributions was to help prevent a sometimes reluctant US administration from backtracking or dragging its feet in the face of domestic opposition.[29] Sir Nicholas Henderson who was then in the Washington embassy argues that 'The Americans were at sea over Europe and needed the British embassy to play their part . . . we helped and made it possible for America to create NATO.'[30] Certainly, this was an instance where Britain successfully acted as a 'bridge' between Europe and the USA, conveying the views of the one to the other, as well as helping to smooth out difficulties created by France.[31]

With the resolution of the crisis over German rearmament in the 1950s, however, the British role lost its prominence. The USA was the undisputed leader of the new Western alliance. Britain remained by European standards a heavy military spender. It was an important and reliable member of the Western team, not least of NATO. It coped with some of the peripheral conflicts 'East of Suez', such as the insurgencies in Malaya and the Dhofar province of Oman, the sultanate which controlled the Arabian side of the Straits of Hormuz at the mouth of the Persian Gulf. British forces were conspicuously much more successful in fighting counter-insurgency warfare than were the Americans. Britain occupied some of the more strategically located territories on the international chessboard, such as Cyprus, which might otherwise, or so the Americans sometimes feared, have been occupied by the Soviet Union. It appears, but the public evidence on such matters must always be treated with some caution, to have provided some very valuable intelligence. Information from a British-run agent, Colonel Penkovsky, in the late 1950s about the Soviet missile programme was important during the Cuban missile crisis; information provided by another British agent, Oleg Gordievsky, helped defuse a potentially dangerous crisis in the early 1980s created by Soviet paranoia over the possibility of an American nuclear attack.[32] And Britain was a prominent part of the Western success story which stood in increasing contrast to what by the 1980s had emerged as the political and economic failure of the Soviet Union. Britain did more than most members of the Atlantic alliance to help win the Cold War. But in the world of nuclear overkill, and against an adversary as militarily strong as the Soviet Union, it was no longer powerful enough to make anything approaching a decisive difference.

Britain's record as an international peacemaker is more impressive in terms of effort than outcome. Some of the failures, notably the Versailles settlement and the Munich accord, where Britain had very conspicu- ously taken the lead in reaching an agreement with Hitler, were both spectacular and counterproductive. Few of the successes were unquali- fied. While Grey's 'remarkable exercise in patient diplomacy' at the 1912 London conference helped defuse a major Balkan crisis, the success proved short-lived.[33] Britain took the initiative in the negotiations resulting in the 1925 Locarno agreement. 'I can see no prospect of the continuance of cordial relations with France in Europe or elsewhere,' the Foreign Secretary, Austen Chamberlain, Neville's half-brother, minuted in January 1925,

> unless we can somehow give her a sense of security. Looking at Germany I see no chance of her settling down to make the best of new conditions unless she is convinced that she cannot hope to divide the Allies or to challenge them with any success for as long a time as any man can look ahead. As long as security is absent, Germany is tempted to prepare for the *Revanche*. 'The Day' will still be the national toast and with far more reason, while French fears, goading France to every kind of folly, will keep alive German hatred and lead us inevitably, sooner or later, to a new catas- trophe.[34]

While Locarno led to a Franco-German *rapprochement*, it was, as already noted, at best a partial settlement which did not provide Europe with the long-term security which Chamberlain had hoped for.

Britain's Cold War diplomacy was not much more productive. One of the main successes was achieved by Eden, who helped convene and then co-chaired the 1954 Geneva conference on Indochina. This defused a crisis created by the French defeat at Dien Bien Phu, which threatened to escalate into a major East–West confrontation. Vietnam was partitioned, and a temporary peace thereby created in the country.[35] Some British diplomats have argued that Macmillan's 1959 visit to Moscow may have had a salutary effect on Khrushchev's handling of the Berlin crisis. Khrushchev had threatened to sign a treaty with East Germany the previous November. Macmillan, it is argued, helped to bring home to the most impetuous of the Soviet Cold War leaders, the gravity of the situation, causing him 'to pause and consider.'[36] But Macmillan's more ambitious hopes of bringing about a larger East–West settlement, which he shared with Churchill and Eden, like Harold Wilson's efforts in the 1960s to mediate between the USA and North Vietnam, came to nothing.

By the time the superpowers were ready for serious negotiations in the early 1970s, Britain was largely out of the picture. The USA and the Soviet Union did not need an independent interlocutor; Britain's nuclear deterrent was too small to give it standing in the Strategic Arms Limitation talks which became the centre point of *détente*; *Ostpolitik* was primarily a German affair. A senior Foreign Office official, Sir Thomas Brimelow, drafted much of the US–Soviet Prevention of Nuclear War agreement of 1972, but this was one of the less important of the agreements of the period.[37] In the mid-1980s, Mrs Thatcher did help facilitate the US–Soviet dialogue which helped bring about the end of the Cold War. Britain appears to have been ahead of the USA in spotting that Mr Gorbachev was a man with whom it was possible to do business, and the fact that the previously hawkish British Prime Minister took this line made it politically easier for Ronald Reagan to do likewise.[38] According to the American ambassador to London, Raymond Seitz, Mrs Thatcher became a 'genuine intermediary' between the superpowers.[39] One of the Prime Minister's advisers puts it slightly differently. Reagan and Gorbachev, he notes, 'had the power; Thatcher had the influence of a well-informed bystander'.[40] A useful rather than a vital role.

Peacemaking is often a thankless business. Breakthroughs are rare and limited; agreements do not always last. Diplomacy might have helped to win a reprieve in 1912; it could no longer do so in 1914, when Germany regarded the prospects for war as far more favourable. It was hardly Eden's fault if the 1954 Geneva conference failed to bring permanent peace to South East Asia. Nor should one necessarily blame British foreign secretaries or prime ministers for trying against the odds. There was a case in the 1950s, when the Cold War was at its frostiest and contact between East and West was minimal, for trying to discover what was on Soviet leaders' minds and seeing whether, in Macmillan's words, it was possible to make 'at least a beginning of reasonable relations' between the blocs.[41] Rigid ideological hostility, as Churchill had argued after Stalin's death, was unproductive as well as dangerous. Eisenhower and Dulles might not agree. Nixon and Kissinger very definitely would.[42] Moreover, as Macmillan privately put it, 'Somebody will have to break the log-jam one day. Why shouldn't we get the credit? If, as is very probable, it all ends in failure to agree, we shall at least have gone through the necessary moral and intellectual exercises to strengthen our resistance.'[43] Public anxiety over the nuclear arms race, coupled with governmental concern to ensure long-term public support for historically unprecedented levels of peacetime military spending, meant that ministers had to be seen to be trying to get a settlement.

That said, there is a case for arguing that Britain did both too little and too much. Peacemaking in Europe after 1918 required a much more substantial commitment than Britain was willing to make. Locarno, as Jon Jacobson notes, marked the limits rather than the beginning of British involvement in Europe. A great deal of work still needed to be done to ease Franco-German relations, but there was little by way of subsequent British diplomatic follow-up. British attention was quickly distracted back to overseas issues; as Chamberlain's successor, Arthur Henderson, rather patronisingly remarked to his German and French colleagues, 'the Foreign Secretary of the British Empire is a very busy man'.[44] On other occasions British ministers were overly eager to reach a settlement in circumstances where either the prospects for success were too remote to justify the costs and risks or agreement could only be achieved by overstepping the borderline between conciliation and appeasement.

This is particularly true of the 1930s. The size of the gap between Neville Chamberlain's hopes and the political realities of the time comes out clearly from R. A. C. Parker's account of the meeting between Chamberlain and Hitler on 30 September 1938, immediately following the agreement on Czechoslovakia. The British Prime Minister

> urged joint action by the "Four Great Powers" to end the Spanish civil war. He suggested the abolition of bombing and bomber aircraft. He argued for reduction of restrictions on trade. To all this Hitler replied amenably if vaguely. Then Chamberlain produced two copies

of a joint statement he and [Sir Horace] Wilson had prepared in advance. Hitler seemed ready enough to sign anything. They put their names to these words. "We regard the agreement signed last night and the Anglo-German Naval Agreement as symbolic of the desire of our two peoples never to go to war again. We are resolved that the method of consultation shall be the method adopted to deal with any other questions that may concern our two countries, and we are determined to continue our efforts to remove possible sources of difference and thus to contribute to assure the peace of Europe."[45]

This remarkable exercise in wishful thinking cannot simply be explained in terms of the Prime Minister's very real desire for peace, his ambition to bring about 'the appeasement of Europe and Asia and the ultimate check to the mad armaments race',[46] underwritten as these were by his awareness of Britain's relative military and economic weakness. There is too a streak of overconfidence bordering on arrogance, which comes across in a speech a few months before Munich. Remarking that neither Fascism nor Communism were in harmony with 'our temper and creed', Chamberlain had gone on to exhort his listeners not to

> forget that we are all members of the human race, and subject to the like passions and affections, and fears and desires. There must be something in common between us, if only we can find it, and perhaps by our very aloofness from the rest of Europe we may have some special part to play as conciliator and mediator. An ancient historian once wrote of the Greeks, that they had made gentle the life of the world. ... I can imagine no nobler ambition for an English statesman than to win the same tribute for his own country.[47]

The element of both personal and national vanity comes out again in a letter to his sisters written in March 1939, just before the Prague coup. 'Like Chatham, "I know that I can save this country and I do not believe that any one else can." '[48] Churchill, who was unkindly, if not unfairly, described by one British diplomat as 'an old man in a hurry',[49] is quoted in 1953 as saying that 'There is a feeling that I am the only person who [can] do anything with Russia.'[50] The Americans attributed similar motives to Macmillan's peacemaking.[51] Writing of Wilson's 1975 visit to Moscow, one of his biographer's notes that the Prime Minister still saw himself as the only man who could communicate on equal terms and with equally good effect between the Soviet Union and the USA.[52]

These ambitions stand in marked contrast to the predominantly pragmatic tradition of British foreign policy, with its distrust of grand designs and preference for the more manageable exercises in problem solving epitomised by Eden's diplomacy at the Geneva and London conferences of 1954. The tension between the two is evident in conflicting approaches to the problem of reforming the international system into something closer to an international society governed by an agreed set of rules and norms. The predominant view among officials and ministers was cautious and sceptical. Few of the most senior British policy makers had anything of the missionary zeal to bring about the abolition of power politics which motivated Woodrow Wilson and Franklin Roosevelt. While George Bush spoke of a 'new world order' emerging in the aftermath of the Cold War, Douglas Hurd saw only a 'slow continuous effort to cope with disaster'.[53] Attlee, however, was a convinced internationalist who genuinely wanted 'to make the success of the United Nations the primary object' of his foreign policy.[54] Michael Stewart, twice Foreign Secretary in the Labour government of the 1960s, looked forward to a world in which international relations were governed by international law, and believed that Britain should be prepared to make sacrifices to bring this about.[55]

Half a century earlier, Robert Cecil, a minister in Lloyd George's wartime government, had championed one of the major innovation of modern international politics, the League of Nations. The bloodletting of the trenches produced the sense that the world could not afford

> To go on with
> The good old rule,
> The simple plan,
> That they should take who have the power
> And they should keep who can.[56]

But while few disputed the need to look for better and more rational ways of conducting international affairs, the majority of officials and ministers had serious reservations about the solutions being proposed. The Foreign Secretary, Arthur Balfour, believed that it 'might be able to do a little good. It symbolised the growth of an international spirit which was definitely desirable, but it could not possibly produce enough of that spirit to generate its own motive power.'[57] Quite apart from the challenge it would present to traditional British strategies, the balance of power and preference to maintain a 'free hand', a League begged as many questions as it answered. Comprehensive international membership would make for an unwieldy body; partial membership for a weak one. Arrangements would have to be made to provide for peaceful change of the status quo. Above all, there was the question of how the norms of international conduct which were eventually laid down in the Covenant could be enforced.[58] 'Collective security' was an immensely appealing slogan, but was it realistic to expect that states would act together in support of a principle when their vital interests were not always engaged? Hard-headed officials such as Maurice Hankey believed that it was not. But Hankey went further, arguing that there was danger in a situation in which the public at large took a more optimistic and, by implication, naive view of the prospects for peace. The creation of a body such as the League would 'put a very strong lever into the hands of the well-meaning idealists who are to be found in almost every Government who deprecate expenditure on armaments, and, in the course of time, it will almost certainly result in this country being caught at a disadvantage'.[59]

No serious attempt was ever made to resolve these dilemmas, and in the circumstances of the time it is arguable that they were in fact unresolvable. The real weakness of British policy and, in the absence of the USA, Britain was the League's most important member, lay therefore in the government's failure to disabuse public opinion of the uncritical faith it quickly came to place in collective security.[60] As W. N. Medicott puts it, although governments knew that in the final analysis force would have to be used, no party had the courage to go to the country with a demand for clear thinking on such unfashionable lines.[61] This did not matter unduly in the 1920s when the international climate was set fair, so that the League was not seriously tested, but with the onset of the predatory international politics of the 1930s it suddenly became critical. When Mussolini attacked Abyssinia in 1935, the government found itself torn between strategic calculations and the political need to support international principle. Italy, as the 1935 Stresa conference had underlined, was, along with France, a potential ally against Germany. Realising that, in the British ambassador in Berlin's words, the Abyssinian imbroglio was 'mere child's play compared with the German problem that will in the not very distant future confront H. M. G',[62] ministers and officials initially settled for a very nineteenth century exercise in *realpolitik*. The Hoare–Laval Pact would have appeased Mussolini at the expense of Ethiopia. Public indignation forced its repudiation and Hoare's resignation, but there was no effective alternative. The imposition of sanctions by the League against Italy alienated the latter without helping Abyssinia, and the prospects of maintaining the European peace were further diminished.

'Collective security', with which British policy became so closely identified in the inter-war years, might be written off as an evasion of the hard realities of international life. It was a predictable failure, which as Hankey had warned actually served to make things worse. This, however, is to take an unduly short-term perspective. The League of Nations, with its Covenant proscribing the use of force other than for purposes of self-defence, established important precedents, beginning the slow twentieth-century process of delegitimising power politics which took a further step forward after the end of the Second World War, and has now come into greater prominence with the end of the Cold War.[63] Plans for the establishment of a successor organisation to the League, which Britain saw as a forum for Great Power cooperation to work for the peaceful settlement of disputes, as well as enhancing its own status as a major power, were set in train during the Second World War. The United Nation's Charter was primarily an Anglo-American document and Britain's part in the formation of the new international body, second only to that of the USA, was recognised by the fact that the first meeting of the General Assembly was held in London.[64] Britain also helped draft the 1948 Universal Declaration of Human Rights and the 1953 European Convention on Human Rights. These were to become increasingly influential with the signature of the 1975 Helsinki agreement, which proved unexpectedly subversive of Soviet power in Eastern Europe.[65] British judges presided over the first international war crimes trial at Nuremberg in 1946.

In the field of international economics, Keynes provided most of the ideas behind the 1944 Bretton Woods accords which established the International Monetary Fund, the World Bank, and later the General Agreement on Tariffs and Trade, the forerunner of the current World Trade Organisation.[66] These provided a new framework for international economic cooperation, conspicuously lacking in the inter-war period, which helped facilitate and regulate the great period of post-war growth. This was not simply a great economic good. It also provided an essential underlying stability for the international system during the the Cold War. Nuclear confrontation in a more volatile economic system would have proved a much more dangerous proposition.

With the onset of the Cold War, the impetus behind the development of international rules and norms outside the areas of international peacekeeping, *détente* and arms control slackened. Here again, though, there were distinctive British contributions. After the completion of Britain's own nuclear test programme, Macmillan worked hard to achieve the first significant arms control agreement of the period, the

1963 test ban treaty. Although not the comprehensive agreement which the Prime Minister had wanted, it was important for environmental reasons, since it ensured that all future tests would be underground. It also took nuclear testing out of the international headlines, thereby removing one of the most prominent nuclear *memento mori* of the Cold War, which had provided part of the impetus behind anti-nuclear movements such as CND.[67] The British part in the negotiation of the nuclear non-proliferation treaty was less prominent, and must be set against the 'bad' example the UK had set, most immediately to France, by its determined pursuit of nuclear status.[68] But Commonwealth connections and influence among new states gave Britain a role as an interlocutor between nuclear and non-nuclear states.[69]

The end of the Cold War again saw a more active British role, initially signalled by the strong British response to the invasion of Kuwait. As the British ambassador to Saudi Arabia, Sir Alan Munro, later put it:

> We were very much aware of finding ourselves at the centre of a drama where, in the first test of the post-Cold War era, the world had its chance to show that aggression would not be tolerated. As the threat to Saudi Arabia itself became evident, it seemed natural as a close friend and partner to offer help with defence. This principle was every bit as important in our minds as the parallel considerations of the security of important Gulf oil resources. Moral arguments carried just as much weight as those derived from expediency.[70]

Britain was subsequently militarily prominent in the Bosnia and Kosovo crises, as well as a number of other peacekeeping operations, where its troops had a reputation for impartiality, professionalism and what the Defence Secretary, Geoffrey Hoon, described as 'no nonsense pragmatism'.[71] No less important than these practical contributions were the ways in which Britain helped to expand the norms of international conduct. The establishment of a safe haven for the Kurds in the aftermath of the Gulf war resulted from an initiative by the Major government, which in turn helped to set one of the most important precedents of the post-Cold War period, that of humanitarian intervention in the affairs of sovereign states.[72] Britain actively supported the International Criminal Tribunals set up in 1993 in the Hague to try Bosnian war criminals, as well as the formal establishment, under the 1998 Rome Statute, of the International Criminal Court.[73] The ruling by the House of Lords that the former Chilean President, Augusto Pinochet was extraditable to Spain to stand trial for alleged human rights abuses in Chile 'was a landmark in the movement towards the concept that inter-national criminal law is universally applicable'.[74] The Kosovo crisis prompted attempts, most publicly outlined in a speech by Tony Blair in Chicago in April 1999, to define international guidelines governing the circumstances where military intervention was appropriate and permissible.[75]

These were typically pragmatic responses to the unforeseen outbreak of disorder which followed the Cold War. The British, along with the rest of the so-called 'international community', found themselves wrestling with the question of what priority to afford to the maintenance of international decency and order in parts of the world which often appeared to have little direct bearing on national security and interests. The dilemmas had been starkly outlined by the outbreak of the Bosnian war in the early 1990s.[76] The issues in Bosnia were nowhere near as clear-cut as they had been in Kuwait, and the military options very unattractive. If firm and rapid action would have stopped the fighting, Douglas Hurd subsequently wrote, 'we would have agreed. Casualties would have been accepted if a quick and favourable outcome could have been assured'.[77] Anxious not to get drawn into a potential military quagmire, but unable to stand aside in the face of the horrors of a televised war in Europe, the government reached the uneasy comprom-ise of sending troops to protect humanitarian operations. But Britain, along with the rest of its EU partners, was in no position to end the war until the Americans were finally willing to intervene.

In his memoirs, John Major accepted, 'as a leader of one member of the international community...the blame that must fall on all our shoulders for the inadequacy of the outside world's response to the crisis', though he also notes that Britain 'did far more than most'.[78] That might serve as a broader verdict on the British approach to the pursuit of order in the final decade of the century, in which inter-national action had sometimes seemed cruelly discriminatory, with some major outbreaks of violence, most notably in Rwanda, being allowed to go virtually unchecked.

This brings us to the final question of Britain's impact on the long-term stability of those parts of the contemporary international system over which it had formerly exercised imperial control or influence. Decolonisation was an inherently destabilising business. Empire had provided security and order, not least because the imperial authority held the ring between potentially hostile communities, Moslems and Hindus in India, Greeks and Turks in Cyprus, between various tribal groups in Africa, and somewhat less successfully between Jews and Arabs in Palestine. Once it became clear that colonies would gain independence, these tensions came to the fore, first in the form of intercommunal violence, then in conflict between successor states. India and Pakistan fought three wars between 1948 and 1971, and at the end of the century were engaged in a low-level but potentially dangerous nuclear arms race. The Arab–Israeli conflict, which erupted immediately after the British withdrawal from Palestine in 1948, subsequently embroiled Lebanon, threatened Jordan with civil war and turned the Middle East into a major theatre of Cold War confrontation. The Middle East was responsible for at least one nuclear crisis in 1973. Cyprus on several occasions brought Greece and Turkey to the brink of war.

While some of these problems pre-dated British rule, others had been created or exacerabated by British policy. The British, like most colonial powers, had drawn their imperial maps to suit their own convenience, with little regard to the long-term cohesion or viability of territorial units whose future independent existence was rarely a matter of much concern. The post-independence problems of Nigeria, as of the former mandatory territory of Palestine and Iraq, have their roots in imperial policy during the earlier part of the twentieth century, although in the latter case officials on the spot did express concern about the viability of the proposed merger of three former Turkish provinces, one of which was largely Shia Arab, another Kurdish. The result, as the civil-commissioner, Colonel Arnold Wilson, warned, 'would be the antithesis of a democratic government'.[79] As already noted, policy in strategically important territories, notably Cyprus and Aden, proved detrimental to the handling of indigenous tensions and instabilities.

Decolonisation also threatened long-term destabilisation for another reason. Although normally well administered, empire had for the most part been run on a shoe-string. There had been no comprehensive programme to prepare countries for self-government. By the time independence loomed, and the decisions, particularly in Africa, were often taken late in the day, there was often relatively little which could be done to ensure that the new states could provide for their own future development and stability. Britain, as the Governor-General of Nigeria, Sir James Robertson, put it in 1959, had

not been allowed enough time: partly this is because we are not strong enough now as a result of two world wars to insist on having longer to build up democratic forms of government, partly because of American opposition to our idea of colonialism by the gradual training of people in the course of generations to run their own show; partly because of dangers from our enemies, the Communists, we have had to move faster than we should have wished.[80]

Against the weaknesses which helped precipitate decolonisation must be set the efforts made to ensure that the actual hand-over of power would occur in a constitutional and peaceful fashion, without the kind of bitter civil war which preceded Algerian independence or the chaos into which the Congo descended immediately after the Belgian departure. This might mean defeating insurgencies, as in Kenya and Malaya, or fighting a war, as in the Falklands. The future of Hong Kong involved complex negotiation, and later serious differences with China, which came to dominate Britain's relations with Beijing in the years prior to the termination of the lease in 1997. It took fifteen years to resolve the Rhodesian problem.

Yet, for all its frustrations, the outcome of the Rhodesian story with the 1980 Lancaster House conference, and the temporary return of a British governor to oversee elections, does eventually underline Lord Carrington's point that 'a responsible Power like Britain did not walk out of its responsibilities'.[81] In the Gulf, where British interests in the form of oil and sterling were much more directly involved, policy makers believed that it was 'right and proper' that they should try to sort out local disputes which threatened long-term stability in the region before they left. And this to some extent they succeeded in doing, helping facilitate the resolution of the Iranian claim to Bahrein and encouraging the merger of the seven independent Trucial States to form the United Arab Emirates.[82]

After independence help continued to be provided, not least in the military sphere in terms of arms, training and more direct forms of British support. Britain came to the help of Kuwait in 1961 and 1990, and provided substantial military assistance to Malaysia in its 'confrontation' with Indonesia. British forces intervened in Kenya and Tanganyika to help quell army mutinies shortly after independence, and provided security for Belize against Honduran pressure. But the capacity to continue to mount such military actions was significantly reduced after 1971. Despite her responsibilities under the Treaty of Guarantee, Britain did not act to prevent the 1974 Turkish invasion which effectively partitioned Cyprus. Nor did Britain have the power and prestige to play an effective long-term peacemaking role in areas such as South Asia and the Middle East. Its most effective diplomatic intervention in the Arab–Israeli conflict came in the aftermath of the 1967 war. Security Council Resolution 242, which became the basis of the subsequent peace negotiations, was drafted and moved by Britain. The carefully crafted wording, in particular the call for 'withdrawal of Israeli armed forces from territories occupied in the recent conflict' (as opposed to *the* territories) provided a constructive diplomatic ambiguity which others could later build on.[83] Although Britain subsequently kept in close touch with key parties to the dispute, helping define the stance of the EEC and EU, and sometimes prodding the USA into greater activity, it was never a primary player.[84]

This is a selective review of the impact of British foreign policy on the international system. Its main focus has been political and strategic, and thus has taken little account of economic, cultural or linguistic impact. It has made no attempt to gauge the longer-term influence of Britain's promotion of democratic government, whether in its former colonies or more recently in the countries of Eastern Europe. Nor has it made allowance for the private or informal initiatives, whether by British NGOs or by opposition politicians, who could on occasion be influential. Churchill's 1946 Zurich speech in which he called for Franco-German reconciliation and the establishment of a united states of Europe, for example, is credited with giving impetus to the European movement.[85] And in the brief space here available, assessment is inevitably circumscribed by the difficulties of identifying a specific British role in complex processes in which many other actors were also involved.

Certain conclusions are nevertheless clear. British foreign policy was conducted with a clear eye to the stability of the international system, with rather less emphasis placed on the justice of that order. It was the eye of a status quo and conservative state which, while ready to innovate, distrusted radical solutions, particularly those involving new institutions.[86] After the Second World War, policy makers looked to the Commonwealth 'as an illustration of how a new form of international relationship could be peacefully carried out',[87] while eschewing the more forward-looking experiments being carried out by the founders of the ECSC and EEC. (Though in this context it is worth noting that British abstention in the early stages may well have served to facilitate the European project. An EEC which Britain had helped to design would probably have been a looser union, less committed to the prospect of 'ever closer union'.[88]) Rather more important, as its declining role in the field of arms control, as well of course as its substantially diminished impact on the stability and security of the post-colonial world underscores, Britain increasingly lacked the means to make a major contribution towards furthering its continuing interest in international order.

There is a further and perhaps more disturbing point. British purposes were by no means always benign. Empire meant domination, and while the effects of this may have been tempered by enlightened administration, they were by no means universally appreciated. On a number of occasions, British policy did real, and long-term, harm. This was as much by its acts of omission, failing to do more to deter Germany in 1914 or to confront her more quickly in the 1930s, than by acts of commission – some of the exercises of imperial map making during the earlier part of the century, trying too hard to get peace, or the Suez operation. Britain did not always behave well or honourably. It was sometimes ready to sacrifice the interests of small nations – Abyssinia in 1935, Czechoslovakia in 1938, and those countries of south-eastern Europe which Churchill effectively assigned to the Soviet Union under the 1944 spheres of influence agreement with Stalin. At Suez, Eden and the Cabinet knowingly broke international law. But while behaviour in the earlier part of the century reflected high-handedness, it was never wilfully malicious in the way that of the main revisionist states was. The Abyssinian affair reflected the muddled and wishful thinking of what Arnold Toynbee described as a 'premature humanism',[89] the peculiar admixture of fear and liberalism which was part of the post 1918 reaction to the bloodletting of the trenches. Czech interests at Munich were sacrificed in what was quite genuinely believed to be the greater European good, while the concessions to Stalin of predominant influence in Romania and Bulgaria were the price of maintaining British, and ultimately democratic, interests in Greece. One should also at least note the fact that Suez, like the Hoare–Laval pact, led to public uproar in Britain, and the resignations of both Sir Samuel Hoare in December 1935 and Eden after Suez (albeit at least formally on grounds of ill-health).[90]

All that said, Britain's positive impact in terms of playing a leading role in containing the most critical imbalances of power and preventing European disaster tipping over into catastrophe, its contribution to the development of a rule-based international society, and managing the dissolution of the world's largest empire in a generally orderly fashion, were significant. Without overstating the case, Britain contributed more than most of the major powers of the period to a more stable, and indeed more civilised world. Its role certainly contrasts dramatically with that of Wilhelmine and Nazi Germany, Imperial Japan and the Soviet Union, at least for the four decades after 1945. While France and West Germany made more striking contributions to long-term European stability after the Second World War, the one power with a significantly larger claim to have exerted a positive impact on the international politics of the twentieth century is of course the United States. The USA had the power, and from 1941 onwards the will, both to ensure the maintenance of an international balance of power and to help establish the basis of more civilised norms of international conduct. The scale of its material contribution, financial as well as military, and the imagination with which it pressed the Marshall Plan, inevitably dwarf what Britain could do. But the Americans did not always act in a wise, timely or measured fashion and, as became increasingly evident towards the end of the century, most obviously through its niggardly approach to the UN, its policy was by no means always internationally minded. The failings of others do not of course excuse the limitations and failings of the British contribution, but they place them in perspective, if only by reminding us that the power which at least broadly identifies its interests with what Eyre Crowe had referred to as the 'general desires and ideals common to all mankind' has historically been the exception rather than the rule.

8
Patterns and Prognoses

Centuries are often arbitrary time-frames, with little obvious relationship to distinctive periods in national or indeed any other kind of history. But the beginning of the twentieth century marked a turning point in British foreign policy. The 1902 Anglo-Japanese alliance and the withdrawal from the western hemisphere were the first signs of the weakness and overextension which were to prove one of the dominant themes of the next seventy years. Their long-term effects were accelerated and accentuated by the repercussions of another and more ominous turn-of-the-century development, the rise of Wilhelmine Germany. Britain's security, its future as a Great Power and its place in the world were in large part determined by the way it handled the successive phases of the German problem between the passage of the first naval bill by the *Reichstag* in 1898, which triggered the Anglo-German naval race, and the rise of Hitler in the 1930s.

On key occasions during this forty-year period, British foreign policy served to make very difficult political and diplomatic situations worse, thereby making it impossible for the country to achieve its primary objectives of avoiding war, or at least ensuring that war should be contained at something approaching a 'tolerable' cost. While the prospects of doing this were never good, several factors stand out in any attempt to explain this, the single most damaging set of failures of modern British foreign policy. The first is the repeated misjudgements of German intentions. Wilhelmine Germany was a powerful, restless and unstable country which, while clearly dissatisfied with the European status quo, had no fixed plans for altering it. Grey appreciated the outlines of the danger which such a power posed, but in the immediate aftermath of the Sarajevo assassination he failed to realise that, in contrast to the last Balkan crisis in 1912, Germany was now willing to risk war. Some of the explanations for this misjudgement have to do with the circumstances of the time, including the relative improvement of Anglo-German relations since 1912, and the way in which previous crises had been overcome. But there was also that streak of liberal naïveté which made it difficult for him, as for his successors in the 1930s, to understand the nature of the 'devilry'[1] afoot in Berlin.

The threat posed by Hitler was at one level again quickly recognised. Already in 1934, the Defence Requirements Committee which had been set up after the Nazi leader's accession to power the previous year had identified Germany as the 'ultimate potential enemy', recommending a five-year deadline for British defence preparations to meet the new danger.[2] At the same time, however, there was now a much greater, and much more widespread, disposition to wishful thinking than there had been before 1914. The apparent extremes of Nazism provoked disbelief among rational people who did not want to face up to the prospect of another great war, and in the case of key policy makers, notably Chamberlain, did not believe that Britain could afford to fight one. Until March 1939, therefore, Britain tried to appease the unappeasable. As late as 23 July 1939, less than six weeks before the outbreak of war, Chamberlain could still write that, 'One thing I think is clear, namely, that Hitler had concluded that we mean business and the time is not ripe for a major war.'[3]

These misreadings of German intentions were accompanied by a deep-seated reluctance to make the necessary military pre-commitments to the maintenance of the balance of power. British policy makers continued to view the problem of security in Europe from a position of insular detachment. Preoccupation with maintaining a 'free hand', as much as concern to avoid polarising yet further European politics, ruled out the kind of unambiguous commitment to France which might have acted as a deterrent to Germany prior to 1914. After the First World War, British policy makers were well aware of the need to try to integrate Germany back into the councils and comity of Europe. But there were clear limits as to the effort they were prepared to put into achieving what, particularly after the Versailles settlement, was a very ambitious, if not impossible, goal. The furthest they were willing to go militarily before 1939 was the very limited guarantees of western European frontiers offered at Locarno, which were not honoured in 1936 when Hitler remilitarised the Rhineland. Indeed, the greater the prospect of war in the 1930s, the more reluctant the government seemed to contemplate anything which might suggest a willingness to fight again on the European mainland.

The repercussions of this combination of diplomatic misjudgement and military underpreparedness made themselves felt both during and after the subsequent conflicts. The level of casualties Britain suffered between 1914 and 1918 can be at least partially explained by the problems of building up a major British army *after* war had broken out, and the inflexibility and lack of imagination of the High Command in adapting quickly to the unforeseen, if not unforeseeable, conditions of trench warfare. While attrition eventually helped win the war, it also helped lose the subsequent peace. The relatively slow pace of rearmament in the mid-1930s meant that over and above its unwillingness to contemplate the prospect of a second major war in a generation, Britain did not feel itself to be militarily ready to confront Hitler before 1939. Even then, other than in terms of air defence, it was ill-prepared for war. These weaknesses did not prevent an 'eleventh hour nation' eventually, in Churchill's words of 1917, from 'muddling through to success' and winning the subsequent wars.[4] Between 1939 and 1945, as in the First World War, Britain fought long and hard. While bombed, it was not invaded and occupied, and thus, unlike the major continental countries, retained both its independence and its self-respect. The importance of this fact, so easily taken for granted, can scarcely be overemphasised.

Nevertheless, Britain's ultimate military successes against Germany, which contrast with the diplomatic failures, have to be qualified. The task it had engaged in in September 1939 proved, as Chamberlain, the Treasury and chiefs of staff had all predicted, beyond its strength, and could only be completed with the help of the great Soviet effort on the Eastern Front, and more familiarly with American financial and military aid. Even then the victory was ambivalent. Just as the victory in 1918 had disoriented foreign policy, making it impossible to retain the balance of power in Europe during the crucial decade of the 1930s, Britain had won at the price of permanent loss of power and status.

These issues were to dominate the next quarter century. While far less traumatic and testing than the preceding forty-five years, they proved in their own ways to be politically and psychologically very difficult years. As the French Foreign Minister, Maurice Couve de Murville, put it:

> La nature humaine, plus encore la nature Britannique, solide et obstinée, n'accepte pas volontiers un changement brutal et radical. C'était donc une longue évolution qui commençait pour que l'Angleterre finisse par s'adapter à l'univers de la seconde partie du 20e siècle.[5]

While the aim of policy after 1945 was to hang on to Britain's remaining status as a 'Great Power', what policy makers actually found themselves engaged in was a series of 'adjustments of great complexity' required by the shift from 'major to lesser power status'.[6] Britain's task was effectively threefold: to conduct an orderly withdrawal from its imperial positions, so as to avoid leaving power vacuums or instability locally or precipitating political crises at home; to recast its security relations with Europe so as to contain the new Soviet threat which emerged as a result of the defeat of Germany; and to come to terms with the economic and political integration movement which emerged in western Europe in the 1950s.

Only the second of these can be regarded as an unqualified success. Britain was a founder member of NATO, and Bevin's role in helping to marshal the western alliance, like Eden's 1954 initiative in resolving the political problem created by West German rearmament, is witness to the creativity and skill of which British diplomacy was capable. The story of imperial withdrawal is less straightforward. Much of the process of decolonisation was indeed orderly, though the reasons for this are by no means entirely a tribute to the skill and good sense of British policy makers. The capacity for pragmatic realism, as already evident in earlier retrenchments, certainly played an important part. British foreign policy across much of the earlier part of the period would have been in far greater difficulty had it not been for the capacity to accept disagreeable facts quickly and go with the grain, as it had previously done in dealing with many of the problems of overstretch. Lansdowne's handling of the 1902 Anglo-Japanese treaty and Curzon's remark *à propos* of Egyptian independence, 'Why worry about the rind if we can obtain the fruit?'[7] are classic examples of this hard-headed flexibility. But one should not overlook the fact that Britain was also lucky. Decolonisation did not seem to be a particularly painful process. The economic losses were relatively small. The empire had few settler colonies other than Rhodesia, and even this, at least when compared with the impact of Algeria on French politics, proved essentially of nuisance value. And the end of formal empire was not perceived as heralding the loss of Great Power status. This was one case where overoptimism, and no doubt an element of wishful thinking about the potential of the Commonwealth as a long-term power base, worked to Britain's advantage.

In other respects the process of losing power proved a confusing, painful and at times disorientating experience. In his account of Suez, Anthony Nutting quoted Kipling:

> Let us admit it fairly as a business people should
> We have had no end of a lesson, it will do us no end of good.[8]

But another, more famous Kipling poem, is perhaps as appropriate:

> If you can keep your head when all about you
> Are losing theirs and blaming it on you...[9]

Suez, however, the one real shout of pain at the only point where retreat seemed to threaten to turn into rout, is very much the exception. For the most part nerve held and, so long as the American safety net was available, decline could normally be managed so as to ensure that neither British, larger Western nor immediate local interests were seriously damaged.

The more persistent danger was of policy being premised on an exaggerated estimate of what Britain could still do. This is evident not just in 1956, but in the decision the year before that Britain could afford to withdraw from the post-Messina negotiations on the formation of a European Common Market, as also in the succession of miscalculations over the viability of major overseas bases. Part of the problem in these latter cases can be attributed to the fact that the loss of power was insufficiently advanced when initial decisions were taken for the long-term dangers to be recognised or admitted. But the necessary adjustments were also hampered by the lack of systematic forward planning and a reluctance to face some of the more obvious and thus unpleasant facts of decline. Breaking Crossman's 'sound barrier', as both Conservative and Labour ministers found out, was very painful. The difficulty is well summarised by Harold Wilson's admission, only three years after the final decision, that he had clung 'to our East of Suez role when facts were dictating a recessional. I was...one of the last to be converted and it needed a lot of hard facts to convince me.'[10]

In the end, however, withdrawal was a finite process. While the links were by no means completely broken, most of the major problems ceased with political and military withdrawal. Establishing a relationship with a Europe committed to 'ever closer union' by contrast involved an open-ended commitment, the difficulties created by which did not end with membership of the EEC in 1973. Britain paid a heavy price for having not so much missed as dismissed the opportunity of founder membership in the mid-1950s. In consequence it found itself having to adjust to rules and institutions which it did not like, but from which it could not afford to stand aside. This was an inherently disagreeable business, which required the discarding of much of the baggage of the country's insular history, the sense of Britain as a place permanently detached and different from the continent. Opposition thus went much deeper and was much more widespread than it had been to some of the landmark withdrawals from imperial positions. The fractious domestic political debates still raging some forty years after the original decision to seek EEC membership provide a graphic illustration of how unpragmatic British foreign policy could, under certain circumstances, be.

If the tendency of heart to overrule head was the main reason why the adjustment to EEC membership proved so difficult, it was by no means the only one. 'Europe' played to other British weaknesses, not least the dislike of radical change. The strengths of British foreign policy were those of ingenuity, of problem solving and adaptation. They are reflected in the idea of an airlift to Berlin in 1948, the formula which provided for the admission of Germany to the WEU and NATO in 1954, the constructive ambiguity of the wording of Security Council Resolution 242 on the resolution of the Arab–Israeli conflict, and the formula which allowed a republican India to join the Commonwealth. British policy makers were not, by contrast, at ease with the kind of grand design represented by the ECSC and EEC, which ran counter to their pragmatic instincts. Mistrusting such methods, officials and ministers underestimated their efficacy in the conditions of post-war Europe which was much more ready for radical changes of direction than they realised.

Judged in terms of these main themes, the record of British foreign policy was a decidedly mixed one. Policy was sometimes highly effective in terms of maximising opportunities ('punching above Britain's weight'), as in its contribution towards a more stable and orderly international system.[11] Vital interests were never compromised and the most serious dangers were all averted. But the margin between success and disaster was at times dangerously thin, and as much was often owed to the help of allies, geography and a certain amount of luck as to diplomatic or military skills. Interests were certainly endangered, objectives were by no means always achieved, and policy was often damagingly slow to adapt; the consequent costs were high. The overall proficiency with which policy, with certain military exceptions, was executed, was not matched by its formulation, particularly in terms of the objectives set.

Inevitably, it is the debit side of the equation which commands attention, and here it is important to maintain a sense of perspective. Britain had no monopoly of miscalculation or misjudgements. No other major European power appreciated the significance of the Sarajevo assassination or foresaw the course and nature of the First World War; no army found it easy to solve the 'riddle of the trenches'. Britain was not alone in appeasing in the 1930s, in overestimating the French army, a mistake shared with the *Wehrmacht*, or in underestimating the growing threat from Japan in 1941, an error also made by the Americans. Britain miscalculated the risks of a Soviet–German understanding in the summer of 1939; Stalin underestimated the risks of a German attack in 1941. Suez was an Anglo-French venture. As the French and after 1989 Russian examples illustrate, others too found Great Power status difficult to give up. America as well as most Arab countries miscalculated Saddam Hussein's intentions in the summer of 1990. Everybody fumbled the earlier stages of the Bosnian crisis.

Foreign policy, as these example illustrate, is an error-prone business, and the challenges facing Britain, as many other countries over the period, were as difficult as they were daunting. Grey spoke the literal truth when he referred on 3 August 1914 to 'the most awful responsibility... resting upon the Government in deciding what to advise the House of Commons to do'.[12] Whatever the criticism of policy in the 1930s, especially of Chamberlain's dogmatic pursuit of Appeasement with Germany, it is difficult not to acknowledge the sense of tragedy in the Prime Minister's heartfelt declaration on the outbreak of a second world war, that 'Everything that I have worked for, everything that I have hoped for, everything that I have believed in my public life has crashed into ruins.'[13] 'All my life,' declared Eden on 3 November 1956, 'I've been a man of peace, working for peace, striving for peace, negotiating for peace. I've been a League of Nations man and a United Nations man and I'm still the same man with the same convictions, the same devotion to peace. I couldn't be other if I wished.'[14]

The scale and nature of external dangers and, no less important of the sense of disorientation which they created, must, as these examples illustrate, be taken into account in any judgement made of the individuals concerned. It certainly mitigates, even if it does exonerate, the blame which attaches in the first place to ministers, but also to senior officials. As *The Dictionary of National Bibliography* entry for Sir Ivone Kirkpatrick, the PUS at the time of Suez, notes, 'He carried great responsibilities through a period of great apparent British power. By 1956 he may have over-estimated what remained of it. Few people did not. But if any one should not, it is the head of the Foreign Office.'[15]

Yet important as the personal factor was in a system in which power was concentrated in so few hands, the main causes of the mishandling of policy must be sought elsewhere. This is clear from what proved the most persistent failure over the period, the pursuit of what turned out to be unrealistic objectives – keeping too great a military and political distance from continental affairs, trying to avoid war in the 1930s, hanging on too long after 1945 to the notion that Britain was still a Great Power. At issue here were facts which politicians and officials did not want to face, or courses of action which the country did not want to take. The delay which this reluctance imposed on the process of adjustment, was facilitated or reinforced by some of the more disfunctional methods, the 'bad habits', outlined in Chapter 1. The machinery of government was not normally good at rethinking policy radically. It did not look sufficiently ahead or go back naturally to 'first principles'. Major policy reappraisals were rare, and even when conducted, they were not necessarily acted on. Options were not always carefully weighed or problems thought through. A number of important decisions were unsound in principle: the Singapore strategy where a two-front war was planned with a one ocean navy; the Balfour declaration which premised British policy in Palestine on a contradictory set of commitments to Arabs and Jews. British policy towards Germany after 1933 was in direct contradiction to the fundamental principle outlined in Eyre Crowe's famous memorandum of 1907:

> To give way to the blackmailer's menaces enriches him, but it has long been proved by uniform experience that, although this may secure for the victim temporary peace, it is certain to lead to renewed molestation and higher demands after ever-shortening periods of amicable forbearance. The blackmailer's trade is generally ruined by the first resolute stand made against his exactions and the determination rather to face all risks of a possibly disagreeable situation than to continue in the path of endless concessions.[16]

These deficiencies might have had less impact given wider public interest and debate. But policy was not systematically scrutinised by independent observers, and where premises or judgements were faulty, correction normally had to wait until the facts had imposed themselves on policy makers in unmistakable fashion, or until change emerged from the consensually, as also often conventionally, minded governmental machine. On the big and usually 'gut' issues, public opinion, admittedly an ill-defined concept, was in fact as likely to reinforce rather than challenge the status quo. In turn, in so far as government recognised the need for change, ministers felt inhibited by public unreadiness to embrace it. While ministers often shared the public's view, there was also a reluctance, as evident over any question of conscription or the acknowledgement of a continental commitment before the First World War as in the Blair government's approach to British membership of the Euro at the end of the century, to expend political capital and risk votes by giving an unpopular lead.

We come back then to the question raised in Chapter 1 as to whether policy could reasonably have been expected to have achieved more than it in fact did. On the face of it the answer must be, yes. Although the scope of the possible was constantly contracting, the British – both decision makers and the public – missed opportunities when different policies might have yielded more favourable outcomes. This was especially true of the handling of the German problem in the run up to and the years after the First and before the Second World War. It is true also of Britain's response to the European integration movement in the 1950s. But for the most part these must be regarded as outside opportunities. Britain's ability to exploit them was severely circumscribed less by material weakness, though this was certainly important in the 1930s, than by the states of mind induced by danger and decline, and mindsets unconducive to the initiatives and changes of policy which alternative policies would have required. To have overcome these would have required exceptional effort. This was achieved in the military sphere, most notably in the Second World War, as more recently in the recapture of the Falklands. The difficulty with foreign policy was that backs were not yet up against the wall and the pressures in consequence were insufficiently acute to focus minds and force change. It would also have required exceptional people – men (there was only one woman Prime Minister and no woman Foreign Secretary) with that rare combination of foresight and determination seen in the case of Churchill, Bevin or Attlee in the case of Indian independence. But exceptional men, by definition, are rare.

In assessing the scope of the possible, therefore, we come back to the fact that external opportunities – Hitler's weakness when he occupied the Rhineland in 1936, the offer of founder membership of the EEC after Messina – were only part of the equation. Opportunities, as we have repeatedly seen, also depended on ideas, culture and opinion. Lord Plowden's distinction between 'opportunity' and 'missed opportunity', quoted in Chapter 1[17] can certainly be regarded as disingenuous, a rationalisation for failures of policy which given a more rational, clear-sighted and intellectually rigorous environment, should not have occurred. But it also reflects the more complex truth that the scope of the possible was circumscribed as much by the way in which events were viewed first and foremost in Whitehall, but also in Westminster, Fleet Street and the constituencies, as by the facts of economic or military power, or by the offers of friends or the vulnerabilities of adversaries. While therefore it is certainly possible to argue individual cases, it is difficult to see that Britain could have done substantially better than it in fact did.

What, if any, lessons does this historical analysis have for the prospect for British foreign policy in the twenty-first century? In key respects the outlook – assuming of course that the United Kingdom does not break up – has become more favourable than at any time since the 1920s. With the collapse of the Soviet Union, the international environment has become more benign. The disorders of Africa, the Balkans and the Middle East are much less threatening to British interests than was the Cold War, and the seemingly endless nuclear arms race which it generated. At the same time Britain's international decline has been halted, and on a limited scale even reversed. The point should not be exaggerated. In key areas such as policy towards Russia, Britain has limited influence over and beyond what can be achieved within alliance frameworks.[18] There is very little Britain on its own can do to encourage China to adopt 'accommodatory' rather than power politics.[19] The discrepancy in power between Britain and the United States remains huge (a GNP of 1.3 as compared with 8.5 trillion dollars.)[20] But with the collapse of the Soviet Union, and the more effective performance of its own economy, Britain has, if only temporarily, again moved up the international power league tables.[21]

This, in other words, is a less dangerous, and certainly a much less disorienting world, in which the temptations to engage in wishful thinking are accordingly reduced. A good deal of the post-Cold War agenda, with its emphasis on functional issues – economic, environmental and security – plays to British pragmatic strengths. Britain has considerable experience with multilateral diplomacy,[22] and multilateral security arrangements have been a British *forte* since the negotiation of the North Atlantic Treaty in the late 1940s. Along with France, the UK is unique in Europe in terms not just of its capabilities, which have been described as those of a 'mini-superpower',[23] but also of the range of its military experience, and its hard-headed approach to the use of force. At the same time Britain retains something of its traditional world view, which is reflected in the military activism of the first post-Cold war decade. As the 1998 Strategic Defence Review put it, the British are by instinct 'an internationalist people. We believe that as well as defending our rights, we should discharge our responsibilities in the world . We do not want to stand idly by and watch humanitarian disasters or the aggression of dictators go unchecked. We want to give a lead, we want to be a force for good.'[24]

Military power is complemented by what has become a well rehearsed list of more intangible assets – the global primacy of the English language, the reputation of the BBC World Service, an unusually long democratic tradition, commitment to the rule of law, and London's role as an international financial centre.[25] In an era of globalisation, Britain has the advantage of a wide range of international contacts, spanning the developed and the developing world. Its membership of some 120 international organisations includes the most important international clubs, NATO, the EU, G-8, the OECD, the Commonwealth and the UN Security Council, of which it has permanent membership. This is an almost unique combination of 'hard' and 'soft' power, only matched by the USA, whose instincts, however, are less positively internationalist.

At the same time, one should not underestimate the amount of unfinished business which remains from the second half of the twentieth century . The necessary adjustments from the old days of international primacy have still to be fully completed. While new arrangements were successfully made between the late 1940s and early 1970s to protect interests, the intangible dimensions of the very demanding combination of decline and reorientation towards Europe have not been fully resolved. The reaction against the loss of empire had not fully worked itself out by the end of the century. The spirit of the Conservative 'Suez Group' could still be detected forty years later among the anti-Maastricht rebels who created so much trouble for John Major's government in the early 1990s.[26] According to Philip Stephens, the relationship with the EU remained 'haunted by the hankering for a lost empire. Euroscepticism has been built on the insecurity of a nation unwilling to own up to its present.'[27]

Three, interrelated issues stand out, all of which are complicated by a tendency for policy to be driven by heart rather than head. The first, and most difficult, is of course the relationship with continental Europe. Paradoxically, this problem has been exacerbated by the resolution of the problem which had caused most of Britain's earlier difficulties. German unification provided much of the impetus for the introduction of a single European currency. Yet, while the Euro scarcely represented the same kind of danger as the *Wehrmacht* or the *Reichswehr*, it has been perceived as constituting a threat to core values, in particular national sovereignty and identity. Rightly or wrongly, the character of the political system, as to some extent the country, is seen to be in question.[28] The strength of the underlying passions in this debate is indicated by Norman Lamont's remark that the idea that, as Chancellor of the Exchequer at the time of Maastricht, he had negotiated away Britain's right to be an independent self-governing country 'literally made me feel physically ill'.[29] An article published in early 2001, at the time of Blair's first visit to see President George W.Bush, cited a Foreign Office memorandum which had warned against any 'weakening of that unquestioning sense of superiority over people of the Continent which forms an essential element in British self-confidence.'[30] Even if these views are regarded as exaggerated, it is clear that Europe involves the kind of 'gut' issues, requiring fundamental change, which Britain has historically found particularly difficult.

Posed in such terms, the prospects are for the old uneasy pattern of relations with Europe to continue. Joining the Euro would not necessarily resolve the relationship if the decision was grudging and the EU then moved further down the integrationist path. The 1975 referendum, despite the large majority it produced for continued British membership of the EEC, did not reconcile the country to the Community. The great danger for British policy thus remains that of irritable and angry drift. Neither geographically nor mentally 'at the heart of Europe', nor at the same time able to establish an alternative power base, Britain may continue as an 'awkward' and an uncomfortable partner, unable to capitalise on the potential advantages of membership of one of the world's most economically powerful and cohesive groupings. This is an unattractive option, which can only engender further frustration, ensuring that 'Europe' continues to have a uniquely divisive impact on domestic politics. It would complicate relations with the USA, and make it more difficult for Britain to define a position for itself in the world. But if the options facing Britain in its relations with an increasingly powerful Union, moving in a direction which Britain does not like but is unable to prevent, cannot be dispassionately analysed and discussed, then the prospect is real.

There are, however, other possibilities in an increasingly complex and potentially fluid situation of the Europe of the early twenty-first century. 'Ever closer union' need not be an inexorable process in a community pledged to a major process of enlargement, and in which for the first time the old Franco-German alliance, which has been at the heart of past progress, comes under strain. Many variables will determine the future of EU developments, some of which may well provide opportunities for Britain to play a more important and prominent role than it was able to do in the twentieth century. Franco-German differences may slow further integration, and offer Britain the prospects of alliances and alignments in EU decision making which were hitherto not available. Were Britain able to establish itself as a leading player, one which helped shape the future of the Union rather than feeling that it was constantly being shaped by it, more favourable public attitudes within Britain might result. Over the long-term, as memories of the Second World War fade, and Brussels comes to be seen as a part of the 'domestic' political process, the 'insular prejudices' to which Major-General Ewart referred in 1907, *à propos* the Channel tunnel, could eventually decline.[31] This may well of course take considerable time; indeed, it may not happen. The integrationist flame will not easily burn itself out and Europe may well continue to develop in ways which go against the British grain. But it would equally be a mistake to assume that the pattern of European development is fixed, and that the politico- economic relationship with the continent must remain a standing refutation of Britain's ability to adapt to new circumstances.

A further possibility, which might follow on from the emergence of a significantly larger European Union in which different groups proceed at varying speeds, is a gradual acceptance that Britain is a *European* rather than a *continental* power. While accepting that Britain has a substantial community of interests and purposes with its partners in the EU, the fact that this community is by no means as extensive as that of the central continental players would be equally clearly recognised. The extent of the difference on any specific issue would continue to be a matter of debate, with pragmatic case-by-case assessments of where the balance of advantage of engagement or abstention lay in any given case. Opting out would be neither an embarrassment nor a norm. The advantages of such an approach are obvious. As a result of accepting frankly that Britain, while an important part of the EU, did not feel itself to be at the 'heart' of the European project, the domestic debate would become easier to defuse, and foreign policy would in consequence gain greater flexibility. As, if not more, important, the spectre of semi-permanent British dissidence on the European issue might finally be banished. This, however, is again very much a long-term prospect. It assumes a willingness to take stock of past history, and a maturity of view which were not in evidence at the beginning of the twenty-first century. It also assumes a domestic consensus on the nature of British identity – and the extent of its Europeanness – which will not be easy to establish.[32]

The issue however is critical, not least because the ability of Britain to sort out its European policy inevitably affects other major elements of its foreign policy. The most obvious of these is whether it can establish a more equitable balance between its key alliances than during the second half of the twentieth century. The late 1990s saw the 'special relationship' with the USA again in good repair, after tensions earlier in the decade over Yugoslavia and Ireland. It also saw a notable effort to improve relations with Britain's main European partners, with cooperation between Britain and France closer than at any stage since the *Entente Cordiale* was signed in 1904. Britain was at the forefront of the fashioning of the European Security and Defence Policy which followed on from the 1998 Anglo-French Saint Malo initiative, the origins of which, at least at the London end, grew out of concern over Europe's overreliance on US military power during the Bosnian and Kosovo crises. While therefore the 'special relationship' continues, as one commentator in 2000 put it, to run in the blood of senior officials,[33] a certain rebalancing of British perceptions seems under way. Though the old instincts to 'consult Washington' may not be in decline, the growing range and intensity of cooperation on foreign policy issues within the EU inevitably has an impact, if only because far more officials are getting to know their European rather than their American opposite numbers.

This does not mean a reversal of alliances. There remains a continued awareness in London of the importance of keeping close to the world's only superpower, as of differences of perception between Paris and London, and indeed of the residual rivalry between the two capitals. One should also be cautious about reading too much into Britain's role as a potential Atlantic 'bridge-builder'. The strains on transatlantic relations created by French suspicions of the USA and US suspicions of a more assertive and independent Europe will provide as many challenges as opportunities for British policy. Mediating differences over security and trade in a world in which the imperatives of Cold War cooperation have weakened will not be an easy task, least of all when it is believed in continental Europe that the traffic across Blair's bridge 'always seems to be travelling in one [that is Atlantic] direction'.[34] Conversely, of course, a more Eurocentric policy, particularly in the area of defence, could strain the 'special relationship'. The danger of falling between the Atlantic and European stools is thus real. But Britain does retain a unique set of links on both sides of the Atlantic, which given skilful diplomacy, represent a significant asset.

Implicit in this role is the view of Britain as something more than a European power. While the term 'Great Power' is now studiously avoided, status remained important for the Britain of the post-Falklands years. Britain's voice still counted internationally and, as John Major wrote in his autobiography, 'I was determined it should continue to do so.'[35] The military dimension was particularly prominent. Despite the withdrawal from East of Suez, British forces were once more operating in the Gulf, and large aircraft carriers, a capability abandoned in the mid-1960s, were again under development. According to the Chief of the Defence Staff, General Sir Charles Guthrie, in 1999 the armed forces experienced 'the greatest operational tempo' since the Second World War.[36] Speaking of British involvement in the initial peacekeeping operation in East Timor the same year, Sir John Kerr, PUS at the Foreign Office, referred to 'the kind of self-confidence which sends in the Gurkhas, which sends in HMS *Glasgow*, permeates through to the man on the street, who understands that we are engaged in something both interesting and exciting'.[37] When, in 2000, British forces were sent to Sierra Leone in an operation which helped save the local UN peacekeeping force, a Downing Street source was quoted as saying that 'Whilst recognising that you can't do everything, and the days of being the global policeman are long gone, it does not mean that you can't show leadership and do what [you] can to help.'[38]

Whether high levels of activity on the diplomatic as well as the military front amounted to a clearly identifiable role is not clear, however. Attempts to define a sustainable and realistic post-imperial role still sound artificial and self-conscious. Thus Tony Blair's declaration:

> No longer do we want to be taken seriously just for our history, but for what we are and what we will become. We have a new role. Not to look back and try to re-create ourselves as the pre-eminent super-power of 1900, nor to pretend to be the Greeks to the Americans' Romans.
>
> It is to use the strengths of our history to build our future not as a super power but as a pivotal power, as a power that is at the crux of the alliances and international politics which shape the world and its future. Engaged, open, dynamic, a partner and where possible, a leader in ideas and in influence, that is where Britain must be.[39]

The issue is at one level semantic. The combination of activist and pragmatic instincts are perhaps sufficient to determine international profile, without straining to find a uniquely British role for a post-imperial era. Britain remains a peculiarly difficult international actor to classify, being neither a superpower

> nor a middle power; it has aspects of a great power, but is caught up in a very complex set of interdependencies; it has to be involved in bargaining within defence and economic alliances and organisations yet it is not a small power. No other country has quite this profile.[40]

Such descriptions suggest that there is little to be gained by continuing to seek a clearly defined role, beyond perhaps characterising Britain as an *active* power. But the term, if descriptively accurate, is hardly emotionally satisfying, and the very fact that Acheson's observation, made back in 1962, that Britain had lost an empire and failed to find a role is still quoted[41] indicates that the failure matters. This is not perhaps surprising given the combination of post-imperial pride and nostalgia which still affects policy and policy makers – witness the extent to which the idea of Britain 'punching above its weight' caught on – and the impossibility of channelling energies more actively into the development of a European role. But there may also now be the further factor of trying to square the country's international profile with a national identity which has become a matter of debate and doubt. The matter is not immediate in the sense that the relationship with Europe or the balance of transatlantic ties are, but when it comes to defining its place in the world in the twenty-first century, Britain is still not a country fully at ease with itself.

Nor has it overcome its old temptation to live beyond the means it is either able or willing to make available. Britain continues to live on the historic capital of old connections which is not being effectively replenished. It does so without having conducted any major post Cold-War reappraisal of its foreign policy, although defence policy was comprehensively reviewed by the incoming Labour government in 1998. To some observers, rather than having found a stable level, British foreign policy is still suffering from 'imperial overhang', the tendency of foreign policy elites to continue to view the world from the old imperial perspectives.[42] Activity on this reading can seem an end in itself, evidence that, in Roy Hattersley's words, the British still think of themselves 'not so much as different but as superior'.[43]

This, however, seems essentially a minority view. Although direct evidence remains difficult to come by in the continued absence of any real public debate, in the absence of major military disaster there is little to suggest general dissatisfaction with an active foreign policy. Nor, however, is there much to suggest that the public is any more willing, or at least that government believes that the public is any more willing, to ensure that ends and means are more comfortably in line than they were in the days of imperial overstretch. Indeed Britain has a significantly smaller number of overseas-based diplomats than France or Germany[44] and lacks the diplomatic staff to engage in prolonged international initiatives. According to Sir John Coles:

> A serious proposal, perhaps to negotiate an end to a conflict or a dispute between two states that want that service, is likely to require a dedicated effort by a team of dedicated experts over months if not years. They would be hard to come by in present circumstances where resources are fully stretched in the handling of more routine diplomacy. In 1996 when the government decided to make a new effort to solve the problem of the divided island of Cyprus, it appointed a retired diplomat, Sir David Hannay, to conduct the effort. It was a sensible use of his outstanding abilities, but his appointment also demonstrated the limited ability of the Foreign Office to conduct initiative diplomacy by using its existing personnel.[45]

Britain's ability to participate in international military operations is limited by constraints on both manpower and the overall defence budget. This is a matter of priorities rather than of economic weakness. The 2.8 per cent of GDP spent on defence in 1998 was less than half the proportion devoted at the height of the Cold War in the mid- and late 1950s. Britain could only field one division during the Gulf war, and even then was left effectively without any reserves. As a senior British commander put it, 'I had the modern British army, there wasn't anything else.'[46] The whole British army, as was noted at the time of the Kosovo war, could be fitted into the Wembley stadium.[47] Parsimony, in other words, continues to vie with international ambition, despite or perhaps rather because of the fact that Britain is an increasingly affluent and peacefully inclined society.

As ever, therefore, it is the continuities of British foreign policy which are important.[48] The early part of the twenty-first century may play more to British foreign policy strengths than did the previous century, with its debilitating combination of loss of power, major security threats and the constant need for change, but the underlying approach to foreign policy is unlikely to alter radically. This is by no means entirely reassuring. For while there is plenty of scope for discussion and argument over the way the foreign policy record of the twentieth century should be read, the existence of weaknesses in the British approach is beyond dispute. Understanding why things went right and wrong, and what the recurrent rather than specific difficulties were, scarcely guarantees more effective policy making in the future. But there are clearly lessons to be learned, and it would be both foolish and irresponsible not to try to learn them.

Appendix I: Outline Chronology, Main Events Relating to British Foreign Policy, 1900–2000

	BRITISH	*INTERNATIONAL*
1902	Anglo-Japanese treaty End of Boer war Committee of Imperial Defence formed	
1904	Anglo-French *Entente Cordiale*	
1905		First Moroccan crisis
1906	Anglo-French Staff talks begin HMS *Dreadnought* launched	
1907	Anglo-Russian *entente* (settles rivalry in Persia, Afghanistan and Tibet) Eyre Crowe, 'Memorandum on the present state of Relations with France and Germany'	
1908		Bosnian crisis
1911	War Book opened	Second Moroccan crisis First Balkan war begins
1912	London conference on Balkans	
1914		Assassination of Archduke Ferdinand, Sarajevo (June) Outbreak of First World War (August)
	First British Expeditionary Force sent to France	
1915	Gallipoli campaign McMahon–Hussein correspondence (future Arab independence in parts of Middle East)	
1916	Battle of the Somme Introduction of conscription Anglo-French Sykes–Picot agreement (partition of Ottoman Empire)	
1917		USA enters war Russian revolution
	Passchendaele (third battle of Ypres) Balfour declaration (national homeland for the Jews)	

1918	Ludendorff breaches British lines on Somme (March) 'Hundred Days' victories (August–November) British intervention in Russian civil war (–1919)	Woodrow Wilson's 'Fourteen Points' German surrender (November)
1919	German fleet scuttled at Scapa Flow Paris peace conference and Versailles treaty 'Ten Year Rule' first instituted Original decision to build Singapore base Irish war of independence begins (–1921)	
1920	First meeting League of Nations (London) Britain given League of Nations mandates for Palestine and Mesopotamia Iraqi revolt Conscription abolished	US Senate rejects Versailles treaty Treaty of Sèvres with Turkey
1922	Britain signs Washington naval treaty Anglo-Japanese treaty terminated Egyptian Protectorate ended Chanak (confrontation between British forces and Kemal Atatürk)	Rapallo Pact (German and Soviet Union)
1923		France reoccupies Ruhr Treaty of Lausanne (revises peace settlement with Turkey)
1924	Britain recognises Soviet Union	Dawes plan scaling down German reparations
1925	Britain returns to gold standard Locarno Pact Dominions Office established	
1926	Balfour definition of Dominion status (refers to 'British Commonwealth of Nations')	
1927	British forces mass at Shanghai	
1928		Kellogg–Briand pact renouncing war

	BRITISH	INTERNATIONAL
1929	Withdrawal of last British forces from Germany	Young plan (German reparations) Wall Street Crash
1930	Iraqi independence	Briand memorandum on united states of Europe
1931	Britain abandons gold standard Statute of Westminster gives legal form to Balfour definition of Commonwealth	Japan attacks Manchuria
1932	Abolition of 'Ten Year Rule'	Geneva disarmament conference opens
1933		Hitler elected German Chancellor Disarmament conference breaks down Japan and Germany leave League of Nations
	Baldwin says, 'the bomber will always get through' Fulham by-election (Conservative candidate supporting rearmament defeated)	
1934	First Defence Requirements Committee report identifies Germany as the 'ultimate potential enemy'	
1935	League of Nations Union 'Peace ballot' Stresa Pact (Britain, France, Italy) Anglo-German naval agreement Abyssinian crisis: Hoare–Laval pact Chiefs of staff warn of 'triple threat' from Germany, Italy, Japan First experiments with radar India Act	
1936		Germany remilitarises Rhineland Outbreak of Spanish civil war
	Arab Revolt in Palestine begins (–1939) Anglo-Egyptian treaty	
1937		Sino-Japanese war begins
1938		German *Anschluss* with Austria (March)

Munich agreement (September)
Anglo-Irish treaty (Britain loses access to
Irish ports)
Singapore base opened (but incomplete)

1939   Tientsin crisis (China)
British guarantees to Poland and
Romania (March)
Introduction of conscription (April)
Anglo-French-Soviet military talks
(August)

Molotov–Ribbentrop pact
(August)
Germany attacks Poland
(September)

Britain declares war on German
(September) British Expeditionary Force to
France (September)

1940   Norwegian campaign (April)
Germany overruns France; BEF evacuated
from Dunkirk (May)
Anglo-French 'union' declaration (June)

Italy declares war on
Britain (June)

Royal Navy bombards French fleet at
Mers el Kebir (July)
Battle of Britain (August–September)
'Destroyer for bases' deal with USA

1941   Atlantic Charter (August)

USA begins 'Lendlease'
(April)
Germany attacks Soviet
Union (June)
Japan attacks Pearl Harbor
(December)

1942   Surrender of Singapore (January)
Battle of El Alamein (November)
Allied troops under Eisenhower land in
North Africa (November)

1943   Casablanca meeting (Churchill and
Roosevelt, January)
British and American troops land in
Sicily (July)
Anglo-American Quebec Agreement on
nuclear cooperation (August)

Tehran conference
(Churchill, Roosevelt,
Stalin, November)

1944   D Day (June)
Churchill's Moscow visit (East European
'spheres of influence' agreement)

	BRITISH	INTERNATIONAL
		Bretton Woods monetary agreement
1945		Yalta conference (February)
		Germany surrenders (May)
		Potsdam conference (July) First atom bombs dropped on Hiroshima and Nagasaki (August) Japan surrenders (August) Inauguration of United Nations
1946	US dollar loan Churchill's Fulton and Zurich speeches	McMahon Act passed in USA, ending nuclear cooperation with Britain
1947	British inform USA of withdrawal from Eastern Mediterranean (February) Anglo-French Dunkirk treaty	Truman Doctrine (February) Marshall's 'Harvard' speech (June)
1948	Brussels Pact signed (Britain,France, Belgium, Holland, Luxembourg) Berlin blockade – airlift begins Palestine mandate abandoned Treaty of Portsmouth (with Iraq) Malayan emergency (–1960)	
		Czech coup
1949	Sterling devaluation	North Atlantic Treaty signed
1950		
		Schumann plan (European Coal and Steel Community) European Convention for Protection of Human Rights signed Korean war begins India becomes Commonwealth Republic
1951	Nationalisation of Anglo-Iranian Oil Company	Establishment of Federal Republic of German

1952	First British A bomb test	
	Mau Mau insurgency Kenya (–1955)	
1953		Death of Stalin
1954		
	London conference agrees German admission to NATO and WEU: Britain pledges to maintain forces on the continent	
	Eden co-chairs Geneva conference on Indochina	SEATO formed
	Anglo-Egyptian agreement on evacuation of Suez Canal Zone base	
	Decision to build British H bomb	
1955		Messina conference
	Britain withdraws from Brussels follow-up talks (November)	Baghdad Pact signed
		Geneva Four Power summit
		Bandung non-aligned summit
	Beginning of Cyprus emergency (–1959)	
1956	Khrushchev and Bulganin visit Britain	
	General Glubb dismissed in Jordan	
	Nationalisation of Suez Canal – Suez operation	Soviet intervention in Hungary
	Cabinet agrees 'Plan G' (17-nation European free trade area)	
1957	Sandys Defence Review, including end of conscription	
	First British H bomb test	
	Anglo-American rapprochement (Bermuda)	
	Macmillan's 'Audit of Empire'	
	Ghanaian (Gold Coast) independence	Treaty of Rome signed
		Soviet Union launches Sputnik
1958	Iraqi coup – British troops to Jordan	
	Malayan independence	
		De Gaulle returns to power in France
		French veto European Free Trade Area negotiations
		Repeal of MacMahon Act
		Khrushchev's Berlin ultimatum – beginning of Berlin crisis

BRITISH	INTERNATIONAL
1959 Macmillan visits Moscow Britain becomes a founder member of seven-nation European Free Trade Area (EFTA) 'Future Policy Study' begun	
1960 Macmillan's 'Winds of Change' speech in Africa	U2 spy plane shot down Collapse of Paris four- power summit
Lee report on Britain's relations with EEC Cyprus independence Nigerian independence Cancellation of Blue Streak missile – agreement to buy American Skybolt instead	
1961 1899 Anglo-Kuwaiti treaty cancelled – Kuwait operation First EEC application	
	Berlin wall (August)
1962 South Arabian Federation formed Ex-US Secretary of State, Dean Acheson, says Britain has lost an empire but not yet found a role US cancels Skybolt missile Nassau conference – Britain obtains Polaris	Cuban missile crisis (October)
1963 De Gaulle vetoes British application to join EEC 'Confrontation' with Indonesia (–1966) Kenyan independence Breakdown of Cyprus agreement Britain signs partial test ban treaty in Moscow (first major East–West arms control agreement)	
1964 British troops join UNFICYP in Cyprus Plowden Report (Committee on Representational Services Overseas) Unified Ministry of Defence formed Title 'Chief of the Imperial General Staff' abolished British troops quell East African mutinies	
	Chinese nuclear test
1965 Rhodesian UDI	
1966 Withdrawal from Aden announced (completed 1967) Next generation aircraft carriers cancelled	

1967	Second de Gaulle veto of British EEC membership Announcement of British withdrawal from Far East by mid-1970s (July)	
		Six Day War in Middle East (June) Security Council Resolution 242 on Arab – Israeli conflict
	Sterling devaluation (November)	
1968	Announcement of final withdrawal form East of Suez (completed 1971) Foreign Office and Commonwealth Offices merged	
		Nuclear Non-proliferation treaty signed
1969	Duncan Report on overseas representation	
1971		Quadripartite agreement on Berlin
1972		Strategic Arms Limitation Treaty (SALT 1) signed
1973	Britain joins EEC	Yom Kippur war/oil crisis
1974		Turkey invades Cyprus
1975	EEC Referendum	Conference on Security and Cooperation in Europe (Helsinki agreement)
1977	CPRS Report (Berrill) on overseas representation	
1979	Britain decides against membership of ERM (Exchange Rate Mechanism) (EEC)	
		Soviet intervention in Afghanistan Iranian revolution
1980	Rhodesian settlement (Lancaster House agreement)	
		Outbreak Iran–Iraq war
1982	Falklands war	
1983	US Cruise missiles deployed in Britain	
1984	Gorbachev visits Britain	
1985	Single European Act	Gorbachev becomes General Secretary, CPSU

	BRITISH	INTERNATIONAL
1987		Intermediate Nuclear Forces (INF) treaty
1989		Collapse of Berlin wall
1990	Britain joins ERM	German unification
		Iraq invades Kuwait
1991	British forces participate in Gulf war	Collapse of Soviet Union
		Maastricht treaty
1992	Britain leaves ERM ('Black Wednesday')	
	British troops sent to Bosnia	
1994	Channel tunnel opened	
1995		Dayton Peace agreement (ex-Yugoslavia)
1997	End of Hong Kong lease	
1998	Strategic Defence Review	
	Anglo-French Saint Malo declaration on European defence	
1999		Kosovo war
		Single European currency established, Britain stays out
		Helsinki European Council authorises European 'Rapid Reaction' Force
2000	British troops to Sierra Leone	

Appendix II British Foreign Secretaries, 1900–2001

1900–5	Lord Lansdowne (C.)
1905–16	Sir Edward Grey (Lib.)
1916–19	Arthur Balfour (C.)
1919–23	Lord Curzon (C.)
1924	Ramsay MacDonald (Lab.)
1924–29	Austen Chamberlain (C.)
1929–31	Arthur Henderson (Lab.)
1931	Marquis of Reading (C.)
1931–35	Sir John Simon (C.)
1935	Sir Samuel Hoare (C.)
1936–38	Anthony Eden (C.)
1938–41	Lord Halifax (C.)
1941–45	Anthony Eden (C.)
1945–51	Ernest Bevin (Lab.)
1951	Herbert Morrisson (Lab.)
1951–55	Anthony Eden (C.)
1955	Harold Macmillan (C.)
1955–61	Selwyn Lloyd (C.)
1961–63	Lord Home (C.)
1963–64	R. A. Butler (C.)
1964	Patrick Gordon-Walker (Lab.)
1965–66	Michael Stewart (Lab.)
1966–68	George Brown (Lab.)
1968–70	Michael Stewart (Lab.)
1970–74	Lord Home (C.)
1974–76	James Callaghan (Lab.)
1976–77	Anthony Crosland (Lab.)
1977–79	David Owen (Lab.)
1979–82	Lord Carrington (C.)
1982–83	Francis Pym (C.)
1983–89	Sir Geoffrey Howe (C.)
1989	John Major (C.)
1989–95	Douglas Hurd (C.)
1995–97	Malcolm Rifkind (C.)
1997–2001	Robin Cook (Lab.)
2001–	Jack Straw

Notes

1 The scope of the possible

1 W. N. Medlicott, Douglas Dakin and M. E. Lambert (eds), *Documents on British Foreign Policy, 1919–1939, Series 1A, Volume 1* (DBFP) (HMSO, London, 1966), p. 846.
2 NB the title of Anthony Clayton, *The British Empire as a Superpower, 1919–39* (University of Georgia Press, Athens, 1986).
3 Cited in David Dutton, *Austen Chamberlain – Gentleman in Politics* (Ross Anderson, Bolton, 1985), p. 239.
4 Charles Grant, *Can Britain Lead in Europe?* (Centre for European Reform, London, 1998), p. 39.
5 *Future Policy Study, 1960–70, Part 111*, CAB21/3841.
6 Paul Kennedy, *The Realities Behind Diplomacy – Background Influences on British External Policy, 1865–1980* (Fontana, London, 1981), p. 318.
7 Lord Plowden, *An Industrialist in the Treasury – The Post War Years* (André Deutsch, London, 1989), p. 96.
8 Ibid., p. 93.
9 Michael Charlton, *The Price of Victory* (BBC, London, 1983), p. 258.
10 Lord Avon, *The Memoirs of Sir Anthony Eden – Vol. 3, Full Circle* (Cassell, London, 1960), p. 3.
11 Alan Bullock, *Hitler and Stalin – Parallel Lives* (HarperCollins, London, 1991), p. 1085.
12 Paul Kennedy, *The Rise and Fall of the Great Powers – Economic Change and Military Conflict from 1500 to 2000* (Fontana Press, London, 1989 edn), p. 259.
13 Ibid., p. 475.
14 Ibid., p. 563.
15 See chapter 5, p. 111
16 David Goldsworthy (ed.), *The Conservative Government and the End of Empire*, (British Documents on the End of Empire, Series A, Vol. 3, HMSO, London, 1994), p. 61.
17 Sir Nicholas Henderson, *Channels and Tunnels – Reflections on Britain and Abroad* (Weidenfeld & Nicolson, London, 1987), p. 143.
18 *The Economist*, 24 February 1962.
19 Cited in Sir Ivone Kirkpatrick, *The Inner Circle – Memoirs of Ivone Kirkpatrick* (Macmillan, London, 1959), p. 268.
20 Harold Nicolson, 'Is War Inevitable?', *The Nineteenth Century and After*, July 1939, p. 2. Cf. also Harold Nicolson, *Diplomacy* (Oxford University Press, London, 3rd edn, 1963), pp. 142–3.
21 Nicolson, 'Is War Inevitable?', p. 2.
22 Aaron Friedberg, *The Weary Titan – Britain and the Experience of Relative Decline, 1895–1905* (Princeton University Press, Princeton, NJ, 1988), pp. 168–9, 189.

23 Cited in Sean Greenwood, *Britain and the Cold War, 1945–91* (Macmillan, Basingstoke, 2000), pp. 91–2. Cf. Marc Trachtenberg, *A Constructed Peace – The Making of the European Settlement, 1945–63* (Princeton University Press, Princeton, NJ, 1999), pp. 216–17.

24 Goldsworthy, *The Conservative Government*, p. 17.

25 Lord Caccia, *The Roots of British Foreign Policy, 1929–65* (Ditchley Foundation Lecture, 1965), p. 7.

26 Francis Williams, *A Prime Minister Remembers* (Heinemann, London, 1961), p. 179.

27 Avon, *Memoirs*, pp. 29, 32. Cf. Plowden, *Industrialist in the Treasury*, p. 119.

28 Cited in Andrew Pierre, *Nuclear Politics – The British Experience with an Independent Strategic Force, 1939–70* (Oxford University Press, Oxford, 1972), p. 245.

29 Royal Institute of International Affairs, *British Interests in the Mediterranean and the Middle East* (London, 1958), p. 35.

30 Caccia, *Roots of British Foreign Policy*, p. 7. See also Sir John Coles, *Making Foreign Policy – A Certain Idea of Britain* (John Murray, London, 2000), p. 49.

31 Michael Kent O'Leary, 'Policy Formulation and Planning', in Robert Boardman and A. J. R. Groom (eds), *The Management of Britain's External Relations* (Macmillan, Basingstoke, 1973), p. 117; Lord Strang, *Britain in World Affairs – Henry VIII to Elizabeth 11* (Faber & Faber and André Deutsch, London, 1961), p. 19; Lord Gladwyn, *The Memoirs of Lord Gladwyn* (Weidenfeld & Nicolson, London, 1972), pp. 226–7; Lord Howe, *Conflict of Loyalty* (Macmillan, London, 1994), p. 325.

32 Lord D'Abernon, *An Ambassador of Peace – Lord D'Abernon's Diary, Vol. 2, The Years of Crisis* (Hodder & Stoughton, London, 1929), p. 15.

33 Cited in Martin Gilbert and Richard Gott, *The Appeasers* (Weidenfeld & Nicolson, London, 2nd edn, 1967), pp. 17–18; Sir Alexander Cadogan, cited in Hugo Young, *This Blessed Plot – Britain and Europe from Churchill to Blair* (Macmillan, London, 1998), p. 34. See also Christopher Thorne, *Allies of a Kind – The United States, Britain and the War Against Japan, 1941–45* (Oxford University Press, Oxford, 1978), p. 118.

34 Notes for Opening Statement by the Prime Minister, Chequers meeting to discuss Study of Future Policy, 7 June 1959, CAB 21/3840. See also *The Plowden Report* (*Committee on Representational Services Overseas, 1962–3*) (Cmnd 2276, HMSO, London, 1964), para. 217.

35 Philip Darby, *British Policy East of Suez, 1947–68* (Oxford University Press, Oxford, 1973), p. 44.

36 Sir Percy Craddock, *In Pursuit of British Interests – Reflections on Foreign Policy under Margaret Thatcher and John Major* (John Murray, London, 1997), p. 36. Coles, *Making Foreign Policy*, pp. 137–8.

37 Kenneth Waltz, *Foreign Policy and Democratic Politics – the American and British Experiences* (Longman, London, 1968), p. 162; Henderson, *Channels and Tunnels*, p. 156.

38 Andrew Shonfield, 'The Pragmatic Illusion – On the British Formula for Muffling Public Purpose', *Encounter*, June 1967, p. 6. See also David Vital, *The Making of British Foreign Policy* (George Allen & Unwin, London, 1968), p. 102.

39 Cited in Anne Orde, *Great Britain and International Security, 1920–26* (Royal Historical Society, London, 1978), p. 161.

40   Cited in Brian Bond, *British Military Policy between the Two World Wars* (Clarendon Press, Oxford, 1980), p. 68.
41   Charlton, *The Price of Victory*, p. 182.
42   Cited in Nicholas Tarling, *Britain, Southeast Asia and the Onset of the Cold War, 1945–50* (Cambridge University Press, Cambridge, 1998), p. 298.
43   Lord Strang, *Home and Abroad* (André Deutsch, London, 1956), p. 311.
44   Peter Unwin, *Hearts, Minds and Interests – Britain's Place in the World* (Profile Books, London, 1998), p. 29.
45   John Buchan, *The Three Hostages* (The Complete Richard Hannay, Penguin Books, Harmondsworth, 1992), p. 712.
46   Cited in Keith Wilson, *Channel Tunnel Visions, 1850–1945* (Hambledon Press, London, 1994), p. 68.
47   Cited by Sabine Lee, 'Staying in the Game? Coming into the Game? Macmillan and European Integration', in Richard Aldous and Sabine Lee, *Harold Macmillan and Britain's World Role* (Macmillan, Basingstoke, 1996), p. 140.
48   Christopher Andrews, *Secret Service – The Making of the British Intelligence Community* (Sceptre, London, 1986 edn), pp. 133–60; G. P. Gooch and Harold Temperley (eds), *British Documents on the Origins of the War, 1898–1914, Vol. 11* (HMSO, London, 1928), pp. 24–5.
49   Keith Robbins, *Sir Edward Grey* (Cassell, London, 1971), p. 291.
50   Hermann Kantarowicz, *The Spirit of British Policy and the Myth of the Encirclement of Germany* (George Allen & Unwin, London, 1931), p. 312.
51   Cited in David Owen, *Time to Declare* (Penguin Books, Harmondsworth, 1992 edn), p. 361.
52   Cited in John Dickie, *Inside the FO* (Chapman, London, 1992), p. 239.
53   Coles, *Making Foreign Policy*, p. 15.
54   Goldsworthy, *The Conservative Government*, p. 17.
55   Craddock, *In Pursuit of British Interests*, p. 64.
56   Young, *This Blessed Plot*, p. 123.

2   Ends beyond means

1   James Callaghan, *Challenges and Opportunities for British Foreign Policy* (Fabian Tract 439, London, 1975), p. 3.
2   Ronald Hyam, 'The British Empire in the Edwardian Age', in William Roger Louis and Judith Brown (eds), *The Oxford History of the British Empire, Vol. 1V* (Oxford University Press, Oxford, 1999), p. 48.
3   Michael Howard, 'Britain's Strategic Problems East of Suez', *International Affairs*, April 1966, p. 179.
4   Cited in Bradford Perkins, *The Great Rapprochement – England and the United States, 1895–1914* (Atheneum, New York, 1968), p. 156.
5   *Foreign Relations of the United States (FRUS) 1958–60, Vol. V11, Part 2, Western Europe* (United States Government Publications Office (USGPO), Washington, 1993), p. 821.
6   'The Future of the United Kingdom in World Affairs', in David Goldsworthy (ed.), *The Conservative Government and the End of Empire* (HMSO, London, 1994), pp. 63–4.

7   Aaron Friedberg, *The Weary Titan* (Princeton University Press, Princeton, NJ, 1988), pp. 89–90.

8   Minute, P. R. Ramsbotham, 28 January 1961, FO371/ 52131.

9   Paul Kennedy, *The Rise and Fall of British Naval Mastery* (Macmillan, Basingstoke, 1983), p. 271.

10   John Darwin, *The End of Empire – the Historical Debate* (Basil Blackwell, Oxford, 1991), pp. 22–3.

11   Phillip Mason, 'The Best of British Bluff', *The Listener*, 7 November 1968, p. 598; John Darwin, *Britain, Egypt and the Middle East – Imperial Policy in the Aftermath of War, 1918–22* (Macmillan, Basingstoke, 1981), p. 221.

12   A. P. Thornton, *The Imperial Idea and its Enemies – A Study in British Power* (Macmillan, Basingstoke, 1985 edn), p. 121.

13   Cited in Friedberg, *The Weary Titan*, pp. 240–1.

14   David Stevenson, *Armaments and the Coming of War – Europe, 1904–14* (Oxford University Press, Oxford, 1996), p. 6.

15   Friedberg, *The Weary Titan*, pp. 92–134.

16   For the naval background, see Zara Steiner, 'Great Britain and the Creation of the Anglo-Japanese Alliance', *Journal of Modern History*, March 1959, p. 30; J. A. S. Grenville, *Lord Salisbury and Foreign Policy – The Close of the Nineteenth Century* (Athlone Press, London, 1970 edn), pp. 389, 400.

17   Samuel Williamson, *The Politics of Grand Strategy – Britain and France Prepare for War, 1904–14* (Harvard University Press, Cambridge, MA, 1969), p. 3.

18   Paul Kennedy, *Strategy and Diplomacy, 1870–1945* (Fontana paperbacks, London, 1983), pp. 16, 20–4.

19   Cited in Kenneth Bourne, *Britain and the Balance of Power in North America, 1815–1908* (Longman, London, 1967), p. 350.

20   Perkins, *The Great Rapprochment*, p. 9. For the shifting balance of economic power between Britain and the United States, see Paul Kennedy, *The Rise and Fall of the Great Powers* (Fontana, London, 1989 edn), p. 259.

21   A. E. Campbell, *Great Britain and the United States, 1895–1903* (Longmans, London, 1960), pp. 42, 45, 84; Perkins, *The Great Rapprochment*, pp. 115, 158.

22   P. M. H. Bell, *France and Britain, 1900–1940 – Entente and Estrangement* (Longman, London, 1996), p. 31.

23   Cited in C. H. D. Howard, *Splendid Isolation* (Macmillan, London, 1967), p. 94.

24   Ibid., pp. 92–5.

25   Cited in Friedberg *The Weary Titan*, p. 204, cf p. 207.

26   John Gallagher, *The Decline, Rise and Fall of the British Empire* (Cambridge University Press, Cambridge, 1982), p. 97.

27   Cited in Jeffrey Pickering, *Britain's Withdrawal from East of Suez – The Politics of Retrenchment* (Macmillan, Basingstoke, 1998), p. 8.

28   David Fromkin, *A Peace to End all Peace – Creating the Modern Middle East, 1914–22* (André Deutsch, London, 1989), p. 499; Robert Holland, *The Pursuit of Greatness – Britain and the World Role, 1900–70* (Fontana, London, 1991), pp. 102–3.

29   Fromkin, *Peace to End all Peace*, p. 499.

30   Gallagher, *Decline, Rise and Fall*, p. 113.

31   Max Beloff, *Britain's Liberal Empire, 1897–1921, Vol 1, Imperial Sunset* (Macmillan, London, 1987 edn), p. 317.

32   William Roger Louis, *British Strategy in the Far East, 1919–39* (Clarendon Press, Oxford, 1971), p. 152.
33   Cited ibid., p. 147.
34   Rohan Butler, J. P. T. Bury and M. E. Lambert (eds), *DBFP, 1919–39*, second series Vol.VIII (HMSO, London, 1960), p. 9.
35   Cited in M. A. Fitzsimons, *Empire by Treaty – Britain in the Middle East in the Twentieth Century* (Benn, London, 1965), p. 29.
36   Lawrence James, *The Rise and Fall of the British Empire* (Little, Brown, London, 1994), p. 390.
37   Cited in Darwin, *End of Empire*, p. 98.
38   Elizabeth Monroe, *Britain's Moment in the Middle East, 1914–56* (Chatto & Windus, London, 1963), pp. 68–9.
39   Darwin, *End of Empire*, pp. 132–6.
40   Ibid., p. 115. Cf. p. 133.
41   Antony Clayton, *The British Empire as a Superpower, 1919–39* (University of Georgia Press, Athens, 1986), p. 469; Oded Eran, 'Negotiating the Anglo-Egyptian Relationship between the World Wars' in Keith Wilson (ed.), *Imperialism and Nationalism in the Middle East – The Anglo-Egyptian Experience, 1882–1982*, (Mansell, London, 1983), p. 70.
42   John Darwin, 'An Undeclared Empire – The British in the Middle East, 1918–39', *Journal of Imperial and Commonwealth History*, May 1999, pp. 170–1.
43   Gallagher, *Decline, Rise and Fall*, p. 144. cf. John Darwin, *Britain and Decolonisation – The Retreat from Empire in the Post-War World* (Macmillan, Basingstoke, 1988), p. 288.
44   Sir Michael Palliser, *Britain and British Diplomacy in a World of Change* (David Davies Memorial Institute, London, 1975), p. 4.
45   Patrick French, *Liberty or Death – India's Journey to Independence and Division* (Flamingo, London, 1998), pp. 138, 189–91.
46   Cited in Frances Williams, *A Prime Minister Remembers* (Heinemann, London, 1961), p. 203.
47   Anita Inder Singh, *The Limits of British Influence – South Asia and the Anglo-American Relationship, 1947–56* (Pinter, London, 1993), p. 23; Peter Hennessy, *Never Again – Britain, 1945–51* (Vintage, London, 1993), pp. 219,232, William Roger Louis, 'The Dissolution of the British Empire', in Louis and Brown, *Oxford History of the British Empire*, p. 227.
48   Cited in Alan Bullock, *Ernest Bevin – Foreign Secretary* (Oxford University Press, Oxford, 1985 edn), pp. 360–1.
49   'The Balance Sheet of Empire', in A. J. Porter, and A. N. Stockwell *British Imperial Policy and Decolonization, 1938–64, Vol. 2, 1951–54* (Macmillan, Basingstoke, 1989), p. 451.
50   Cited in Harold Macmillan, *Pointing the Way, 1959–61* (Macmillan, London, 1972), p. 119.
51   Cited in Robert Shepherd, *Ian Macleod* (Hutchinson, London, 1994), p. 162.
52   Darwin, *Britain and Decolonisation*, p. 252; Shepherd, *Ian Macleod*, p. 256; Sir William Jackson, *Withdrawal from Empire – A Military View* (Batsford, London, 1986), pp. 114,180; Ritchie Ovendale, 'Macmillan and the Winds of Change in Africa, 1957–60', *Historical Journal*, vol.38, no.2, 1995, pp. 455–77.
53   Harold Macmillan, *Pointing the Way*, p. 156.

54 Cited in Christopher Thorne, *Allies of a Kind* (Oxford University Press, Oxford, 1979), pp. 210–11; Macmillan, *Pointing the Way*, pp. 116–17.

55 Lord Strang, *Britain in World Affairs* (André Deutsch and Faber, London, 1961), p. 388; Kenneth Morgan, *The People's Peace – British History, 1945–90* (Oxford University Press, Oxford, 1992), p. 48.

56 Darwin, *Britain and Decolonisation*, pp. 244, 303–7.

57 Charles Feinstein, 'The End of Empire and the Golden Age', in Peter Clarke and Charles Trebilcock (eds), *Understanding Decline – Perceptions and Realities of British Economic Performance*, (Cambridge University Press, Cambridge, 1997), pp. 216–17.

58 James, *Rise and Fall of the British Empire*, p. 595. See also Denis Judd, *Empire – the British Imperial Experience – From 1765 to the Present* (Harper Collins, London, 1996), p. 366.

59 Cited in Paul Gillespie (ed.), *Britain's European Question – the Issue for Ireland* (Institute of European Affairs, Dublin, 1996), p. 12; Peter Marshall, 'Imperial Britain', *Journal of Imperial and Commonwealth History*, September 1995, p. 385. For a more detailed argument of this case, see Linda Colley, *Britons – Forging the Nation, 1707–1837* (Pimlico, London, 1992).

60 Enoch Powell, 'The Spell of England', reprinted in *The Daily Telegraph*, 9 February 1998.

61 Robert Holland, *Britain and the Revolt in Cyprus, 1954–59* (Clarendon Press, Oxford, 1998), pp. 328–9.

62 Judd, *Empire*, p. 366; John Turner, *Macmillan* (Longman, London, 1994), p. 199; Holland, *The Pursuit of Greatness*, p. 301.

63 W.David McIntyre, *The Rise and Fall of the Singapore Naval Base, 1919–42* (Macmillan, Basingstoke, 1979), p. 53.

64 Cited in James Neidpath, *The Singapore Naval Base and the Defence of Britain's Eastern Empire, 1919–41* (Clarendon Press, Oxford, 1981), p. 215.

65 Ibid., p. 77.

66 Ibid., p. 90.

67 Raymond Callahan, 'The Illusion of Security – Singapore, 1919–42', *Journal of Contemporary History*, April 1974, p. 91.

68 McIntyre, *Rise and Fall of the Singapore Naval Base*, p. 123.

69 Cited in Bradford Lee, *Britain and the Sino-Japanese War, 1937–39 – A Study in the Dilemmas of British Decline* (Stanford University Press, Stanford, CA, 1973), pp. 169–70.

70 Cited in Neidpath, *The Singapore Naval Base*, p. 175.

71 Ibid., pp. 163, 175; Callahan, 'Illusion of Security', p. 120.

72 Major-General Stanley Kirby, *Singapore – The Chain of Disaster* (Cassell, London, 1971), p. 119.

73 Elisabeth Barker, *The British between the Superpowers, 1945–50* (Macmillan, London, 1983), p. 37.

74 Neidpath, *The Singapore Naval Base*, pp. 180–1.

75 Piers Dixon, *Double Diploma – the Life of Sir Pierson Dixon* (Hutchinson, London, 1968), p. 232.

76 Bullock, *Ernest Bevin*, pp. 506–7. See also William Roger Louis, *The British Empire in the Middle East, 1945–51 – Arab Nationalism, the United States and Postwar Imperialism* (Oxford University Press, Oxford, 1984), pp. 336–40.

77 Sir Charles Johnson, Valedictory Despatch, Aden 26 August 1963, CO ADN 164/56/01.
78 John Kent, 'The Egyptian Base and the Defence of the Middle East, 1945–54', *Journal of Imperial and Commonwealth History*, September 1993, p. 55.
79 Cited ibid., p. 51.
80 For a good account of the Suez Group's view of the issue, see Sue Onslow, *Backbench Debate within the Conservative Party and its Influence on British Foreign Policy, 1948–57* (Macmillan, Basingstoke, 1997), pp. 166–71.
81 See, for example, Lloyd George, cited in David Fromkin, *A Peace to End all Peace* (André Deutsch, London, 1989), p. 509.
82 William Roger Louis, 'Churchill and Egypt, 1946–56', in Robert Blake and William Roger Louis (eds), *Churchill* (Oxford University Press, Oxford, 1994), pp. 480–81; *Hansard*, vol.531, col. 726, 29 July 1954.
83 'Egypt; The Alternatives', in Porter and Stockwell, *British Imperial Policy*, p. 199.
84 Harold Macmillan, *Tides of Fortune, 1945–55* (Macmillan, London, 1969), p. 505.
85 *Hansard*, vol. 531, cols. 731, 729, 29 July 1954.
86 *Hansard*, vol. 531, col. 496, 28 July 1954.
87 Darwin, *Britain and Decolonisation*, p. 194.
88 Cited in Robin Edmonds, *Setting the Mould – the United States and Britain* (Oxford University Press, Oxford, 1986), p. 121.
89 Holland, *Britain and the Revolt in Cyprus*, pp. 53–4. For contrasting political and strategic views about the importance of sovereignty, see Goldsworthy, *The Conservative Government*, pp. 134, 147, 148–9.
90 Captain A. O. Shipley, 'Imperial Defence and the Rise of Nationalism in Colonial Territories', *Journal of the Royal Artillery*, October 1957, p. 243.
91 *Aspects of UK Strategic Policy – the Next Fifteen Years*, CAB 21/3840.
92 Holland, *Britain and the Revolt in Cyprus*, pp. 330, 331.
93 William Wallace, *The Foreign Policy Process in Britain* (RIIA, London, 1975), p. 133.
94 Jackson, *Withdrawal from Empire*, p. 173.
95 Glen Balfour-Paul, *The End of Empire in the Middle East – Britain's Relinquishment of Power in her Last Three Arab Dependencies* (Cambridge University Press, Cambridge, 1991), pp. 70–73.
96 William Roger Louis, 'The Dissolution of the British Empire', in Louis and Brown, *Oxford History of the British Empire*, p. 344.
97 Kennedy Trevaskis, *Shades of Amber – A South Arabian Episode* (Hutchinson, London, 1968), p. 159.
98 Cited in Balfour-Paul, *The End of Europe in the Middle East*, p. 84. Cf. Denis Healey, *The Time of My Life* (Michael Joseph, London, 1989), p. 284; Karl Pieragostini, *Britain, Aden and South Arabia – Abandoning Empire* (Macmillan, Basingstoke, 1991), pp. 131–43, 157–73.
99 Lord Carver, *Tightrope Walking – British Defence Policy Since 1945* (Hutchinson, London, 1992), p. 76; Michael Stewart, *Life and Labour – An Autobiography* (Sidgwick & Jackson, London, 1986), p. 232.
100 Patrick Gordon-Walker, *The Cabinet* (Heinemann, London, 1972 edn), p. 143.
101 Cited in Healey, *Time of My Life*, p. 279.

102 Christopher Mayhew, *Britain's Role Tomorrow* (Hutchinson, London, 1967), p. 28.

103 Philip Darby, *British Defence Policy East of Suez, 1947–68* (Oxford University Press, Oxford, 1973), p. 328

104 Cited in Sean Greenwood, *Britain and the Cold War, 1945–91* (Macmillan, Basingstoke, 2000), p. 169.

105 Pickering, *Britain's Withdrawal*, pp. 170–1.

106 Gordon-Walker, *The Cabinet*, p. 144.

107 Richard Neutstadt, *Report to JFK – The Skybolt Crisis in Perspective* (Cornell University Press, Ithaca, 1999), p. 110. See also Morgan, *The People's Peace*, p. 197; P. M. H. Bell, *France and Britain, 1940–94 – The Long Separation* (Longman, London, 1997), pp. 183–5.

108 Philip Larkin, 'Homage to a Government', *Collected Poems* (Faber & Faber, London, 1988), p. 171.

109 Douglas Hurd, *An End to Promises – Sketch of a Government, 1970–74* (Collins, London, 1979), p. 46.

110 Ibid., p. 56.

111 Foreword to Balfour-Paul, *The End of Empire in the Middle East*, p. xvi.

112 Healey, *Time of My Life*, p. 300. See also Gordon-Walker, *The Cabinet*, pp. 147–8.

113 Darby, *British Defence*, pp. 138–42; William Wallace, *The Foreign Policy Process*, pp. 139–40.

3   The limits of pragmatism

1 Robert Gibson, *Best of Enemies – Anglo-French Relations since the Norman Conquest* (Sinclair Stevenson, London, 1995), p. 318.

2 Cited in James Joll, *The Origins of the First World War* (Longman, London, 1984), p. 65.

3 Robert Bunselmeyer, *The Cost of the War – British Economic War Aims and the Origins of Reparations* (Archon Books, Hamden, CI, 1975), pp. 145,184; Michael Dockrill and J.Douglas Gould, *Peace Without Promise – Britain and the Peace Conferences, 1919–23* (Batsford, London, 1981), pp. 75, 84.

4 P. M. H. Bell, *France and Britain, 1900–40* (Longman, London, 1996), p. 151.

5 Cited in David Dutton, *Austen Chamberlain* (Ross Anderson Publications, Bolton, 1985), p. 252.

6 Cited in Brian Bond, *British Military Policy between the Two World Wars* (Clarendon Press, Oxford, 1980), p. 306.

7 Ibid., p. 328.

8 Michal Howard, *The Continental Commitment* (Temple Smith, London, 1972), p. 130.

9 PREM 11 / 1333, November 1955.

10 Ibid.

11 Cited in Michael Charlton, *The Price of Victory* (BBC, London, 1983), p. 184. Cf., John Young, 'The Parting of the Ways? Britain, the Messina Conference and the Spaak Committee, June-December 1955', in Michael Dockrill and John Young, *British Foreign Policy, 1945–56* (Macmillan, Basingstoke, 1989), p. 202.

12 Cited in Alistair Horne, *Harold Macmillan, Vol. 2* (Macmillan, London, 1989), p. 260.

13 Sir Arthur Irvine, *Hansard*, vol. 823, col.1542, 26 October 1971.

14 Ibid., col.1271, 25 October 1971.

15 Raymond Seitz, *Over Here* (Weidenfeld & Nicolson, London, 1998), p. 304.

16 Lord Howe, *Conflict of Loyalties* (Macmillan, London, 1994), p. 631; John Major, *John Major: The Autobiography* (HarperCollins, London, 1999), p. 268.

17 Margaret Thatcher, *The Downing Street Years, 1979–90* (HarperPerennial, New York, 1993), p. 743.

18 Philip Stephens, 'Own Goals', *Financial Times*, 4 December 1998.

19 *Financial Times*, 24 February 2000, 2–3 December 2000.

20 C. Seymour (ed.), *The Intimate Papers of Colonel House, Vol.1* (Ernest Benn, London, 1926), p. 255.

21 Grey of Fallodon, *Twenty-Five Years, 1892–1916, Vol.2* (Hodder & Stoughton, London, 1928), p. 144.

22 Anthony Adamthwaite, *France and the Coming of the Second World War* (Frank Cass, London, 1977), p. 180.

23 Gitta Sereny, *Albert Speer – His Battle with Truth* (Picador, London, 1996), p. 208.

24 Cited in Niall Fergusson, *The Pity of War* (Allen Lane, London, 1998), p. 74.

25 Cited in C. J. Lowe and M. L. Dockrill, *The Mirage of Power – British Foreign Policy Vol.1* (Routledge & Kegan Paul, London, 1972), p. 27.

26 Cited in Harold Nelson, *Land and Power – Britain and Allied Policy on Germany's Frontiers, 1916–19* (Routledge & Kegan Paul, London, 1963), pp. 94–5.

27 'Final Draft of the Fontainebleau Memorandum' reprinted in Martin Gilbert, *The Roots of Appeasement* (Weidenfeld & Nicolson, London, 1966), pp. 189, 193.

28 Adamthwaite, *France*, p. 23.

29 Cited in Keith Robbins, *Sir Edward Grey* (Cassell, London, 1971), p. 192.

30 Grey, *Twenty-Five Years*, p. 145.

31 Zara Steiner, *Britain and the Origins of the First World War* (Macmillan, London, 1977), pp. 254–5.

32 Keith Feiling, *The Life of Neville Chamberlain* (Macmillan, London, 1947), p. 358.

33 C. P. Snow, *The Affair* (Penguin, Harmondsworth, 1962), p. 230. Cf. Sir Percy Craddock, *In Pursuit of British Interests* (John Murray, London, 1997), p. 42; Keith Middlemas and John Barnes, *Baldwin : A Biography*, (Weidenfeld & Nicolson, London, 1969), pp. 757–8.

34 E. L. Woodward and Rohan Butler (eds), *DBFP., 1919–1939* (2nd. Series, 1933, Vol. V.) (HMSO, London, 1956), p. 53.

35 Sir Ivone Kirkpatrick, *The Inner Circle* (Macmillan, London, 1959), p. 91.

36 Martin Gilbert and Richard Gott, *The Appeasers* (Weidenfeld & Nicolson, London, 1963), p. 42.

37 Simon Burgess and Geoffrey Edwards, 'The Six plus One: British Policy-Making and the Question of European Economic Integration, 1955', *International Affairs*, Summer 1988, pp. 401–2.

38 Paul-Henri Spaak, *The Continuing Battle – Memoirs of a European, 1936–66* (Weidenfeld & Nicolson, London, 1971), p. 230.

39 Lord Gore-Booth, *With Great Truth and Respect* (Constable, London, 1974), pp. 248–9; Young, 'The Parting of the Ways?', p. 217; Sir Roy Denman, *Missed*

Chances – Britain and Europe in the Twentieth Century (Cassell, London, 1996), p. 191.

40 Minute Coulson, 6 August; letter Boothby, 9 August 1955, FO371/116045; Charlton, *The Price of Victory*, p. 194.

41 Roger Bullen and M. A. Pelly (eds), *Documents on British Policy Overseas (DBPO), Series 11, Vol 1, 1950–52* (HMSO, London, 1986), p. 108.

42 Cited in Edmund Dell, *The Schumann Plan and the British Abdication of Leadership in Europe* (Oxford University Press, Oxford, 1995), p. 152; Charlton, *The Price of Victory*, p. 83.

43 Hugo Young, *This Blessed Plot* (Macmillan, London, 1998), p. 73; Charlton, *The Price of Victory*, p. 139.

44 Thatcher, *Downing Street Years*, p. 552.

45 Cited in R. A. C. Parker, *Chamberlain and Appeasement – British Policy and the Coming of the Second World War* (Macmillan, Basingstoke, 1993), p. 169.

46 David Dilks (ed.), *The Diaries of Sir Alexander Cadogan, 1938–1945* (Cassell, London, 1971), p. 161 (emphasis added). Cf., also Sir Neville Henderson's account of his embassy in Berlin, *Failure of a Mission, Berlin 1937–39* (Hodder & Stoughton, London, 1940), pp. vi, 102, 201.

47 Cited in Keith Wilson, *The Policy of the Entente – Essays on the Determinants of British Foreign Policy, 1904–14* (Cambridge University Press, Cambridge, 1965), p. 114.

48 W. N. Medlicott and Douglas Dakin (eds), *DBFP, 1919–39, Vol.XXV11* (HMSO, London, 1986), p. 316.

49 *Saturday Evening Post*, 15 February 1930

50 Cited in Denman, *Missed Chances*, p. 189.

51 'Memorandum on the Present State of Britain's Relations with France and Germany' in G. P. Gooch and Harold Temperley (eds), *British Documents on the Origins of the War, 1898–1914, Vol 3* (HMSO, London, 1928), p. 403.

52 Cited in Harold Nicolson, *Diplomacy* (Oxford University Press, London, 3rd edn, 1963), p. 137.

53 Samuel Williamson, *The Politics of Grand Strategy* (Harvard University Press, Cambridge, MA, 1969), pp. 82–4.

54 Cited in Neville Waites (ed.), *Troubled Neighbours – Franco-British Relations in the Twentieth Century* (Weidenfeld & Nicolson, London, 1971), p. 33.

55 Bell, *France and Britain*, p. 150.

56 Cited in Alan Bullock, *Ernest Bevin* (Oxford University Press, Oxford, 1985), p. 645.

57 Cited in Maurice Bruce, *British Foreign Policy – Isolation or Intervention?* (Thomas Nelson, London, 1938), p. 7.

58 Cited in Henry Kissinger, *Diplomacy* (Simon & Schuster, London, 1995), p. 252.

59 Cited in Denman, *Missed Chances*, p. 149.

60 Bond, *British Military Policy*, p. 208; Cf. Peter Dennis, *Decision by Default – Peacetime Conscription and British Defence, 1919–39* (Routledge & Kegan Paul, London, 1972), pp. 47, 69.

61 Bell, *France and Britain*, p. 185.

62 Ibid.

63 Uria Bialer, *The Shadow of the Bomber – The Fear of Air Attack and British Politics, 1932–39* (Royal Historical Society, London, 1980), p. 133.

64 Dennis, *Decision by Default*, p. 111.
65 Eric Newby, *Love and War in the Apennines* (Picador, London, 1971), p. 19.
66 *Richard 11* (Act Two, Scene 1), William Shakespeare, *The Complete Works* (Collins, London and Glasgow, 1951 edn), p. 454.
67 Sir Nicholas Henderson, *Channels and Tunnels* (Weidenfeld & Nicolson, London, 1987), p. 7.
68 Cited in Keith Wilson, *Channel Tunnel Visions, 1850–1945* (Hambledon Press, London, 1994), p. 192.
69 Philip Bell, 'A Historical Cast of Mind – Some Eminent English Historians and Attitudes to Continental Europe in the Middle of the Twentieth Century', *Journal of European Integration History*, 1996, Vol 2; Jeremy Black, *Convergence or Divergence? Britain and the Continent* (Macmillan, Basingstoke, 1994), pp. 195, 196.
70 Lord Plowden, *An Industrialist in the Treasury* (André Deutsch, London, 1989), p.93. Charlton, *The Price of Victory*, p. 62.
71 Jacqueline Tratt, *The Macmillan Government and Europe – a Study in the Process of Policy Development* (Macmillan, Basingstoke, 1996), p. 119.
72 Bernard Donoghue, 'Harold Wilson and the Renegotiation of the EEC Terms of Membership, 1974–5; a Witness Account', in Brian Brivati and Harriet Jones (eds), *From Reconstruction to Integration – Britain and Europe since 1945* (Leicester University Press, Leicester, 1993), p. 204.
73 Craddock, *In Pursuit of British Interests*, p. 125.
74 David Sanders, *Losing an Empire, Finding a Role – British Foreign Policy since 1945* (Macmillan, Basingstoke, 1990), p. 119.
75 Stephen George, *An Awkward Partner – Britain in the European Community* (Oxford University Press, Oxford, 3rd edn, 1998), pp. 70, 152.
76 Thatcher, *Downing Street Years*, p. 727.
77 Major, *Autobiography*, p. 583.
78 Cited ibid., p. 363.
79 Charlton, *The Price of Victory*, p. 194; cited in Anthony Nutting, *No End of a Lesson* (Constable, London, 1967), p. 46.
80 Philip Larkin, 'Homage to a Government', *Collected Poems* (Faber & Faber, London, 1988), p. 171.
81 Cited in 'Undoing Britain?', *Economist*, 6 November 1999.
82 Cited in Charlton, *The Price of Victory*, pp. 106, 90; P. M. H. Bell, *France and Britain 1940–94* (Longman, London, 1997), p. 117.
83 Charlton, *The Price of Victory*, p. 151.
84 Ibid., p. 159.
85 Ibid., p. 160
86 Spenser Mawby, 'From Distrust to Despair: Britain and the European Army, 1950–54', *European History*, October 1998, pp. 502–3.
87 Cited in George Ball, *The Past Has Another Pattern* (W. W. Norton, New York, 1982), p. 213.
88 Hugo Young, *This Blessed Plot*, pp. 245–51.
89 Linda Colley, *Britons – Forging the Nation, 1707–1837* (Pimlico, London, 1994 edn), p. 375.
90 Harold Evans, *Downing Street Diary – The Macmillan Years, 1957–62*, (Hodder & Stoughton, London, 1981), p. 200.
91 Major, *Autobiography*, pp. 202, 583–4.

92   Steiner, *Britain and the Origins of the First World War*, p. 255.
93   Cited in George Monger, *The End of Isolation – British Foreign Policy, 1900–07* (Thomas Nelson, London, 1963), p. 273.
94   Keith Wilson, 'The Foreign Office and the "Education" of Public Opinion before the First World War', *The Historical Journal*, vol.26, no.2, 1983, p. 408.
95   Ibid., p. 405. Cf. Lord Strang, *Britain and World Affairs* (Faber & Faber and André Deutsch, London, 1961), pp. 277–8.
96   Cited in Howard, *The Continental Commitment*, p. 115.
97   Bond, *British Military Policy*, p. 217.
98   Tratt, *The Macmillan Government*, p. 123.
99   Horne, *Harold Macmillan*, p. 256.
100 Piers Ludlow, *Dealing with Britain – the Six and the First UK Application to the EEC* (Cambridge University Press, Cambridge, 1997), pp. 245–7.
101 Denman, *Missed Chances*, p. 225; Miriam Camps, *Britain and the European Community, 1955–63* (Princeton University Press, Princeton, NJ, 1964), pp. 370–1.
102 David Allen, 'Britain and Western Europe', in Michael Smith, Steve Smith and Brian White (eds), *British Foreign Policy – Tradition, Change and Transformation* (Unwin Hyman, London, 1988), pp. 173–4.
103 Major, *Autobiography*, p. 269.
104 *Times*, 15 April 1999.
105 Philip Stephens, 'A Risky Way to Play it Safe', *Financial Times*, 26 May 2000.
106 Lord Avon, *Full Circle* (Cassell, London, 1960), p. 168.
107 *Hansard*, vol.547, col.38, 5 December 1955.

4   Kinds of allies

1   Cited in Michael Glover, *Invasion Scare, 1940* (Leo Cooper, London, 1990), p. 52.
2   *Future Policy Study, 1960–70, Part 111*, CAB 21/3841.
3   Sir Curtis Keeble, *Britain and the Soviet Union, 1917–89* (Macmillan, Basingstoke, 1990), p. 8.
4   Martin Kitchen, *British Policy towards the Soviet Union during the Second World War* (Macmillan, Basingstoke, 1986), p. 152; Richard Overy, *Why the Allies Won* (Jonathan Cape, London, 1995), pp. 1, 321.
5   David Reynolds, *Britannia Overruled – British Policy and World Power in the Twentieth Century* (Longman, London, 1991), p. 151; David Reynolds, 'Roosevelt, Churchill and the Wartime Anglo-American Alliance, 1939–45', in William Louis and Hedley Bull, *The 'Special Relationship' – Anglo-American Relations since 1945* (Clarendon Press, Oxford, 1986), p. 39; Christopher Thorne, *Allies of a Kind* (Oxford University Press, Oxford, 1978), p. 702.
6   Cited in Corelli Barnett, *The Lost Victory, British Dreams and Realities, 1945–50* (Pan Books, London, 1996), pp. 10–11.
7   Nicholas Clifford, *Retreat from China: British Policy in the Far East, 1937–41* (Longman, London, 1971), p. 25; Anthony Adamthwaite, *France and the Coming of the Second World War* (Frank Cass, London, 1977), pp. 69–70.

8   Anthony Clayton, *The End of Empire – the Experience of Britain, France and the Soviet Union/Russia Compared* (Strategic and Combat Studies Institute, Camberley, 1996), p. 7.

9   Geoffrey Smith, *Reagan and Thatcher* (Bodley House, London, 1990), p. 263.

10   Cited in Ben Pimlott, *Hugh Dalton* (Jonathan Cape, London, 1985), pp. 434, 436.

11   Andrew Pierre, *Nuclear Politics* (Oxford University Press, Oxford, 1972), p. 316.

12   Max Beloff, 'The Special Relationship: an Anglo-American Myth', in Martin Gilbert (ed.), *A Century of Conflict, 1850–1950 – Essays for A. J. P. Taylor* (Hamish Hamilton, London, 1966), pp. 164–5.

13   Reynolds, *Britannia Overruled*, p. 23.

14   Ibid., p. 40; Alex Danchev *On Specialness – Essays in Anglo-American Relations* (Macmillan, Basingstoke, 1998), pp. 21, 28.

15   Cited in William Clarke, *From Three Worlds – Memoirs* (Sidgwick & Jackson, London, 1986), p. 38.

16   Pierre, *Nuclear Politics*, p. 63.

17   Cited in Warren Kimball, *Forged in War – Churchill, Roosevelt and the Second World War* (HarperCollins, London, 1997), p. 13.

18   Thorne, *Allies of a Kind*.

19   Ibid., pp. 280–81, 391,293.

20   Cited in Sean Greenwood, *Britain and the Cold War, 1945–51* (Macmillan, Basingstoke, 2000), p. 95.

21   Sue Onslow, *Backbench Debate Within the Conservative Party and its Influence on British Foreign Policy* (Macmillan, Basingstoke, 1997), pp. 120–1.

22   David Dutton, *Anthony Eden – A Life and Reputation* (Edward Arnold, London, 1997), pp. 353–4. See also Victor Feske, 'The Road to Suez: the British Foreign Office and the Quai d'Orsay, 1951–57', in Gordon Craig and Francis Loewenheim (eds), *The Diplomats, 1939–79* (Princeton University Press, Princeton, NJ, 1986), p. 172.

23   Sir Evelyn Shuckburgh, *Descent to Suez* (Weidenfeld & Nicolson, London, 1986), p. 27. See also W. Scott Lucas, 'The Cost of Myth: Macmillan and the Illusion of the Special Relationship', in Richard Aldous and Sabine Lee (eds), *Harold Macmillan – Aspects of a Political Life* (Macmillan, Basingstoke, 1999), p. 18. Ritchie Ovendale, *Britain, the United States and the Transfer of Power in the Middle East, 1945–62* (Leicester University Press, London, 1996), p. 150.

24   Marc Trachtenberg, *A Constructed Peace* (Princeton University Press, Princeton, NJ, 1999), pp. 216–17.

25   Michael Beschloss (ed.), *Taking Charge, The Johnson White House Tapes, 1963–4* (Simon & Schuster, New York, 1997), p. 191; John Dickie, *'Special' No More – Anglo-American Relations: Rhetoric and Reality* (Weidenfeld & Nicolson, London, 1994), p. 161.

26   Cited in John Gearson, *Harold Macmillan and the Berlin Wall Crisis, 1958–62–The Limits of Interests and Force* (Macmillan, Basingstoke, 1998), p. 141.

27   Ernest May and Philip Zelikow, *The Kennedy Tapes – Inside the White House During the Cuban Missile Crisis* (Harvard University Press, Cambridge, MA, 1997), p. 66.

28   Keith Neilson, 'Wishful Thinking: the Foreign Office and Russia, 1907–17', in B. J. C. McKercher and D. J. Moss, *Shadow and Substance in British Foreign Policy, 1895–1939* (University Press of Alberta, Alberta, 1984), pp. 152,158.

29 Keeble, *Britain and the Soviet Union*, p. 144.
30 Cited in Keith Feiling, *The Life of Neville Chamberlain* (Macmillan, London, 1947), p. 403.
31 Robert Manne, 'The British Decision for Alliance with Russia, May 1939', *Journal of Contemporary History*, July 1974, p. 20.
32 Williamson Murray, *The Change in the European Balance of Power, 1938–39 – The Paths to Ruin* (Princeton University Press, Princeton, NJ, 1984), p. 305.
33 P. M. H. Bell, 'The Implications of the Soviet–German Pact for Great Britain (August–December 1939)', in David Wingeate Pike (ed.), *The Opening of the Second World War* (Peter Lang, New York, 1991), p. 154.
34 Kitchen, *British Policy*, pp. 194–200, 244.
35 Peter Mangold, *From Tirpitz to Gorbachev* (Macmillan, Basingstoke, 1998), pp. 86–7.
36 Bell, *France and Britain, 1900–40*, pp. 228–9.
37 P. M. H. Bell, *France and Britain, 1940–94* (Longman, London, 1997), pp. 155–8.
38 Cited in John Cairns, 'Great Britain and the Fall of France – A Study of Allied Disunity', *Journal of Modern History*, December 1955, p. 379.
39 John Cairns, 'A Nation of Shopkeepers in Search of a Suitable France', *The American Historical Review*, June 1974, p. 718.
40 Bell, *France and Britain, 1900–40*, pp. 121, 138; William Laird Kleiene-Ahlbrandt, *The Burden of Victory – Britain, France and the Enforcement of the Versailles Peace, 1919–25* (University Press of America, Lanham, MD, 1995), p. 137.
41 Richard Davis, '*Mésentente Cordiale*: the Failure of the Anglo-French Alliance – Anglo-French Relations during the Ethiopian and Rhineland Crises, 1934–36', *European History*, October 1993, p. 517.
42 Ibid., p. 514.
43 Adamthwaite, *France and the Coming of the Second World War*, p. 86.
44 Cited in Robert Gibson, *Best of Enemies* (Sinclair Stevenson, London, 1995), p. 300.
45 Cited in R. A. C. Parker, *Chamberlain and Appeasement* (Macmillan, Basingstoke, 1993), p. 16.
46 Cited in Davis, '*Mésentente Cordiale*', p. 518.
47 Sean Greenwood, *The Alternative Alliance: Anglo-French Relations before the Coming of NATO, 1944–48* (Minerva Press, London, 1996), p. 298.
48 Cited in Alistair Horne, *Macmillan Vol.2* (Macmillan, London, 1989), p. 319. Cf. pp. 285, 287.
49 Jean Lacouture, *De Gaulle – The Ruler, 1945–70* (Harvill, London, 1991), p. 333; Charles Williams, *The Last Great Frenchman – A Life of General de Gaulle* (Abacus, London, 1983), pp. 423–4.
50 Bell, *France and Britain, 1940–94*, pp. 196–7.
51 Jacqueline Tratt, *The Macmillan Government and Europe* (Macmillan, Basingstoke, 1996), p. 153; Harold Macmillan, *At the End of the Day, 1961–63* (Macmillan, London, 1973), p. 120; Alain Peyrefitte, *C'Etait de Gaulle – 'La France redevient la France'* (Editions de Fallois, Fayard, Paris, 1995), pp. 302–4, 325.
52 Piers Ludlow, '*Ne Pleurez pas, Milord*: Macmillan and France from Algiers to Rambouillet', in Richard Aldous and Sabine Lee (eds), *Harold Macmillan*

(Macmillan, Basingstoke, 1999), p. 103; Richard Davis, ' "Why did the General Do It?" De Gaulle, Polaris and the French Veto of Britain's Application to Join the Common Market', *European History*, July 1998, p. 375.

53　Peyrefitte, *C'Etait de Gaulle*, p. 325.

54　Harold Macmillan, *At the End of the Day*, p. 367; Horne, *Macmillan, Vol.2*, pp. 450,448.

55　For an account of French thinking behind the second veto see Alain Peyrefitte, *C'Etait de Gaulle – Tout le Monde a besoin d'une France qui marche* (Editions de Fallois, Fayard, Paris, 2000), pp. 266–74.

56　For a usefully concise account, see Bell, *France and Britain, 1940–94*, pp. 215–17.

57　Sir Nicholas Henderson, *Mandarin – The Diaries of an Ambassador, 1969–82* (Weidenfeld & Nicolson, London, 1994), pp. 132, 213.

58　*Britain and France – Partners for the Millennium* (Agenda Publishing, London, 1999), p. 7; Flora Lewis, 'Closing a Colonial Divide Holds Hope for Africa', *International Herald Tribune*, 23 April 1999.

59　John Major, *John Major* (HarperCollins, London, 1999), p. 504; Douglas Hurd, 'The "Entente Cordiale" Ninety Years On', *Journal of the Royal United Services Institute*, October 1995; *Britain and France* (Agenda Publishing, London, 1999), p. 5.

60　Cited in Anne Deighton, 'Memory and Power in International Relations' in *Memory and Power in International Relation* (Cambridge University Press, forthcoming)

61　Henderson, *Mandarin*, p. 38. See also Sabine Lee, 'Pragmatism versus Principle? Macmillan and Germany', in Aldous and Lee, *Harold Macmillan*, pp. 114–15.

62　Cited in George Bush and Brent Scowcroft, *A World Transformed* (Vintage Books, New York, 1999 edn), p. 249. See also Margaret Thatcher, *The Downing Street Years* (HarperPerennial, New York, 1993), pp. 790–99.

63　Cited in Bush and Scowcroft, *A World Transformed*, p. 253.

64　Sir Percy Craddock, *In Pursuit of British Interests* (John Murray, London, 1997), pp. 32, 112–15.

65　Hans-Peter Schwarz, *Konrad Adenauer*, Vol. 2 (Berghahn, Providence and Oxford, 1997), pp. 396, 401.

66　Piers Ludlow, *Dealing with Britain* (Cambridge University Press, Cambridge, 1997), pp. 162, 174–80; George Ball, *The Past has Another Pattern* (W. W. Norton, New York, 1982), p. 270; Schwarz, *Adenauer*, p. 119; Willy Brandt, *My Life in Politics* (Hamish Hamilton, London, 1992), p. 36.

67　'Allies of Convenience who would Now be Better Friends', *The Independent*, 8 July 1988.

68　Cited in William Roger Louis, *British Strategy in the Far East, 1919–39* (Clarendon Press, Oxford, 1971), p. 58.

69　Sir Austen Chamberlain, *Down the Ages* (Cassell, London, 1935), pp. 231–2; cf. Churchill, cited in Robin Renwick, *Fighting with Allies – America and Britain in Peace and War* (Macmillan, Basingstoke, 1996), p. 59.

70　*FRUS, Vol. X111, Western Europe and Canada* (USGPO, Washington, 1994), p. 1034.

71　Harold Macmillan, *Riding the Storm* (Macmillan, London, 1971), p. 281.

72　Cited in Richard Neustadt, *Report to JFK – the Skybolt Crisis in Perspective* (Cornell University Press, Ithaca, 1999), pp. 72–3.

73　Ibid., pp. 36, 60.

74 *FRUS, 1961–63*, p. 1089.
75 'Witness Seminar: the Role of the British Embassy in Washington', *Contemporary British History*, Autumn 1998, p. 117; Geoffrey Warner, 'The Anglo-American Special Relationship', *Diplomatic History*, Fall 1989, p. 496.
76 Renwick, *Fighting with Allies*, p. 276.
77 Sir Solly Zuckerman, *Monkeys, Men and Missiles – an Autobiography, 1946–88* (Collins, London, 1988), p. 320.
78 Cited in Louise Richardson, *When Allies Differ – Anglo-American Relations during the Suez and Falklands Crises* (Macmillan, Basingstoke, 1996), p. 128.
79 Robin Edmonds, *Setting the Mould* (Oxford University Press, Oxford, 1986), pp. 255–6.
80 James Cable, 'Interdependence; a Drug of Addiction', *International Affairs*, Summer, 1983, pp. 370, 373, 376. Cf. Henry Kissinger, *Years of Renewal* (Weidenfeld & Nicolson, London, 1999), p. 607.
81 Charles Maechling, 'Too Special a Relationship makes Britain a Feeble Ally', *International Herald Tribune*, 18 December 1997.
82 Roger Bullen and M. A. Pelly (eds), *DBPO Series 2, Vol. 2* (HMSO, London, 1987), p. 115.
83 Cited in Davis, 'Why Did the General Do It?', p. 385.
84 Harold Macmillan, *Pointing the Way, 1959–61* (Macmillan, London, 1972), p. 112.
85 Ibid., pp. 112–14.
86 Constantine Pagedas, *Anglo-American Strategic Relations and the French Problem, 1960–63 – A Troubled Partnership* (Cass, London, 2000), pp. 163–4, 168.
87 Ibid., pp. 209–12, 216; Ludlow, '*Ne Pleurez Pas Milord*', in Aldous and Lee, *Harold Macmillan*, pp. 106–7.
88 *FRUS, 1961–63*, p. 1069; Ludlow, '*Ne Pleurez Pas Milord*', p. 104.
89 Ludlow, *Dealing with Britain*, p. 118–19; Davis 'Why did the General Do It?', pp. 381–2.
90 Cited in John Campbell, *Edward Heath*, (Jonathan Cape, London, 1993), p. 344; Henry Kissinger, *Years of Upheaval* (Weidenfeld & Nicolson/Michael Joseph, London, 1982), p. 141.
91 *Hansard*, vol. 823, col. 2204, 28 October 1971.
92 Campbell, *Edward Heath*, p. 350; Cable, 'Interdependence', p. 377; Kissinger, *Years of Upheaval*, p. 189.
93 Ibid., pp. 191–2.
94 'Those Perfidious Anglo Spies', *The Economist*, 29 April 2000.
95 Robin Renwick, 'Why their Man in London is our Man too', *The Times*, 29 January 1998; 'US warns EU over Joint Action on Security', *The Guardian*, 23 November 1999.
96 Renwick, *Fighting with Allies*, p. 276. See also Edmonds, *Setting the Mould*, p. 54; John Turner, *Macmillan* (Longman, London, 1994), p. 271.
97 Cited ibid., p. 156.
98 Kenneth Harris, *Attlee* (Weidenfeld & Nicolson, London, 1984 edn), p. 465.
99 Dickie, *'Special' No More*, pp. 106–7.
100 May and Zelikow, *The Kennedy Tapes*, p. 692.
101 Ibid., p. 483.

102   Gary Rawnsly, 'How Special is Special? The Anglo- American Alliance during the Cuban Missile Crisis', *Contemporary History*, Winter 1995, p. 590; Michael Hopkins, 'Focus of a Changing Relationship: The Washington Embassy and Britain's World Role since 1945', *Contemporary British History*, Autumn 1998, p. 110; Sir Oliver Wright, 'Macmillan – A View from the Foreign Office', in Aldous and Lee, *Harold Macmillan*, p. 9; L. V. Scott, *Macmillan, Kennedy and the Cuban Missile Crisis – Political, Military and Intelligence Aspects* (Macmillan, Basingstoke, 1999).
103   Kissinger, *Years or Renewal*, p. 210.
104   *FRUS, 1961–63*, p. 1073. Cf. Pagedas, *Anglo-American Strategic Relations*, pp. 187, 196.
105   Wright, 'Macmillan', p. 9
106   Richardson, *When Allies Differ*, pp. 125; Wright, *Macmillan*, p. 10.
107   Smith, *Reagan and Thatcher*, p. 262.
108   Dean Rusk, *As I Saw It – A Secretary of State's Memoirs* (I. B. Tauris, London, 1991), p. 239; 'Witness Seminar', p. 122.
109   Nigel Ashton, 'Managing Transition: Macmillan and the Utility of Anglo-American Relations' in Aldous and Lee, *Harold Macmillan*, pp. 246–7.
110   Sir James Eberle, 'The Military Relationship', in Louis and Bull, *The 'Special Relationship'*, p. 151.
111   Cited in *The Economist*, 29 April 2000.
112   Dean Acheson, *Present at the Creation – My Years in the State Department* (Hamish Hamilton, London, 1969), p. 323.
113   Cited in John Newhouse, *De Gaulle and the Anglo- Saxons* (André Deutsch, London, 1970), p. 102; Dickie, *'Special' No More*, p. 113; Hopkins, 'Focus of a Changing Relationship', p. 110.
114   Kissinger, *The White House Years*, p. 96.
115   Edmonds, *Setting the Mould*, p. 166.
116   *FRUS, 1955–57, Vol. XXV11, Western Europe and Canada* (USGPO, Washington, 1992), p. 617.
117   *FRUS, 1958–60, Vol. V11 Part 2, Western Europe* (USGPO, Washington, 1993), p. 821.
118   Pierre, *Nuclear Politics*, p. 144.
119   Ibid.
120   David Reynolds, 'A "Special Relationship?" America, Britain and the International Order since the Second World War', *International Affairs*, Winter 1985–6, p. 15.
121   Richard Aldrich, 'British Intelligence and the Anglo-American "Special Relationship" during the Cold War', *Review of International Studies*, July 1998, pp. 348–50; Raymond Seitz, *Over Here* (Weidenfeld & Nicolson, London, 1998), pp. 298–9.
122   Seitz, *Over Here*, p. 299.
123   Cited in Alistair Horne, 'The Macmillan Years and Afterwards', in Louis and Bull, *The 'Special Relationship'*, p. 88. See also Kissinger, *The White House Years*, p. 90
124   Treverton and May, in Louis and Bull, *The 'Special Relationship'*, p. 177.
125   Kissinger, *The White House Years*, p. 90.
126   Dickie, *'Special' No More*, 259. Danchev, *On Specialness*, ch. 6, 'In the Backroom: Defence Cooperation'.

127   Ian Clarke, *Nuclear Diplomacy and the Special Relationship* (Oxford University Press, Oxford, 1994), pp. 433–4. Zuckerman, *Monkeys, Men and Missiles*, pp. 251, 253.

128   Macmillan, *Riding the Storm*, p. 252. Cf. Anne Deighton, *The Impossible Peace* (Clarendon Press, Oxford, 1993), p. 199.

129   Macmillan, *Pointing the Way*, p. 338.

130   Cited in Anita Inder Singh, *The Limits of British Influence* (Pinter, London, 1993), p. 170.

131   Cited in Philip Ziegler, *Wilson – The Authorised Life of Lord Wilson of Rievaulx* (Weidenfeld & Nicolson, London, 1995), p. 459.

132   Treverton and May, in Louis and Bull, *'The Special Relationship'*, p. 181. Renwick, *Fighting with Allies*, p. 110.

133   Cited in Michael Charlton, *The Price of Victory* (BBC, London, 1983), pp. 212–13. Something of this last factor is perhaps also reflected in Kennedy's comment that Macmillan was somebody whom he could share his loneliness with (Horne, *Macmillan, Vol. 2*), p. 305.

134   William Wallace, 'Foreign Policy and National Identity in the UK', *International Affairs*, January 1991, p. 77.

135   Cited in Christopher Goldsmith, 'In the Know? Sir Gladwyn Jebb: Ambassador to France', in Saul Kelly and Anthony Gorst, *Whitehall and the Suez Crisis* (Frank Cass, London, 2000), p. 8.

136   Cited in Danchev, *On Specialness*, pp. 3–4.

137   Kissinger, *Years of Renewal*, p. 210.

138   Richardson, *When Allies Differ*, pp. 25–6; Geoffrey Warner, 'The US and the Suez Crisis', *International Affairs*, April 1991, pp. 313–14.

139   See Chapter 5, p. 105.

140   *International Herald Tribune*, 31 March 1999.

141   Renwick, *Fighting with Allies*, p. 276.

142   Cited in Tratt, *The Macmillan Government and Europe*, p. 182; interview, Tony Blair, *International Herald Tribune*, 18 November 1998.

5   The strategic dimension

1   Paul Kennedy, *The Rise and Fall of the Great Powers* (Fontana, London, 1989 edn), pp. 344, 354; W. K. Hancock and Margaret Gowing, *The British War Economy – History of the Second World War* (HMSO, London, 1949), p. 199; David Stevenson, *Armaments and the Coming of War* (Oxford University Press, Oxford, 1996), p. 6; *The Military Balance, 1999–2000* (International Institute for Strategic Studies, London, 1999), p. 300.

2   Anthony Clayton, *The British Empire as a Superpower, 1919–39* (University of Georgia Press, Athens, 1986), p. 189.

3   Malcolm Rifkind, 'Peacekeeping or Peacemaking? Implications and Prospects', *Journal of the Royal United Services Institute*, April 1993, p. 1.

4   A. J. P. Taylor, *English History, 1914–45* (Oxford University Press, Oxford, 1965), p. 600.

5   Michael Crawshaw, 'The Impact of Technology on the BEF and its Commander', in Brian Bond and Nigel Cave (eds), *Haig – A Reappraisal Seventy Years On* (Leo Cooper, London, 1999), p. 158.

6   Alan Bullock, *Ernest Bevin* (Oxford University Press, Oxford, 1985), p. 854.
7   Williamson Murray, 'British Military Effectiveness in the Second World War', in Allan Millet and Williamson Murray, *Military Effectiveness, Vol. 3, The Second World War* (Allen & Unwin, Boston, 1988), pp. 92–3.
8   Williamson Murray, *Luftwaffe* (George Allen & Unwin, London, 1985), p. 47. Michael Glover, *Invasion Scare, 1940* (Leo Cooper, London, 1990), pp. 101, 194–200; Jehuda Wallach, 'The Sea Lion that did not Roar: Operation Sea Lion and its Limitations', in John Hattendorf and Malcolm Murfet (eds), *The Limitations of Military Power* (Macmillan, Basingstoke, 1990), pp. 197, 199. See also David Reynolds, *Britannia Overruled* (Longman, London, 1991), p. 147.
9   Clayton, *The British Empire as a Superpower*, p. 80; Jafna Cox, 'A Splendid Training Ground: the Importance to the RAF of its Role in Iraq, 1919–32', *Journal of Imperial and Commonwealth History*, January 1985, p. 159; David Omissi, *Air Power and Colonial Control – the Royal Air Force, 1919–39* (Manchester University Press, Manchester, 1990), p. 212.
10   Clayton, *The British Empire as a Superpower*, p. 80.
11   Anthony Clayton, ' "Deceptive Might": Imperial Defence and Security, 1900–68', in William Roger Louis and Judith Brown, *The Oxford History of the British Empire, Vol. 1V* (Oxford University Press, Oxford, 1999), p. 303.
12   Clayton, *The British Empire as a Superpower*, p. 15.
13   Thomas Mockaitis, *British Counterinsurgency, 1919–60* (Macmillan, Basingstoke, 1990), p. 23.
14   Clayton, 'Deceptive Might', p. 303; Frank Furedi, 'Creating a Breathing Space: the Political Management of Colonial Emergencies', in Robert Holland (ed.), *Emergencies and Disorders in the European Empires after 1945* (Frank Cass, London, 1994), p. 97.
15   Cited in Denis Healey, *The Time of My Life* (Michael Joseph, London, 1989), p. 287.
16   Mockaitis, *British Counterinsurgency*, pp. 52, 55–7.
17   Cited in *British Foreign Policy – A Brief Collection of Fact and Quotation* (Central Office of Information, London, 1954), p. 6.
18   Cited in Keith Kyle, 'The Mandarin's Mandarin: Sir Norman Brook, Secretary of the Cabinet', in Saul Kelly and Anthony Gorst, *Whitehall and the Suez Crisis* (Frank Cass, London, 2000), p. 68.
19   Cited in Anthony Adamthwaite, 'Suez Revisited', *International Affairs*, Summer 1988, p. 453.
20   Peter Mangold, 'The Role of Force in British Policy towards the Middle East, 1957–66' (unpublished PhD thesis, University of London, 1973), pp. 270, 272.
21   Healey, *Time of My Life*, p. 287. Thomas Mockaitis, *British Counterinsurgency in the Post-Imperial Era* (Manchester University Press, Manchester, 1995), pp. 34–7.
22   William Roger Louis, 'The Dissolution of the British Empire' in Louis and Brown, *Oxford History*, p. 339.
23   William Roger Louis, *The British Empire in the Middle East, 1945–51* (Oxford University Press, Oxford, 1984), p. 675.
24   Ibid., pp. 687–8.
25   David Goldsworthy (ed.), *The Conservative Government and the End of Empire, 1951–57* (HMSO, London, 1994), pp. 179–83.

26 Barbara Castle, *The Castle Diaries, 1964–70* (Weidenfeld & Nicolson, London, 1984), pp. 257–8.

27 Malcom Rifkind, 'Peacekeeping', p. 3. See also Douglas Hurd, *Hansard*, Sixth Series, vol. 219, col. 785, 23 February 1993.

28 Sir William Jackson, *Withdrawal from Empire* (Batsford, London, 1986), p. 114.

29 Margaret Thatcher, *The Downing Street Years, 1979–1990* (HarperPerennial, New York, 1993), p. 235.

30 Cited in Norman Rose, *Churchill – an Unruly Life* (Simon & Schuster, London, 1994), p. 113.

31 Ibid.

32 Robert Rhodes-James, *Churchill – a Study in Failure* (Weidenfeld & Nicolson, London, 1990), pp. 74–5.

33 Sir Curtis Keeble, *Britain and the Soviet Union, 1917–89* (Macmillan, Basingstoke,1990), p. 36.

34 Ibid., p. 37.

35 John Darwin, *Britain and Decolonisation* (Macmillan, Basingstoke, 1988), p. 119.

36 See Naomi Shepherd, *Ploughing Sand – British Rule in Palestine, 1917–48* (John Murray, London, 1999), pp. 7–13.

37 David Fromkin, *A Peace to End All Peace*, (André Deutsch, London, 1989), pp. 297; William Roger Louis, *In the Name of God, Go! Leo Amery and the British Empire in the Age of Churchill* (W. W. Norton, New York, 1992), p. 82. For the text of the Balfour Declaration, see Avi Shlaim, *The Iron Wall – Israel and the Arab World* (Allen Lane, The Penguin Press, London, 2000), p. 7.

38 Cited in Robert Holland, *Britain and the Revolt in Cyprus, 1954–59* (Oxford University Press, Oxford, 1998), p. 57.

39 Cited in Sean Faughnan, 'The Politics of Influence – Churchill, Eden and Soviet Communism 1951–7' (unpublished PhD thesis, University of Cambridge, 1993), p. 374.

40 Evelyn Shuckburgh, *Descent to Suez* (Weidenfeld & Nicolson, London, 1986), p. 347.

41 Ibid., p. 350.

42 Brian Lapping, *The End of Empire* (Paladin, London, 1989), p. 316. See also interview with Anthony Nutting, transcripts, *End of Empire* (Middle East Archive, St Antony's College, Oxford).

43 Cited in Alistair Horne, *Macmillan, Vol. 1* (Macmillan, London, 1988), p. 416. Cf. Shuckburgh, *Descent to Suez*, pp. 360–1.

44 Horne, *Macmillan, Vol. 1*, pp. 410.

45 Ibid., p. 411.

46 Keith Kyle, *Suez* (Weidenfeld & Nicolson, London, 1991), p. 208.

47 Cited in Ann Lane, 'The Past as Matrix: Sir Ivone Kirkpatrick, Permanent Under-Secretary for Foreign Affairs', in Kelly and Gorst, *Whitehall*, p. 202.

48 Cited in Peter Calvocoressi (ed.), *Suez Ten Years After* (BBC, London, 1967), p. 45.

49 Kyle, *Suez*, pp. 257–8; Horne, *Macmillan, Vol. 1*, pp. 420–25. See also Lewis Johnman, 'Playing the Role of a Cassandra: Sir Gerald Fitzmaurice, Senior Legal Counsel to the Foreign Office', in Kelly and Gorst, *Whitehall*.

50 Horne, *Macmillan, Vol. 1*, p. 427.

51 Cited ibid., p. 447.

52   D. R. Thorpe, *Selwyn Lloyd* (Cape, London, 1989), p. 267. Kyle, *Suez*, pp. 210–11, 335; Michael Thornhill, 'Alternatives to Nasser; Humphrey Trevelyan, Ambassador to Egypt', in Kelly and Gorst, *Whitehall*, pp. 11–25.

53   Harold Macmillan, *Riding the Storm* (Macmillan, London, 1971), p. 511.

54   General André Beaufre, *The Suez Expedition* (Faber & Faber, London, 1969) p. 127. Lapping, *End of Empire*, pp. 334–40.

55   Sean Greenwood, *Britain and the Cold War, 1945–91* (Macmillan, Basingstoke, 2000), p. 139.

56   Cited in William Roger Louis, 'The Dissolution of the British Empire', in Louis and Brown, *Oxford History*, p. 343. See also Sir Charles Johnson, *The Brink of Jordan* (Macmillan, London, 1972), p. 171. Nigel John Ashton, 'A Microcosm of Decline. British Loss of Nerve and Military Intervention in Jordan and Kuwait, 1958 and 1961', *The Historical Journal*, vol. 40, no. 4, 1997, pp. 1069–73.

57   Richard Lamb, *The Macmillan Years, 1957–63 – The Emerging Truth* (John Murray, London, 1995), pp. 35–6; Nigel John Ashton, *Eisenhower, Macmillan and the Problem of Nasser – Anglo-American Relations and Arab Nationalism, 1955–59* (Macmillan, Basingstoke, 1996), pp. 170–71.

58   Ibid., pp. 170–72.

59   Macmillan, *Riding the Storm*, p. 517.

60   Ibid., pp. 271, 277, 516–21. Cf. Ashton, 'A Microcosm of Decline', p. 1083.

61   Kyle, *Suez*, pp. 559–60; James Callaghan, *Time and Chance* (William Collins, London, 1987), p. 356.

62   Michael Parsons (ed.), *Looking Back: the Wilson Years, 1964–70* (Publications de L'Université de Pau, Pau, 1999), pp. 63–4.

63   Bullock, *Ernest Bevin*, p. 51.

64   Michael Charlton, *The Price of Victory* (BBC, London, 1983), p. 307.

65   Paul Kennedy, 'Britain in the First World War', in Allan Millett and Williamson Murray (eds), *Military Effectiveness, Vol. 1, The First World War* (Unwin, Hyman, Boston, 1988), p. 72.

66   Ibid., p. 63.

67   Peter Mangold, *From Tirpitz to Gorbachev* (Macmillan, Basinstoke, 1998), ch. 3.

68   *Journal of the Royal United Service Institute*, vol. XLIII, 15 December 1899, no.262.

69   Mangold, *Tirpitz to Gorbachev*, pp. 35–6.

70   Michael Geyer, 'German Strategy in the Age of Machine Warfare', in Peter Paret (ed.), *Masters of Modern Strategy* (Oxford University Press, Oxford, 1986), p. 536.

71   Cited in Trevor Wilson, *The Myriad Faces of War – Britain and the Great War, 1914–18* (Polity Press, Cambridge, 1986), p. 99.

72   Michael Howard, *The Continental Commitment* (Temple Smith, London, 1972), p. 45.

73   Colonel Seely, *Hansard*, Fifth Series, vol. XXXV, col. 1020, 12 March 1912. See also Crawshaw, 'The Impact of Technology', p. 157.

74   Samuel Williamson, *The Politics of Grand Strategy* (Harvard University Press, Cambridge, MA, 1969), pp. 112, 369; Paul Guinn, *British Strategy and Politics, 1914–18* (Oxford University Press, Oxford, 1965), pp. 22–3.

75   David French, *British Strategy and War Aims, 1914–16* (Allen & Unwin, London, 1986), pp. 13–14.

76 Cited in Williamson, *Grand Strategy*, p. 24.
77 Cited in R. J. Q. Adams and Philip Poirier, *The Conscription Controversy in Great Britain, 1900–18* (Ohio State University Press, Ohio, 1987), pp. 16, 248.
78 John Gooch, 'The Weary Titan – Strategy and Policy in Great Britain, 1890–1918', in Williamson Murray, Macgregor Knox and Alvin Bernstein (eds), *The Making of Strategy – Rulers, States and War*, (Cambridge University Press, Cambridge, 1994), p. 299.
79 Wilson, *Myriad Faces of War*, p. 318.
80 Denis Winters, *Haig's Command – A Reassessment* (Penguin, Harmondsworth, 1992), p. 136.
81 Tim Travers, *The Killing Ground – the British Army, the Western Front and the Emergence of Modern Warfare, 1900–18* (Routledge, London, 1993 edn), pp. 85–97; C. S. Forester, *The General* (Penguin Books, Harmondsworth, 1956), p. 173; Kennedy, 'Britain in the First World War', pp. 52–5.
82 Martin Samuels, *Doctrine and Dogma – German and British Infantry Tactics in the First World War* (Greenwood Press, New York, 1992), pp. 49–50, 88–9, 97.
83 Williamson Murray, 'Armoured Warfare', in Williamson Murray and Allan Millet (eds), *Military Innovation in the Interwar Period* (Cambridge University Press, Cambridge, 1996) p. 47.
84 Cited in Elizabeth Kier, *Imagining War – French and British Military Doctrine between the Wars* (Princeton University Press, Princeton, NJ, 1997), p. 137.
85 Cited in Murray, *Military Innovation*, p. 22.
86 David Fraser, *Alanbrooke* (Harper Collins, London, 1997), pp. 105–6.
87 See C. N. Barclay, *On their Shoulders – British Generalship in the Lean Years, 1939–42* (Faber & Faber, London, 1964).
88 Brian Bond, *British Military Policy between the Two World Wars* (Clarendon Press, Oxford, 1980), p. 25.
89 Cited in John Ferris, *Men, Money and Diplomacy: The Evolution of British Policy, 1919–26* (Cornell University Press, Ithaca, 1989), pp. 111–12.
90 R. A. C. Parker, *Chamberlain and Appeasement* (Macmillan, Basingstoke, 1993), pp. 272, 285; Paul Kennedy, *The Rise and Fall of British Naval Mastery* (Macmillan, London, 1983), p. 315. See also G. C. Peden, *British Rearmament and the Treasury, 1932–39* (Scottish Academic Press, Edinburgh, 1979), pp. 63, 65. N. H. Gibbs, *Grand Strategy – Vol. 1* (HMSO, London, 1976), pp. 283–5.
91 Peter Dennis, *Decision by Default: Peacetime Conscription and British Defence Policy, 1919–39* (Routledge & Kegan Paul, 1972), pp. 32–3, 57.
92 Gibbs, *Grand Strategy*, p. 98.
93 Lord Lloyd, 'The Need for the Rearmament of Great Britain: Its Justification and Scope', *International Affairs*, January/February 1936, p. 70; Neville Thompson, *The Anti-Appeasers – Conservative Opposition to Appeasement in the 1930s* (Oxford University Press, Oxford, 1971), p. 106.
94 Cited in Keith Middlemas and John Barnes, *Baldwin* (Weidenfeld & Nicolson, London, 1969), p. 722.
95 Cited in Philip Williamson, *Stanley Baldwin, Conservative Leadership and National Values* (Cambridge University Press, Cambridge, 1999), p. 300.
96 *Hansard*, vol. 275, cols 1817, 1824, 14 March 1933; Middlemas and Barnes, *Baldwin*, pp. 732, 735–6.
97 See Murray, *The Change in the European Balance of Power*, pp. 152–3, 222, 262–3.

98   Cited in Lord Strang, *Britain in World Affairs* (Faber & Faber and André Deutsch, London, 1961), p. 324.

99   Murray, *The Change in the European Balance of Power*, p. 91.

100 David Owen, *Time to Declare* (Penguin, Harmondsworth, 1992), p. 361.

101 Michael Charlton, *The Little Platoon – Diplomacy and the Falklands Dispute* (Basil Blackwell, Oxford, 1989), p. 28.

102 Ibid., pp. 92, 95.

103 Ibid., p. 57.

104 Ibid., p. 138; Alex Danchev, 'Introduction', *The Franks Report – Lord Franks et al.* (Pimlico, London, 1982), p. xx. See also Lord Carrington, *Reflect on Things Past* (Fontana, London, 1989), p. 357.

105 Charlton, *The Little Platoon*, p. 138.

106 Danchev, 'Introduction', p. 30.

107 Thatcher, *The Downing Street Years*, p. 179.

108 Michael Stewart, *Life and Labour* (Sidgwick & Jackson, London, 1986), pp. 169–70.

109 Jackson, *Withdrawal from Empire*, pp. 227–8.

110 General Sir Charles Guthrie, 'Bringing the Armed Forces into the New Millennium', *Journal of the Royal United Services Institute*, February 2000, p. 3.

111 Williamson, *The Politics of Grand Strategy*, pp. 187–93, 369.

112 David French, *Raising Churchill's Army – the British Army and the War Against Germany* (Oxford University Press, Oxford, 2000), pp. 284–5.

113 *The Economist*, 25 November 2000.

114 'The East of Suez Decision', *Journal of Contemporary History*, Winter 1993, p. 634.

6   The sound barrier

1   *FRUS, 1961–63, Vol. XIII, Western Europe and Canada* (USGPO, Washington, 1994), p. 1064.

2   Cited in Robert Boardman and A. J. R. Groom, *The Management of Britain's External Relations* (Macmillan, Basingstoke, 1973), p. 6; John Campbell, *Edward Heath* (Cape, London, 1993), p. 334; John Young, 'The Heath Government and British Entry into the European Community', in Stuart Ball and Anthony Seldon (eds), *The Heath Government, 1970–74 – A Reappraisal* (Longman, London, 1996), p. 261.

3   William Wallace, 'Foreign Policy' in Denis Kavanagh and Anthony Seldon (eds), *The Major Effect* (Macmillan, London, 1994), p. 285.

4   Anne Deighton 'British Imperial Memories and the European Question' in *Memory and Power in International Relations* (Cambridge University Press, forthcoming).

5   William Fox, *The Super-Powers* (Harcourt, Brace and Co., New York, 1944), pp. 12, 20–21.

6   Geoffrey Warner, 'The Impact of the Second World War upon British Foreign Policy', in Brian Brivati and Harriet Jones (eds), *What Difference did the War Make?* (Leicester University Press, Leicester, 1993), pp. 99–100.

7   Cited in David Reynolds, 'Britain and the New Europe: the Search for Identity since 1940', *Historical Journal*, 1988, vol. XXX1, p. 225;

Robin Edmonds, *Setting the Mould* (Oxford University Press, Oxford, 1986), p. 29.

8 Cited in Corelli Barnett, *The Lost Victory – British Dreams, British Realities, 1945–50* (Pan Books, London, 1996), p. 89.

9 Cited in John Baylis, *Ambiguity and Deterrence – British Nuclear Strategy, 1945–65* (Clarendon Press, Oxford, 1995), p. 86.

10 Cited in Barnett, *The Lost Victory*, p. 54.

11 Cited in Anthony Adamthwaite, 'The Foreign Office and Policy-Making' in John Young (ed.), *The Foreign Policy of Churchill's Peacetime Administration, 1951–55* (Leicester University Press, Leicester, 1988), p. 9. See also Anthony Adamthwaite, 'Overstretched and Overstrung: Eden, the Foreign Office and the Making of Policy, 1951–55', *International Affairs*, Spring 1988, p. 243.

12 Lord Franks, *Britain and the Tide of World Affairs* (BBC Reith Lectures, 1954) (Oxford University Press, London, 1955), p. 5.

13 Cited in David Reynolds, 'Roosevelt, Churchill and the Wartime Anglo-American Alliance, 1939–45', in William Roger Louis and Hedley Bull (eds), *The 'Special Relationship'* (Clarendon Press, Oxford, 1986), p. 29.

14 Cited in Dennis Austin, *Malta and the End of Empire* (Cass, London, 1971), p. 67.

15 Roy Douglas, *World Crisis and British Decline, 1929–56* (Macmillan, Basingstoke, 1986), p. 254.

16 Cited in Sir John Coles, *Making British Foreign Policy* (John Murray, London, 2000), p. 72.

17 Franks, *Britain and the Tide of World Affairs*, p. 6.

18 Sean Greenwood, *Britain and the Cold War, 1945–91* (Macmillan, Basingstoke, 2000), p. 194.

19 Lord Carrington, *Reflect on Things Past* (Fontana, London, 1989), p. 311; Michael Charlton, *The Price of Victory* (BBC, London, 1983), p. 171.

20 Charles de Gaulle, *The Complete War Memoirs* (Simon & Schuster, New York, 1972 edn), p. 1; Paul Sharp, *Thatcher's Diplomacy – the Revival of British Foreign Policy* (Macmillan, Basingstoke, 1997), p. 73.

21 Cited in Sean Faughnan 'The Politics of Influence' (unpublished PhD thesis, Cambridge University, Cambridge 1993), p. 274.

22 Richard Crossman, *The Crossman Diaries, Vol. 2* (Hamish Hamilton and Jonathan Cape, London, 1976), p. 639.

23 Enoch Powell, 'The Spell of England', *The Daily Telegraph*, 9 February 1998. See also Michael Blackwell, *Clinging to Grandeur: British Attitudes and Foreign Policy in the Aftermath of the Second World War* (Greenwood, Westport, CT, 1993), p. 119.

24 Sir Charles Johnson, valedictory despatch, Aden, 26 August 1963, CO ADN 164/56/01; Sir Evelyn Shuckburgh, transcripts, *Granada – End of Empire* (Middle East Archive, St Antony's College, Oxford); Joseph Frankel, *British Foreign Policy, 1945–73* (Royal Institute of International Affairs/Oxford University Press, Oxford, 1975), p. 118. Cf. W. David McIntyre, *British Decolonisation, 1946–97 – When, Why and How did the British Empire Fall?* (Macmillan, Basingstoke, 1998), p. 129.

25 Lord Plowden, *An Industrialist in the Treasury* (André Deutsch, London, 1989), p. 162. See also Blackwell, *Clinging to Grandeur*, pp. 66–8, 77; Frankel, *British Foreign Policy*, pp. 91–2; John Darwin, *Britain and Decolonisation* (Macmillan, Basingstoke, 1988), p. 130.

26 'The Future of the UK in World Affairs', in David Goldsworthy (ed.), *The Conservative Government and the End of Empire* (HMSO, London, 1994), p. 63.

27 Cited in Blackwell, *Clinging to Grandeur*, p. 121.

28 *Future Policy Study, 1960–70, Part 3*, CAB21/3841.

29 Charles Feinstein, 'The End of Empire and the Golden Age', in Peter Clarke and Clive Trebilcock (eds), *Understanding Decline* (Cambridge University Press, Cambridge, 1997), p. 213.

30 *Future Policy Study, Part 2 The Resources of the UK*, CAB21/3841.

31 Paul Kennedy, *The Realities behind Diplomacy* (Fontana, London, 1981), p. 341.

32 Andrew Pierre, *Nuclear Politics* (Oxford University Press, Oxford, 1972), p. 198.

33 *Hansard*, vol. 622, cols 288–9, 27 April 1960.

34 Ibid., col. 259.

35 Charlton, *The Price of Victory*, pp. 303–4. Cf. Sir Ivone Kirkpatrick, cited in Anthony Adamthwaite, 'Overstretched and Overstrained', p. 254; Lord Strang, cited in Victor Feske, 'The Road to Suez: the British Foreign Office and the Quai d'Orsay, 1951–57', in Gordon Craig and Francis Loewenheim (eds), *The Diplomats, 1939–79* (Princeton University Press, Princeton, NJ, 1994), p. 170.

36 Goldsworthy, *The Conservative Government*, p. 60.

37 Tony Hopkins, 'Macmillan's Audit of Empire', in Clarke and Trebilcock (eds), *Understanding Decline*, p. 259.

38 Minute, Sir Norman Brooke, 25 November 1957, PREM 11/2321.

39 FO371/143702; Lord Carver, *Tightrope Walking – British Defence Policy since 1945* (Hutchinson, London, 1992), p. 63.

40 Coles, *Making British Foreign Policy*, pp. 68–9.

41 *Future Policy Study, 1960–70*, CAB 21/3841.

42 Cited in Greenwood, *Britain and the Cold War*, p. 54; see also p. 72.

43 Cited in Frankel, *British Foreign Policy*, p. 157; Peter Hennessy, *Never Again* (Vintage, London, 1983 edn), pp. 342–3. See also Anne Deighton, 'Britain and the Three Interlocking Circles' in Antonio Varsori (ed.), *Europe, 1945–90 – The End of an Era?* (Macmillan, Basingstoke, 1995).

44 Simon Burgess and Geoffrey Edwards, 'The Six Plus One', *International Affairs*, Summer 1988, p. 407.

45 Cited in Philip Darby, *British Defence Policy East of Suez, 1947–68* (Oxford University Press, Oxford, 1993), p. 152.

46 William Wallace, *The Foreign Policy Process in Britain* (Royal Institute of International Affairs, London, 1975), p. 133.

47 James Wyllie, *The Influence of British Arms – An Analysis of British Military Intervention since 1956* (George Allen & Unwin, London, 1986), p. 1.

48 Andrew Shonfield, 'The Pursuit of Prestige – A Guide to Post-war British Policy', *Encounter*, January 1957, p. 44.

49 Cited in Frankel, *British Foreign Policy*, p. 163. See also L. A. Seidentop, 'Mr.Macmillan and the Edwardian Style', in Vernon Bogdanor and Robert Skidelsky (eds), *The Age of Affluence* (Macmillan, London, 1970), p. 34; Leon Epstein, 'Britain and the H-bomb', *The Review of Politics*, July 1959, p. 518.

50 James Callaghan, *Challenges and Opportunities for British Foreign Policy* (Fabian Tract no.439, London, 1975), p. 10. Cf. Sir Alec Douglas-Home, cited in Kenneth Waltz, *Foreign Policy and the Democratic Process* (Longman, London, 1968), p. 241.

51 Tony Blair, 'The Principles of a Modern British Foreign Policy', *International Herald Tribune*, 10 November 1997; 'Britain is now a Pivotal Power, Claims Blair', *The Guardian*, 23 November 1999.

52 Cited in *Report of the Committee on Representation Overseas* (the Plowden Report) Cmnd 2276, (HMSO, London 1964), para. 9.

53 Harold Macmillan, *Pointing the Way* (Macmillan, London, 1972), p. 195; Richard Aldous, 'A Family Affair – Macmillan and the Art of Personal Diplomacy', in Richard Aldous and Sabine Lee (eds), *Harold Macmillan and Britain's World Role* (Macmillan, Basingstoke, 1996), p. 22.

54 Shuckburgh, *Granada-End of Empire*, p. 274. Cf. Faughnan, *The Politics of Influence*, pp. 258, 274.

55 Cited in John Gearson, *Harold Macmillan and the Berlin Wall Crisis* (Macmillan, Basingstoke, 1998), p. 77.

56 Cited in Horne, *Macmillan*, Vol. 2, p. 231; John Turner, *Macmillan* (Longman, London, 1994,) pp. 146, 150.

57 Shonfield, *The Pursuit of Prestige*, p. 40; Malcolm Chalmers, *Paying for Defence – Military Spending and British Decline* (Pluto, London,1985), p. 26.

58 Margaret Gowing, *Independence and Deterrence – Britain and Atomic Energy, 1945–52, Vol. 1 Policy-Making* (Macmillan, London, 1974), p. 184; Peter Hennessy, *Muddling Through – Power, Politics and the Quality of Government in Postwar Britain* (Indigo edn, London,1997), pp. 98, 104.

59 Cited in Michael Dockrill, 'Restoring the Special Relationship – the Bermuda and Washington Conferences, 1957', in Dick Richardson and Glyn Stone (eds), *Decisions and Diplomacy – Essays in Twentieth Century International History* (Routledge, London, 1995), p. 207.

60 Cited in William Wallace, 'World Status Without Tears' in Bogdanor and Skidelsky, *The Age of Affluence*, pp. 219–20.

61 Cited in Jeffrey Pickering, *Britain's Withdrawal from East of Suez* (Macmillan, Basingstoke, 1998), p. 95. Cf. Philip Ziegler, *Wilson* (Weidenfeld & Nicolson, London, 1995), p. 210.

62 *FRUS, 1961–62, Vol. X111*, p. 1109.

63 Susan Strange, *Sterling and British Policy – A Political Study of an International Currency in Decline* (Oxford University Press, Oxford, 1971); David Sanders, *Losing an Empire, Finding a Role* (Macmillan, Basingstoke, 1990), p. 206.

64 *Future Policy Study, 1960–70, Pt 2.*, CAB21/3841.

65 Hennessy, *Never Again*, p. 416.

66 Ibid., p. 415. For an alternative view, see Jihang Park, 'Wasted Opportunities? The 50s Rearmament Programme and the Failure of the British Economy', *Journal of Contemporary History*, July 1997.

67 Chalmers, *Paying for Defence*, pp. 116–20.

68 Callaghan, *Challenges and Opportunities for British Foreign Policy*, p. 1; Sir Alec Douglas-Home, *Britain's Changing Role in World Affairs* (David Davies Memorial Institute, London, 1974), p. 2.

69 Raymond Seitz, *Over Here* (Weidenfeld & Nicolson, London, 1998), pp. 300–1.

70 Henry Kissinger, *The White House Years* (Weidenfeld & Nicolson/Michael Joseph, London, 1979), p. 421.

71 Sir Nicholas Henderson, 'Britain's Decline: its Causes and Consequences', reprinted in *Channels and Tunnels* (Weidenfeld & Nicolson, London, 1987), p. 154.

72 Callaghan, *Challenges and Opportunities for British Foreign Policy*, p. 4.
73 'Record of the Final Session of the Annual Conference of the Commissioner-General, South East Asia', 19 January 1958, PREM11/2219.
74 Cited in Wolfram Kaiser, *Using Europe, Abusing the Europeans – Britain and European Integration, 1945–63* (Macmillan, Basingstoke, 1996), p. 2.
75 Cited in Lord Carver, *Out of Step – Memoirs of a Field Marshal* (Hutchinson, London, 1989), p. 288.
76 Hugo Young, *This Blessed Plot* (Macmillan, London, 1998), pp. 101–3, 176.
77 Attlee cited in John Baylis, *The Diplomacy of Pragmatism – Britain and the Formation of NATO, 1942–49* (Macmillan, Basingstoke, 1993), p. 76.
78 Adamthwaite, 'Overstretched and Overstrung', p. 248.
79 Darwin, *Britain and Decolonisation*, p. 290; Richard Neustadt, *Report to JFK* (Cornell University Press, Ithaca, 1999), p. 110.
80 Pierre, *Nuclear Politics*, pp. 221–2.
81 David Dutton, *Anthony Eden* (Edward Arnold, London, 1997), p. 328; Robert Rhodes-James, *Anthony Eden* (Weidenfeld & Nicolson, London, 1986), p. 353.
82 Macmillan, *Pointing the Way*, pp. 79–80.
83 *Hansard*, vol. 622, col. 259, 27 April 1960.
84 Lawrence Martin and John Garnett, *British Foreign Policy – Challenges and Choices for the Twenty-First Century* (Royal Institute of International Affairs, London, 1997), p. 16.
85 Willy Brandt, *My Life in Politics* (Hamish Hamilton, London, 1992), p. 420; Kaiser, *Using Europe*, p. 74; John Young, 'The Heath Government and British Entry into the European Community', in Ball and Seldon, *The Heath Government*, p. 261.
86 F. S. Northedge, *The Troubled Giant – Britain among the Great Powers, 1916–39* (LSE, London, 1966), p. 629.
87 Wallace, op. cit., p. 274.
88 See Chapter 1, p. 4–5.
89 Waltz, *Foreign Policy and the Democratic Process*, p. 306–7. Cf. also Frankel, *British Foreign Policy*, p. 110.

7   International impact

1 G. P. Gooch and Harold Temperley, 'Memorandum on the Present State of British Relations with France and Germany', *British Documents on the Origins of the War, 1989–1914, Vol. 3* (HMSO, London, 1928), pp. 402–3.
2 Cited in W. N. Medlicott, *British Foreign Policy since Versailles, 1918–63* (Methuen, London, 2nd edn, 1968), p. 334.
3 'Memorandum on the Foreign Policies of His Majesty's Government', in W. N. Medlicott and Douglas Dakin (eds), *DBFP, 1919–39 Series 1A, Vol. 1* (HMSO, London, 1966), p. 846. See also Michael Stewart, cited in Joseph Frankel, *British Foreign Policy, 1945–73* (Royal Institute of International Affairs/Oxford University Press, London, 1975), p. 86.
4 *The Essential Interests of the United Kingdom, Vol. 1* (Royal Institute of International Affairs, London, 1938), p. 3. Cf. James Joll, *Britain and Europe, 1793–1940* (A. C. Black, London, 1961 edn), p. 11.

5 *FRUS, 1958–60, Vol. V11, Pt. 2 Western Europe* (USGPO, Washington, 1993), p. 846. See also Peter Boyle, 'The British Government's View of the Cuban Missile Crisis', *Contemporary History*, Autumn 1996, p. 29.

6 Michael Howard, *War and the Liberal Conscience* (Temple Smith, London, 1978), p. 31.

7 Cited in R. A. C. Parker, *Chamberlain and Appeasement* (Macmillan, Basingstoke, 1992), p. 336. See also Peter Ludlow, 'The Unwinding of Appeasement' in Lothar Kettenacker, *Das 'Andere Deutschland' im Zweiten Weltkrieg* (Ernst Klett Verlag, Stuttgart, 1977), pp. 17–18.

8 Lord Beloff, *The Future of British Foreign Policy* (Secker & Warburg, London, 1969), p. 116.

9 *Hansard*, Sixth Series, vol. 219, col. 783, 23 February 1993.

10 'Cook makes Pledge on Human Rights', *Financial Times*, 13 May 1997.

11 Henry Kissinger, 'Reflections on a Partnership: British and American Attitudes to Postwar Foreign Policy', *International Affairs*, Autumn 1982, p. 572.

12 PREM 11/3775. See inter alia D. C. Watt, 'British Reactions to the Assassination at Sarajevo', *European Studies Review*, July 1971, pp. 238–9; Sean Lynn-Jones, 'Détente and Deterrence – Anglo-German Relations, 1911–14', *International Security*, Fall 1986.

13 For further discussion of these points, see Peter Mangold, *From Tirpitz to Gorbachev* (Macmillan, Basingstoke, 1998), pp. 32–3.

14 Cited in Michael Stuermer, *Die Grenzen der Macht – Begegnung der Deutschen mit der Geschichte* (Siedler Verlag, Berlin, 1992), p. 98.

15 Parker, *Chamberlain and Appeasement*, pp. 261–2.

16 Michael Howard, 'British Grand Strategy in World War One', in Paul Kennedy (ed.), *Grand Strategies in War and Peace* (Yale University Press, New Haven and London, 1991), p. 34.

17 Cited in David Fraser, *Alanbrooke* (HarperCollins, London, 1997 edn), p. 46.

18 Paul Kennedy, *The Rise and Fall of the Great Powers* (Fontana, London, 1989), p. 354.

19 Ibid., p. 458.

20 David Reynolds, '1940: Fulcrum of the Twentieth Century?', *International Affairs*, April 1990, p. 346.

21 Richard Overy, *Why the Allies Won* (Jonathan Cape, London, 1995), p. 131.

22 Corelli Barnett, *Britain and her Army, 1509–1970* (Allen Lane, The Penguin Press, Harmondsworth, 1970), p. 426.

23 Sir Michael Alexander, 'Does Better Intelligence Improve Foreign Policy Decisions?', *Journal of the Royal United Services Institute*, October 1999, p. 4.

24 See Ian Turner, *Reconstruction in Post-War Germany, British Occupation and the Western Zones, 1945–55* (Berg, Oxford and New York, 1989); Anne Deighton, 'Britain and the Cold War; an Overview', in Brian Brivati and Harriet Jones (eds), *From Reconstruction to Integration – Britain and Europe since 1954* (Leicester University Press, Leicester, 1993), p. 11. See also Anne Deighton, *The Impossible Peace – Britain, the Division of Germany, and the Origins of the Cold War* (Clarendon Press, Oxford, 1993).

25 Sean Greenwood, *Britain and the Cold War, 1945–91* (Macmillan, Basingstoke, 2000), pp. 126–7; P. M. H. Bell, *France and Britain, 1940–94* (Longman, London, 1997), pp. 125–6; Anne Deighton, 'Britain and the Creation of the

WEU, 1954', in Anne Deighton (ed.), *WEU, 1954–97 – Deterrence, Security, Integration* (European Interdependence Research Unit, St Antony's College, Oxford, 1997), pp. 11,22.

26 Deighton, *The Impossible Peace*, p. 206; John Baylis, *The Diplomacy of Pragmatism* (Macmillan, Basingstoke, 1993), p. 4.

27 Alan Bullock, *Ernest Bevin* (Oxford University Press, Oxford, 1985), pp. 575–6; Avi Shlaim, 'Britain, the Berlin Blockade and the Cold War', *International Affairs*, Winter 1983–4, pp. 5–6; Stuart Croft, *The End of Superpower – British Foreign Office Conceptions of a Changing World, 1945–51* (Dartmouth, Aldershot, 1994), pp. 127–8.

28 Greenwood, *Britain and the Cold War*, p. 194.

29 Martin Folly, 'Breaking the Vicious Circle – Britain, the United States and the Genesis of the North Atlantic Treaty', *Diplomatic History*, Winter 1988, p. 60; Baylis, *Diplomacy of Pragmatism*, p. 129. Cf. Bullock, *Ernest Bevin*, pp. 672, 848; Robin Edmonds, *Setting the Mould* (Oxford University Press, Oxford, 1986), p. 177.

30 'Witness Seminar: The Role of the British Embassy in Washington', *Contemporary British History*, Autumn 1998, p. 116.

31 Folly, 'Breaking the Vicious Circle', pp. 60–1; Baylis, *Diplomacy of Pragmatism*, p. 129.

32 L. V. Scott, *Macmillan, Kennedy and the Cuban Missile Crisis* (Macmillan, Basingstoke, 1999), pp. 120–30. Gordon Brooke-Shepherd, *The Storm Birds – Soviet Post-War Defectors* (Weidenfeld & Nicolson, London, 1988), pp. 267–71.

33 R. G. Compton, 'The Balkans, 1909–14' in F. H. Hinsley (ed.), *British Foreign Policy under Sir Edward Grey* (Cambridge University Press, Cambridge, 1977), p. 261.

34 W. N. Medlicott and Douglas Dakin (eds), *D.B.F.P., 1919–39, First Series, Vol. XXVII, 1925* (HMSO, London, 1986), p. 256.

35 James Cable, *The Geneva Conference of 1954 on Indochina* (Macmillan, Basingstoke, 1986), p. 2.

36 Sir Curtis Keeble, 'Macmillan and the Soviet Union', in Richard Aldous and Sabine Lee, *Harold Macmillan – Aspects of a Political Life* (Macmillan, Basingstoke, 1999), pp. 210–11; John Gearson, 'British Policy and the Berlin Wall Crisis, 1958–61', *Contemporary Record*, Summer 1992, pp. 137–8.

37 Henry Kissinger, *Years of Upheaval* (Weidenfeld & Nicolson and Michael Joseph, London, 1982), pp. 285–6.

38 *The Cold War*, BBC 2, 25 April 1999.

39 Raymond Seitz, *Over Here* (Weidenfeld & Nicolson, London, 1998), p. 319. See also Lord Howe, *Conflict of Loyalties* (Macmillan, London, 1994), p. 542.

40 Cited in John Dickie, *'Special' No More* – (Weidenfeld & Nicolson, London, 1994), p. 193.

41 Harold Macmillan, *Pointing the Way* (Macmillan, London, 1972), p. 195; Harold Macmillan *Riding the Storm* (Macmillan, London, 1971), pp. 495, 585–6.

42 John Young, *Winston Churchill's Last Campaign – Britain and the Cold War, 1951–5* (Clarendon Press, Oxford, 1996), pp. 325–7.

43 Keeble, 'Macmillan and the Soviet Union', p. 207.

44 Jan Jacobson, *Locarno Diplomacy – Germany and the West, 1925–29* (Princeton University Press, Princeton, NJ), p. 376.

45 Parker, *Chamberlain and Appeasement*, p. 180.
46 Cited in Andrew Roberts, *Holy Fox – A Life of Lord Halifax* (Papermac, London, 1992), p. 63.
47 Cited in Keith Feiling, *The Life of Neville Chamberlain* (Macmillan, London, 1947), p. 321.
48 Cited in John Charmley, *Chamberlain and the Lost Peace* (Ivan R.Dee, Chicago, 1989), p. 166.
49 Cited in Sean Faughnan, 'The Politics of Influence' (unpublished PhD thesis, Cambridge University, Cambridge, 1993), p. 19.
50 Cited in Young, *Winston Churchill's Last Campaign*, p. 216.
51 *FRUS, 1961–63, Vol X111, Western Europe and Canada* (USGPO, Washington, 1994), pp. 1066–7.
52 Philip Ziegler, *Wilson* (Weidenfeld & Nicolson, London, 1995), p. 461. Cf., Sir Michael Palliser, 'Foreign Policy: in Europe, Continuity, Elsewhere Change', in Michael Parsons (ed.), *Looking Back: the Wilson Years* (L'Université de Pau, Pau, 1999), p. 25.
53 Cited in Mark Stuart, *Douglas Hurd – The Public Servant* (Mainstream Publishing, Edinburgh and London, 1998), p. 451.
54 Kenneth Harris, *Attlee* (Weidenfeld & Nicolson, London, 1984), pp. 293–4.
55 Sir Nicholas Henderson, *The Private Office* (Weidenfeld & Nicolson, London, 1984), p. 89.
56 Robert Cecil, *A Great Experiment – an Autobiography* (Cape, London, 1941), pp. 58–9.
57 Cited in Jason Tome, *Balfour and Foreign Policy – the International Thought of a Conservative Statesman* (Cambridge University Press, Cambridge, 1997), p. 283.
58 George Egerton, *Great Britain and the Creation of the League of Nations – Strategy, Politics and International Organisation, 1914–19* (University of North Carolina Press, Chapel Hill, 1978), pp. 39–43,100, 102–3, 159.
59 Stephen Roskill, 'Lord Hankey – The Creation of the Machinery of Government, *Journal of the Royal United Services Institute*, September 1975, p. 13.
60 Anne Orde, *Great Britain and International Security, 1920–26* (Royal Historical Society, London, 1978), p. 209.
61 Medlicott, *British Foreign Policy since Versailles*, p. 79.
62 Cited in Richard Lamb, *Mussolini and the British* (John Murray, London, 1997), p. 137. See also R.A.C.Parker, 'Great Britain, France and the Ethiopian Crisis, 1935–36', *English Historical Review*, vol. 89, 1974, p. 296.
63 Mangold, *From Tirpitz to Gorbachev*, p. 66.
64 Eric Jensen, 'Introduction' and Lord Gladwyn, 'Founding the United Nations: Principles and Objects', in Erik Jensen and Thomas Fisher (eds), *The United Kingdom – the United Nations* (Macmillan, Basingstoke, 1990), pp. 3, 21.
65 Sally Morphet, 'British Foreign Policy and Human Rights – From Law to High Politics', in David Forsyth (ed) *Human Rights and Comparative Foreign Policy* (United Nations University Press, Tokyo, New York, Paris, 2000).
66 Hans Singer, 'The Vision of Keynes: the Bretton Woods Institutions', in Jensen and Fisher, *The United Kingdom – the United Nations*, p. 235.
67 Kendrick Oliver, *Kennedy, Macmillan and the Nuclear Test-Ban Treaty* (Macmillan, Basingstoke, 1998).

68 Andrew Pierre, *Nuclear Politics* (Oxford University Press, Oxford, 1972), pp. 312–13.
69 J. P. G. Freeman, *Britain's Nuclear Arms Control Policy in the Context of Anglo-American Relations, 1957–68* (Macmillan, Basingstoke, 1986), p. 224.
70 Sir Alan Munro, *An Arabian Affair* (Brasseys, London, 1996), p. 59; John Major, *John Major* (HarperCollins, London, 1999), p. 536.
71 Geoffrey Hoon, 'Kosovo: One Year After', *Journal of the Royal United Services Institute*, April 2000, p. 5.
72 Munro, *An Arabian Affair*, p. 339.
73 Foreign Affairs Commitee, *First Annual Report on Human Rights, 1999* (HC41, 25 January 2000, Stationery Office, London, 2000), p. xii.
74 *Strategic Survey,1999/2000* (International Institute for Strategic Studies, London, 2000), p. 32.
75 Tony Blair, speech in Chicago, *The Times*, 23 April 1999. See also Malcolm Rifkind, 'Peacekeeping or Peacemaking? Implications and Prospects', *Journal of the Royal United Services Institute*, April 1993, pp. 2–5; Douglas Hurd, *Hansard*, Sixth Series, vol.219, 23 February 1993.
76 Major, *John Major*, p. 536.
77 Douglas Hurd, *The Search for Peace* (Little, Brown, London, 1997), p. 130.
78 Major, *John Major*, pp. 548, 549. Hurd, *The Search for Peace*, p. 127.
79 Munro, *An Arabian Affair*, pp. 2–3.
80 Cited in Roger Louis, 'The Dissolution of the British Empire', in Roger Louis and Judith Brown (eds), *The Oxford History of the British Empire, Vol. 1V* (Oxford University Press, Oxford, 1999), p. 350.
81 Cited in Paul Sharp, *Thatcher's Diplomacy* (Macmillan, Basingstoke, 1997), p. 61.
82 Glen Balfour-Paul, *The End of Empire in the Middle East* (Cambridge University Press, Cambridge, 1991), pp. 130–36.
83 George Brown, *In My Way – The Memoirs of Lord George-Brown* (Gollancz, London, 1971), p. 233.
84 David Owen, *Time to Declare* (Penguin, Harmondsworth, 1992), p. 261.
85 Michael Charlton, *The Price of Victory* (BBC, London, 1983), pp. 40–41.
86 Ibid., p. 72.
87 Ibid., p. 31.
88 David Owen, 'Britain and the United States', in *Britain and the United States – Four Views to Mark the Silver Jubilee* (Heinemann, London, 1979), p. 77.
89 Cited in F.S.Northedge, *Freedom and Necessity in British Foreign Policy* (London School of Economics, London, 1972), p. 22.
90 Elizabeth Monroe, *Britain's Moment in the Middle East* (Chatto & Windus, London, 1963), p. 206.

8   Patterns and prognoses

1 See Chapter 1, p. 16.
2 Welsey Wark, *The Ultimate Enemy – British Intelligence and Nazi Germany, 1935–39* (I.B.Tauris, London, 1985), p. 31.
3 Cited in D. C. Watt, *How War Came – the Immediate Origins of the Second World War, 1938–9* (Pantheon Books, New York, 1989), p. 372.

4 Churchill, cited in Peter Hennessy, *Muddling Through* (Indigo, London, 1997); Michael Charlton, *The Little Platoon* (Basil Blackwell, Oxford, 1989), p. 183.
5 Maurice Couve de Murville, *Une Politique Etrangère, 1958–69* (Plon, Paris, 1971), p. 388.
6 See Chapter 6, p. 117.
7 See Chapter 1, p. 29.
8 Cited in Anthony Nutting, *No End of a Lesson* (Constable, London, 1967), p. 7.
9 Rudyard Kipling, 'If', first published in *American Magazine*, October 1910.
10 Cited in Sir Michael Palliser, 'Foreign Policy', in Michael Parsons (ed.), *Looking Back: The Wilson Years, 1964–70* (Publications de L'Université de Pau, Pau, 1999), p. 25.
11 Cf. verdicts in John Young, *Britain in the World in the Twentieth Century* (Arnold, London, 1997), pp. 221–4, 229; David Reynolds, *Britannia Overruled* (Longman, London, 1991), p. 304; Elizabeth Barker, *The British Between the Superpowers, 1945–50* (Macmillan, Basingstoke, 1983), p. 242.
12 *Hansard*, vol.LXV, col.1823, 3 August 1914.
13 Cited in Watt, *How War Came*, pp. 601–2.
14 Cited in Peter Hennessy, *The Prime Minister* (Allen Lane, London, 2000), p. 247.
15 *Dictionary of National Bibliography, 1961–70* (Oxford University Press, Oxford, 1971), p. 617.
16 'Memorandum on the Present State of British Relations with France and Germany', in G. P. Gooch and Harold Temperley (eds), *British Documents on the Origins of the War, 1989–1914, Vol. 3* (HMSO, London, 1928), p. 416.
17 See p. 4.
18 Peter Unwin, *Hearts, Minds and Interests* (Profile Books, London, 1997), p. 154.
19 For the concept of 'accommodatory politics', see Peter Mangold, *From Tirpitz to Gorbachev* (Macmillan, Basingstoke, 1998), p. 123.
20 *The Military Balance, 1999/2000* (International Institute for Strategic Studies, London, 1999), pp. 20,75.
21 Julian Lindly-French, 'Paying for the Privilege – Why an Ethical Foreign Policy Needs an Increase in Defence Expenditure', *Journal of the Royal United Services Institute*, October 1999, p. 7.
22 Sir David Hannay, *The Growth of Multilateral Diplomacy* (Occasional Papers, No.13, FCO Historians, London, 1996), p. 13; Hennessy, *Muddling Through*, p. 162.
23 Lawrence Martin and John Garnett, *Challenges and Choices for the Twenty-First Century* (Royal Institute of International Affairs, London, 1997) p. 107.
24 *The Strategic Defence Review* (Cmnd, 3999, Stationery Office, London, 1998), p. 4. See also Tony Blair, speech, Lord Mayor's Banquet, 22 November 1999 (1999 Guildhall speech).
25 See, for example, Unwin, *Hearts, Minds and Interests*, ch. 4.
26 Sue Onslow, *Backbench Debate within the Conservative Party and its Influence on British Foreign Policy* (Macmillan, Basingstoke, 1997), p. 235.
27 Philip Stephens. *'Rip it up and Start Again'*, *Financial Times*, 25–6 April 1998.
28 Sir John Coles, *British Influence and the Euro* (New Europe, London, 1999), pp. 6–7.
29 Norman Lamont, *In Office* (Little, Brown, London, 1999), p. 125.

30 Roy Denman, 'Coming Attraction: Mr. Blair Goes to Washington', *International Herald Tribune* 14 February 2001.

31 See Chapter 1, p. 16.

32 See Timothy Garton-Ash, 'Is Britain European?', *International Affairs*, January 2001.

33 Charles Grant, *Intimate Relations – Can Britain Play a Leading Role in European Defence – and Keep its Special Links to US Intelligence?* (Centre for European Reform, London, 2000), p. 13.

34 *Financial Times*, 16 February 2001.

35 John Major, *John Major* (HarperCollins, London, 1999), p. 496.

36 General Sir Charles Guthrie, 'Bringing the Armed Services into the New Millennium', *Journal of the Royal United Services Institute*, February 2000, p. 1.

37 Sir John Kerr, 'My Job: Bringing the Foreign Office into the New Millennium', ibid., p. 11.

38 Cited in 'Flawed Evidence Led to "Mission Creep"', *Guardian*, 16 May 2000.

39 Blair, 1999 Guildhall speech.

40 Cited in Sir John Coles, *Making Foreign Policy* (John Murray, London, 2000), p. 179.

41 Blair, 1999 Guildhall speech. Patrick Wormwald, 'The Eternal Angle' *Times Literary Supplement*, 16 March 2001.

42 David Sanders, *Losing an Empire, Finding a Role* (Macmillan, Basingstoke, 1990), p. 290.

43 Roy Hattersley, 'What Are We Good For?', *Guardian*, 7 March 2000; 'The Foreign Office Must Shrug Off the Burdens of the Past', *Independent*, 14 January 1999. See also Unwin, *Hearts, Minds and Interests* pp. 184–5.

44 Kerr, 'My Job', p. 8.

45 Coles, *Making Foreign Policy*, pp. 9, 148–9.

46 Cited in Colin McInnes, *Hot War, Cold War – The British Army's Way in Warfare* (Brasseys, London, 1996), p. 96.

47 Roger Bootle, 'Defending the Indefensible', *Times*, 12 April 2000. See also James Thomas, *The Military Challenges of Transatlantic Coalitions* (Adelphi Paper 333, International Institute for Strategic Studies, London, 2000), pp. 13–17. See also Michael Alexander and Timothy Garten, 'The Arithmetic of Defence Policy', *International Affairs*, July 2001.

48 Joseph Frankel, 'The Intellectual Framework of British Foreign Policy', in Karl Kaiser and Roger Morgan (eds), *Britain and West Germany – Changing Societies and the Future of Foreign Policy* (Oxford University Press, Oxford, 1971), p. 87.

Select Bibliography

Adamthwaite, Anthony, *France and the Coming of the Second World War* (Frank Cass, London, 1977).

Aldous, Richard and Sabine Lee, *Harold Macmillan and Britain's World Role* (Macmillan, Basingstoke, 1996).

—— *Harold Macmillan – Aspects of a Political Life* (Macmillan, Basingstoke, 1999).

Ashton, Nigel John, *Eisenhower, Macmillan and the Problem of Nasser – Anglo-American Relations and Arab Nationalism* (Macmillan, Basingstoke, 1996).

Balfour-Paul, Glen, *The End of Empire in the Middle East – Britain's Relinquishment of Power in Her Last Three Arab Dependencies* (Cambridge University Press, Cambridge, 1991).

Barclay, Brigadier C. N., *On Their Shoulders – British Generalship in the Lean Years, 1939–42*, (Faber, London, 1964).

Barker, Elisabeth, *The British between the Superpowers* (Macmillan, Basingstoke 1983).

Barnett, Corelli, *The Audit of War – the Illusion and Reality of Britain as a Great Nation* (Macmillan, London, 1986).

—— *Britain and Her Army, 1509–1970* (Allen Lane, London, 1970).

—— *The Lost Victory – British Dreams, British Realities, 1945–50* (Macmillan, London, 1995).

Bartlett, C. J. *British Foreign Policy in the Twentieth Century* (Macmillan, Basingstoke, 1989).

Baylis, John, *Ambiguity and Deterrence – British Nuclear Strategy, 1945–64* (Oxford University Press, Oxford, 1995).

—— *Anglo-American Relations Since 1939 – the Enduring Alliance* (Manchester University Press, Manchester, 1997).

—— *The Diplomacy of Pragmatism – Britain and the Formation of NATO, 1942–49* (Macmillan, Basingstoke, 1993).

Bell, Peter, *Chamberlain, Germany and Japan, 1933–34* (Macmillan, Basingstoke, 1996).

Bell, Philip, *A Certain Eventuality – Britain and the Fall of France* (Saxon House, Farnborough, 1974).

—— *France and Britain, 1900–1940 – Entente and Estrangement* (Longman, London, 1996).

—— *France and Britain, 1940–94 – The Long Separation* (Longman, London, 1997).

Beloff, Max, *Britain's Liberal Empire, 1897–1921, Vol. 1, Imperial Sunset*, 2nd edn (Macmillan, Basingstoke, 1987).

—— *Britain's Liberal Empire, 1921–42, Vol.2, Dream of Commonwealth* (1989).

—— *The Future of British Foreign Policy* (Secker & Warburg, London, 1969).

Bennett, G. H., *British Foreign Policy During the Curzon Period, 1919–24* (Macmillan, Basingstoke, 1995).

Best, Anthony, *Britain, Japan and Pearl Harbor – Avoiding War in East Asia, 1936–41* (Routledge, London, 1995).

Bialer, Uri, *The Shadow of the Bomber – the Fear of Air Attack and British Politics, 1932–39* (Royal Historical Society, London, 1980).

Blackwell, Michael, *Clinging to Grandeur – British Attitudes and Foreign Policy in the Aftermath of the Second World War* (Greenwood, Westport, Conn., 1993).

Boardman, Robert and A. J. R. Groom (eds), *The Management of Britain's External Relations* (Macmillan, Basingstoke, 1973).

Bogdanor, Vernon and Robert Skidelsky (eds), *The Age of Affluence, 1951–64* (Macmillan, London, 1970).

Bond, Brian, *British Military Policy Between the Two World Wars* (Clarendon Press, London, 1980).

Brivati, Brian and Harriet Jones, *From Reconstruction to Integration – Britain and Europe Since 1954* (Leicester University Press, Leicester, 1993).

Bruce, Maurice, *British Foreign Policy – Isolation or Intervention?* (Nelson, London, 1938).

Buffet, Cyril and Beatrice Heuser (eds), *Haunted by History – Myths in International Relations* (Berghahn Books, Providence, Oxford, 1998).

Bullock, Alan, *Ernest Bevin – Foreign Secretary, 1945–51* (Oxford University Press, Oxford, 1985).

Cable, James, *The Geneva Conference of 1954 on Indochina* (Macmillan, Basingstoke, 1986).

Callaghan, Lord, *Time and Chance* (Collins, London, 1987).

Campbell, A. E., *Britain and the United States, 1895–1903* (Longmans, London, 1960).

Campbell, John, *Edward Heath* (Jonathan Cape, London, 1993).

Camps, Miriam, *Britain and the European Community, 1955–63* (Princeton University Press, Princeton, NJ, 1964).

Carlton, David, *Anthony Eden – A Biography* (Allen Lane, London, 1981).

Carrington, Lord, *Reflect on Things Past – The Memoirs of Lord Carrington* (Fontana, London, 1989).

Carver, Lord, *Out of Step – Memoirs of a Field Marshal* (Hutchinson, London, 1989).

—— *Tightrope Walking – British Defence Policy Since 1945* (Hutchinson, London, 1992).

Central Office of Information, *British Foreign Policy – A Brief Collection of Fact and Quotation* (COI, London, 1954).

Chalmers, Malcolm, *Paying for Defence – Military Spending and British Decline* (Pluto, London, 1985).

Charlton, Michael, *The Little Platoon – Diplomacy and the Falklands Dispute* (Basil Blackwell, Oxford, 1989).

—— *The Price of Victory* (BBC, London, 1983).

Charmley, John, *Chamberlain and the Lost Peace* (Ivan R. Dee, Chicago, 1989).

—— *Churchill – The End of Glory* (Hodder & Stoughton, London, 1993).

Clark, Ian, *Nuclear Diplomacy and the Special Relationship* (Oxford University Press, Oxford, 1994).

Clarke, Michael, *British External Policy-Making in the 1990s* (Macmillan, Basingstoke, 1992).

Clayton, Anthony, *The British Empire as a Superpower, 1919–39* (University of Georgia Press, Athens, 1986).

Clifford, Nicholas, *Retreat from Asia – British Policy in the Far East, 1937–41* (Longmans, London, 1971).

Coles, Sir John, *Making Foreign Policy – A Certain Idea of Britain* (John Murray, London, 2000).

Craddock, Sir Percy, *In Pursuit of British Interests – Reflections on Foreign Policy under Margaret Thatcher and John Major* (John Murray, London, 1997).

Croft, Stuart, *The End of Superpower – British Foreign Office Conceptions of a Changing World, 1945–51* (Dartmouth, Aldershot, 1994).

Crossman, Richard, *The Crossman Diaries*, condensed edn (Magnum Books, London, 1979).

d'Abernon, Lord, *An Ambassador of Peace – Lord d'Abernon's Diary, Vol. 1 From Spa to Rapallo* (Hodder & Stoughton, London, 1929).

——Vol.2 The Years of Crisis, June 1922–December 1923 (1929).

——Vol.3 The Years of Recovery (1930).

de Madariaga, Salvador, *Englishmen, Frenchmen, Spaniards*, 2nd edn (Pitman, London, 1970).

Danchev, Alex (ed.) *The Franks Report* (Pimlico, London, 1992).

——*Oliver Franks – Founding Father* (Oxford University Press, Oxford, 1993).

——*On Specialness – Essays in Anglo-American Relations* (Macmillan, Basingstoke, 1998).

Darby, Philip, *British Defence Policy East of Suez, 1947–68* (Oxford University Press, Oxford, 1973).

Darwin, John, *Britain, Egypt and the Middle East – Imperial Policy in the Aftermath of the War, 1918–22* (Macmillan, Basingstoke, 1981).

——*Britain and Decolonisation – the Retreat from Empire in the Post-War World* (Macmillan, Basingstoke, 1988).

——*The End of the British Empire – The Historical Debate* (Basil Blackwell, Oxford, 1991).

Deighton, Anne, *The Impossible Peace – Britain, the Division of Germany and the Origins of the Cold War* (Clarendon Press, Oxford, 1993).

——(ed.), *Britain and the First Cold War* (Macmillan, Basingstoke, 1990).

Dell, Edmund, *The Schuman Plan and the British Abdication of Leadership in Europe* (Oxford University Press, Oxford, 1995).

Denman, Roy, *Missed Chances – Britain and Europe in the Twentieth Century* (Cassell, London, 1996).

Dennis, Peter, *Decision by Default – Peacetime Conscription and British Defence, 1919–39* (Routledge & Kegan Paul, London, 1972).

Dickie, John, *Inside the Foreign Office* (Chapmans, London, 1997).

——*'Special' No More – Anglo American Relations: Rhetoric and Reality* (Weidenfeld & Nicolson, London, 1994).

Dobson, Alan, *Anglo-American Relations in the Twentieth Century – Of Friendship, Conflict and the Decline of Superpower* (Routledge, London, 1995).

Dockrill, Michael and John Young, *British Foreign Policy, 1945–56* (Macmillan, Basingstoke, 1989).

Dockrill, Michael and J. Douglas Gould, *Peace Without Promise – Britain and the Peace Conference, 1919–23* (Batsford, London, 1981).

Douglas, Roy, *The World Crisis and British Decline, 1929–56* (Macmillan, Basingstoke, 1986).

Dutton, David, *Anthony Eden – A Life and Reputation* (Arnold, London, 1997).

——*Austen Chamberlain – Gentleman in Politics* (Ross Anderson Publications, Bolton, 1985).

—— (ed.), *Twentieth Century Statecraft and Diplomacy: Essays Presented to P. M. H. Bell* (Liverpool University Press, Liverpool, 1995).

Eden, Sir Anthony, *Full Circle* (Cassell, London, 1960).

Edmonds, Robin, *Breaking the Mould – the United States and Britain* (Oxford University Press, Oxford, 1986).

Egerton, George, *Great Britain and the Creation of the League of Nations – Strategy, Politics and International Organisation, 1914–19* (University of South Carolina Press, Chapel Hill, 1978).

Ferris, John, *Men, Money and Diplomacy – the Evolution of British Strategic Policy, 1919–21* (Cornell University Press, Ithaca, 1989).

Fitzsimons, M. A., *Empire by Treaty – Britain and the Middle East in the Twentieth Century* (Benn, London, 1965).

Frankel, Joseph, *British Foreign Policy, 1945–68* (Oxford University Press, London, 1975).

Franks, Lord *Britain and the Tide of World Affairs* (1954 Reith Lectures, Oxford University Press, London, 1955).

French, David, *British Strategy and War Aims, 1914–16* (Allen & Unwin, London, 1986).

—— *The Strategy of the Lloyd George Coalition, 1916–18* (Oxford University Press, Oxford, 1995).

Friedberg, Aaron, *The Weary Titan – Britain and the Experience of Relative Decline, 1895–1905* (Princeton University Press, Princeton, NJ, 1988).

Fromkin, David, *A Peace to End All Peace – Creating the Modern Middle East, 1914–22* (André Deutsch, London, 1989).

Gallagher, John, *The Decline, Revival and Fall of the British Empire* (ed. Anil Seal) (Cambridge University Press, Cambridge, 1982).

Gates, Eleanor, *End of the Affair – the Collapse of the Anglo-French Alliance, 1939–40* (Allen & Unwin, London, 1981).

Gearson, John, *Harold Macmillan and the Berlin Wall Crisis – the Limits of Interests and Force* (Macmillan, Basingstoke, 1998).

George, Stephen, *An Awkward Partner – Britain in the European Community*, 3rd edn (Oxford University Press, Oxford, 1998).

George-Brown, Lord, *In My Way – the Political Memoirs of Lord George-Brown* (Gollancz, London, 1971).

Gibbs, N. H., *Grand Strategy, Vol.1 – Rearmament Policy* (HMSO, London, 1976).

Gilbert, Martin, *The Roots of Appeasement* (Weidenfeld & Nicolson, London, 1966).

Gilbert, Martin and Richard Gott, *The Appeasers* (Weidenfeld & Nicolson, London, 1963).

Goldstein, Erik, *Winning the Peace – British Diplomatic Strategy, Peace Planning, and the Paris Peace Conference, 1916–20* (Oxford University Press, Oxford, 1991).

Goldsworthy, David, *The Conservative Government and the End of Empire – British Documents on the End of Empire Series A, Vol.3* (HMSO, London, 1994).

Gordon Walker, Patrick, *The Cabinet* (Fontana, London, 1972).

Gore-Booth, Lord, *With Great Truth and Respect* (Constable, London, 1974).

Greenwood, Sean, *Britain and the Cold War, 1945–91* (Macmillan, Basingstoke, 2000).

Grenville, J. A. S., *Lord Salisbury and Foreign Policy – the Close of the Nineteenth Century* (Athlone Press, London, 1970 edn).

Grey of Fallodon, *Twenty Five Years, 1892–1916* (Hodder & Stoughton, London, 1928).

Griffiths, Richard and Stuart Ward, *Courting the Common Market – the First Attempt to Enlarge the European Community, 1961–63* (Lothian Foundation Press, London, 1996).

Harris, Kenneth, *Attlee* (Weidenfeld & Nicolson, London, 1982).

Healey, Denis, *The Time of My Life* (Michael Joseph, London, 1989).

Heath, Sir Edward, *The Course of My Life – an Autobiography* (Hodder & Stoughton, London, 1998).

Henderson, Sir Neville, *Failure of a Mission – Berlin, 1937–39* (Hodder & Stoughton, London, 1940).

Henderson, Sir Nicholas, *The Birth of NATO* (Weidenfeld & Nicolson, London, 1987).

—— *Channels and Tunnels – Reflections on Britain and Abroad* (Weidenfeld & Nicolson, London, 1987).

—— *The Private Office* (Weidenfeld & Nicolson, London, 1986).

Hennessy, Peter, *Muddling Through – Power, Politics and the Quality of Government in Postwar Britain* (Indigo, London, 1997).

—— *Never Again – Britain, 1945–51* (Vintage, London, 1993).

—— *The Prime Ministers – The Office and its Holders Since 1945* (Allen Lane, London, 2000).

Hinsley, F. H. (ed.), *British Foreign Policy Under Sir Edward Grey* (Cambridge University Press, Cambridge, 1977).

Holland, R. F., *Britain and the Revolt in Cyprus, 1954–59* (Clarendon Press, Oxford, 1998).

—— *Emergencies and Disorder in the European Empires After 1945* (Frank Cass, London, 1994).

—— *European Decolonization, 1918–81 – An Introductory Survey* (Macmillan, Basingstoke, 1985).

—— *The Pursuit of Grandeur – Britain and the World Role, 1900–70* (Fontana, London, 1991).

Horne, Alistair, *Macmillan, Vol.1 1894–1956* (Macmillan, London, 1988).

—— *Macmillan, Vol.2 1957–86* (Macmillan, London, 1989).

Howard, Michael, *The Continental Commitment* (Temple Smith, London, 1972).

Howe, Sir Geoffrey, *Conflict of Loyalty* (Macmillan, London, 1994).

Hurd, Douglas, *The End of Promises – Sketch of a Government, 1970–74* (Collins, London, 1979).

—— *The Search for Peace* (Little, Brown, London, 1997).

—— *The Shape of Ice* (Warner, London, 1999).

Hyam, Ronald, *Britain's Imperial Century, 1815–1914 – A Study of Empire and Expansion*, 2nd edn (Macmillan, Basingstoke, 1993).

Jackson, Sir William, *Withdrawal from Empire – A Military Review* (Batsford, London, 1986).

Jacobson, Jon, *Locarno Diplomacy – Germany and the West, 1925–29* (Princeton University Press, Princeton, NJ, 1972).

James, Alan, *Britain and the Congo Crisis, 1960–63* (Macmillan, Basingstoke, 1996).

James, Lawrence, *The Rise and Fall of the British Empire* (Little, Brown, London, 1994).

Jensen, Erik and Thomas Fisher, *The United Kingdom – the United Nations* (Macmillan, London, 1990).

Judd, Denis, *Empire – The British Imperial Experience – From 1765 to the Present* (HarperCollins, London, 1996).

Kaiser, Wolfram, *Using Europe, Abusing the Europeans – Britain and European Integration, 1945–64* (Macmillan, Basingstoke, 1996).

Keeble, Sir Curtis, *Britain and the Soviet Union, 1917–89* (Macmillan, Basingstoke, 1990).

Keir, Elizabeth, *Imagining War – French and British Military Doctrine Between the Wars* (Princeton University Press, Princeton, NJ, 1997).

Kelly, Saul and Anthony Gorst (eds), *Whitehall and the Suez Crisis* (Frank Cass, London, 2000).

Kennedy, Paul, *The Realities Behind Diplomacy – Background Influences on British External Policy, 1865–1980* (Fontana, London, 1981).

—— *The Rise and Fall of British Naval Mastery* (Macmillan, Basingstoke, 1983).

—— *The Rise and Fall of the Great Powers – Economic Change and Military Conflict from 1500–2000* (Fontana, London, 1989).

—— *The Rise of Anglo-German Antagonism, 1860–1914 (George Allen & Unwin, London, 1980).*

—— *Strategy and Diplomacy, 1870–1945* (Fontana, London, 1984).

Kimball, Warren, *Forged in War – Churchill, Roosevelt and the Second World War* (HarperCollins, London, 1997).

Kirby, Major-General S.Woodburn, *Singapore – the Chain of Disaster* (Cassell, London, 1971).

Kirkpatrick, Sir Ivone, *The Inner Circle – Memoirs of Ivone Kirkpatrick* (Macmillan, London, 1959).

Kissinger, Henry, *Diplomacy* (Simon & Schuster, London, 1995).

—— *The White House Years* (Weidenfeld & Nicolson and Michael Joseph, London, 1979).

—— *Years of Upheaval* (Weidenfeld & Nicolson and Michael Joseph, London, 1982).

—— *Years of Renewal* (Weidenfeld & Nicolson, London, 1999).

Kitchen, Martin, *British Policy Towards the Soviet Union During the Second World War* (Macmillan, Basingstoke, 1986).

Kleine-Ahlbrandt, William Laird, *The Burden of Victory – Britain, France and the Enforcement of the Versailles Peace, 1919–25* (University Press of America, Lanham, Maryland, 1995).

Kupchan, Charles, *The Vulnerability of Empire* (Cornell University Press, Ithaca, 1994).

Kyba, Patrick, *Covenants Without the Sword – Public Opinion and British Defence Policy, 1931–35* (Wilfred Laurier Press, Waterloo, Ontario, 1983).

Kyle, Keith, *Suez* (Weidenfeld & Nicolson, London, 1991).

Lamb, Richard, *The Failure of the Eden Government* (Sidgwick & Jackson, London, 1987).

—— *The Macmillan Years – The Emerging Truth, 1957–63* (John Murray, London, 1995).

—— *Mussolini and the British* (John Murray, London, 1997).

Lapping, Brian, *End of Empire* (Paladin, London, 1989).

Lee, Bradford, *Britain and the Sino-Japanese War, 1937–39 – A Study in the Dilemma of British Decline* (Standford University Press, Stanford 1973).

Lloyd, Christopher, *British Entry Into the European Community Under the Heath Government of 1970–74* (Dartmouth, Aldershot, 1993).

Louis, William Roger, The *British Empire in the Middle East, 1945–51 – Arab Nationalism, the United States and Post-War Imperialism* (Oxford University Press, Oxford, 1984).

——*British Strategy in the Far East, 1919–39* (Oxford University Press, Oxford, 1971).

Louis, William Roger and Robert Blake, *Churchill* (Oxford University Press, Oxford, 1994).

Louis, William Roger and Judith Brown, *The Oxford History of the British Empire, Vol.IV, The Twentieth Century* (Oxford University Press, Oxford 1999).

Louis, William Roger and Hedley Bull (eds), *The 'Special Relationship': Anglo-American Relations Since 1945* (Clarendon Press, Oxford, 1986).

Louis, William Roger and Roger Owen (eds), *Suez 1956 – The Crisis and its Consequences* (Clarendon Press, Oxford, 1989).

Ludlow, N. Piers, *Dealing with Britain – the Six and the First UK Application to the EEC* (Cambridge University Press, Cambridge, 1997).

Macmillan, Harold, *Riding the Storm,1956–59* (Macmillan, London, 1971).

——*Pointing the Way, 1959–61* (Macmillan, London, 1972).

——*At the End of the Day, 1961–63* (Macmillan, London, 1973).

Major, John, *John Major – the Autobiography* (HarperCollins, London, 1999).

Mangold, Peter, *From Tirpitz to Gorbachev – Power Politics in the Twentieth Century* (Macmillan, Basingstoke, 1998).

Martin, Lawrence and John Garnett, *British Foreign Policy – Challenges and Choices for the Twenty-First Century* (Chatham House Papers, London 1997).

Mayhew, Christopher, *Britain's Role Tomorrow* (Hutchinson, London, 1967).

McInnes, Colin, *Hot War, Cold War – the British Army's Way in Warfare* (Brasseys, London, 1996).

McIntyre, David W., *British Decolonization, 1946–97 – When, Why and How did the British Empire Fall?* (Macmillan, Basingstoke, 1998).

——*The Rise and Fall of the Singapore Naval Base, 1919–42* (Macmillan, Basingstoke, 1979).

McKercher, B. J. C., (ed.) *Anglo-American Relations in the 1920s – The Struggle for Supremacy* (Macmillan, Basingstoke, 1991).

Medlicott, W. N., *British Foreign Policy since Versailles, 1919–39*, 2nd edn (Methuen, London, 1968).

Melissen, Jan, *The Struggle for Nuclear Partnership – Britain, the United States and the Makings of an Ambiguous Alliance, 1952–9* (Styx Publications, Groningen, 1993).

Middlemas, Keith and John Barnes, *Baldwin – a Biography* (Weidenfeld & Nicolson, London, 1969).

Millett, Allan and Williamson Murray (eds), *Military Effectiveness, Vol.1* (Allen & Unwin, Boston, 1988).

——*Vol. 2 The Interwar Period* (Allen & Unwin, Boston, 1988).

——*Vol. 3 The Second World War* (Allen & Unwin, Boston, 1988).

Mockaitis, Thomas, *British Counterinsurgency, 1919–60* (Macmillan, London, 1990).

——*British Counterinsurgency in the Post-Imperial Era* (Manchester University Press, Manchester, 1995).

Monger, George, *The End of Isolation – British Foreign Policy, 1900–07* (Thomas Nelson, London, 1963).

Monroe, Elizabeth, *Britain's Moment in the Middle East, 1914–56* (Chatto & Windus, London, 1963).

Morgan, Kenneth, *Callaghan – A Life* (Oxford University Press, Oxford, 1997).

—— *The People's Peace – British History, 1945–90* (Oxford University Press, Oxford, 1992).

Munro, Alan, *An Arabian Affair – Politics and Diplomacy Behind the Gulf War* (Brasseys, London, 1996).

Murray, Williamson, *The Change in the European Balance of Power – the Paths to Ruin* (Princeton University Press, Princeton, NJ, 1984).

—— and Millett, Allen (eds), *Military Innovation in the Interwar Period* (Cambridge University Press, Cambridge, 1996).

Neidpath, James, *The Singapore Naval Base and the Defence of Britain's Eastern Empire, 1919–41* (Oxford University Press, Oxford, 1981).

Nelson, Harold, *Land and Power – Britain and Allied Policy on German Frontiers, 1916–19* (Routledge & Kegan Paul, London, 1963).

Neustadt, Richard, *Report to JFK – the Skybolt Crisis in Perspective* (Cornell University Press, Ithaca, 1999).

Newhouse, John, *De Gaulle and the Anglo-Saxons* (André Deutsch, London, 1970).

Nicolson, Harold, *Diplomacy*, 3rd edn (Oxford University Press, London, 1963).

Nish, Ian, *Anglo-Japanese Alienation, 1919–52 (Cambridge University Press, Cambridge, 1982).*

—— *The Anglo-Japanese Alliance – The Diplomacy of Two Island Empires, 1894–1907,* 2nd edn (The Athlone Press, London, 1985).

Northedge, F. S, *British Foreign Policy – the Process of Readjustment, 1945–61* (George Allen & Unwin, London, 1962).

—— *The Troubled Giant: Britain Among the Great Powers, 1900–45* (George Bell & Sons, London, 1966).

Nutting, Anthony, *No End of a Lesson* (Constable, London, 1967).

Oliver, Kendrick, *Kennedy, Macmillan and the Nuclear Test Ban Debate, 1961–63* (Macmillan, Basingstoke, 1998).

Onslow, Sue, *Backbench Debate Within the Conservative Party and its Influence on British Foreign Policy, 1948–57* (Macmillan, London, 1997).

Orde, Anne, *Great Britain and International Security, 1920–26* (Royal Historical Society, London, 1978).

Ovendale, Ritchie (ed.), *Britain's Defence Policy Since 1945* (Manchester University Press, Manchester, 1994).

—— *Britain, the United States and the Transfer of Power in the Middle East, 1945–62* (Leicester University Press, London, 1996).

—— *The English-Speaking Alliance – Britain, the United States, the Dominions and the Cold War, 1945–51* (George Allen & Unwin, London, 1985).

—— *The Foreign Policy of the Labour Government, 1945–51* (Leicester University Press, Leicester, 1984).

Owen, David, *Time to Declare* (Penguin, Harmondsworth, 1992).

Pagedas, Constantine, *Anglo-American Relations and the French Problem, 1960–63* (Frank Cass, London, 2000).

Parker, R. A. C., *Chamberlain and Appeasement – British Policy and the Coming of the Second World War* (Macmillan, Basingstoke, 1993).

Parsons, Michael (ed.), *Looking Back: the Wilson Years, 1964–70* (Publications de l'Université de Pau, Pau, 1999).

Peden, G. C., *British Rearmament and the Treasury: 1932–39* (Scottish Academic Press, Edinburgh, 1979).

Perkins, Bradford, *The Great Rapprochement – England and the United States, 1895–1914* (Atheneum, New York, 1968).

Peyrefitte, Alain, *C'Etait de Gaulle* (Fayard, Paris, 1995 and 2000).

Pickering, James, *Britain's Withdrawal from East of Suez – the Politics of Retrenchment* (Macmillan, Basingstoke, 1998).

Pieragostini, Karl, *Britain, Aden and South Arabia – Abandoning Empire* (Macmillan, Basingstoke, 1991).

Pierre, Andrew, *Nuclear Politics – the British Experience with an Independent Strategic Force, 1939–70* (Oxford University Press, Oxford, 1970).

Plowden, Lord, *An Industrialist in the Treasury* (André Deutsch, London 1989).

Porter, A. N. and A. J. Stockwell, *British Imperial Policy and Decolonization, 1938–64 Vol.2 1951–54* (Macmillan, Basingstoke, 1989).

Porter, Bernard, *The Lion's Share – A Short History of British Imperialism, 1850–1995*, 3rd edn (Longman, London).

Pratt, Lawrence, *East of Malta, West of Suez – Britain's Mediterranean Crisis, 1936–39* (Cambridge University Press, Cambridge, 1975).

Renwick, Robin, *Fighting with Allies – America and Britain in Peace and War* (Macmillan, Basingstoke, 1996).

Reynolds, David, *Britannia Overruled – British Policy and World Power in the Twentieth Century* (Longman, London, 1991).

Rhodes-James, Robert, *Anthony Eden* (Weidenfeld & Nicolson, London 1986).

Richardson, Louise, *When Allies Differ – Anglo-American Relations During the Suez and Falklands Crises* (Macmillan, Basingstoke, 1996).

Robbins, Keith, *Sir Edward Grey* (Cassell, London, 1971).

Roberts, Andrew, *'The Holy Fox' – A Life of Lord Halifax* (Papermac, London, 1991).

Rothwell, Victor, *Britain and the Cold War, 1941–47* (Cape, London, 1982).

Samuels, Martin, *Doctrine and Dogma – German and British Infantry Tactics in the First World War* (Greenwood Press, New York, 1992).

Sanders, David, *Losing an Empire, Finding a Role – British Foreign Policy Since 1945* (Macmillan, London 1990).

Scott, L. V., *Macmillan, Kennedy and the Cuban Missile Crisis – Political, Military and Intelligence Aspects* (Macmillan, Basingstoke, 1999).

Seitz, Raymond, *Over Here* (Weidenfeld & Nicolson, London, 1998).

Sharp, Paul, *Thatcher's Diplomacy – the Revival of British Foreign Policy* (Macmillan, Basingstoke, 1997).

Shuckburgh, Evelyn, *Descent to Suez – Diaries, 1951–56* (Weidenfeld & Nicolson, London, 1986).

Singh, Anita Inder, *The Limits of British Influence – South Asia and the Anglo-American Relationship, 1947–56* (Pinter, London, 1993).

Smith, Geoffrey, *Reagan and Thatcher* (Bodley Head, London, 1990).

Smith, Michael, Steve Smith and Brian White (eds), *British Foreign Policy – Tradition, Change and Transformation* (Unwin Hyman, London, 1988).

Steiner, Zara, *Britain and the Origins of the First World War* (Macmillan, Basingstoke, 1977).

Stephens, Philip, *Politics and the Pound – the Tories, the Economy and Europe* (Macmillan, London, 1996).

Stephens, Robert, *Ian Macleod* (Hutchinson, London, 1994).

Stewart, Michael, *Life and Labour – an Autobiography* (Sidgwick & Jackson, London, 1986).

Strang, Lord, *Britain in World Affairs – Henry VIII-Elizabeth II* (Faber and Deutsch, London, 1961).

—— *Home and Abroad* (Deutsch, London, 1956).

Strange, Susan, *Sterling and British Policy – A Political Study of an International Currency in Decline* (Oxford University Press, Oxford, 1971).

Stuart, Mark, *Douglas Hurd – the Public Servant* (Mainstream Publishing, Edinburgh and London, 1998).

Thatcher, Margaret, *The Downing Street Years, 1979–90* (HarperCollins, London, 1993).

Thompson, Neville, *The Anti-Appeasers – Conservative Opposition to Appeasement in the 1930s* (Oxford University Press, Oxford, 1971).

Thorne, Christopher, *Allies of a Kind – the United States, Britain and the War Against Japan, 1941–45* (Oxford University Press, Oxford, 1978).

Thornton, A. P, *The Imperial Ideas and its Enemies – A Study in British Policy* (Macmillan, London, 1985 edn).

Thorpe, D. R., *Alec Douglas-Home* (Sinclair Stevenson, London, 1996).

—— *Selwyn Lloyd* (Jonathan Cape, London, 1989).

Tomes, Jason, *Balfour and Foreign Policy – the International Thought of a Conservative Statesman* (Cambridge University Press, Cambridge, 1997).

Tratt, Jacqueline, *The Macmillan Government and Europe – A Study in the Process of Policy Development* (Macmillan, Basingstoke, 1996).

Travers, Tim, *The Killing Ground – the British Army, the Western Front and the Emergence of Modern Warfare, 1900–18* (Routledge, London, 1993 edn).

Turner, Ian, *Reconstruction in Post-War Germany – British Occupation Policy and the Western Zones, 1945–55* (Berg, Oxford, 1989).

Turner, John, *Macmillan* (Longman, London, 1994).

Unwin, Peter, *Hearts, Minds and Interests – Britain's Place in the World* (Profile Books, London, 1998).

Vital, David, *The Making of British Foreign Policy* (George Allen & Unwin, 1968).

Waites, Neville (ed.), *Troubled Neighbours – Franco-British Relations in the Twentieth Century* (Weidenfeld & Nicolson, London, 1971).

Wallace, William, *The Foreign Policy Process in Britain* (Royal Institute of International Affairs, London, 1975).

Waltz, Kenneth (ed.), *Foreign Policy and Democratic Politics – the American and British Experience* (Longmans, London, 1968).

Watt, D. C., *How War Came – the Immediate Origins of the Second World War, 1938–39 (Pantheon Books, New York, 1989).*

—— *Succeeding John Bull – America in Britain's Place, 1900–75* (Cambridge University Press, Cambridge, 1984).

Williamson, Samuel, *The Politics of Grand Strategy – Britain and France Prepare for War, 1904–14* (Harvard University Press, Cambridge, Mass., 1969).

Wilson, Harold, *The Labour Government, 1964–70 – A Personal Record* (Weidenfeld & Nicolson, London, 1971).

Wilson, Keith, *Channel Tunnel Visions, 1850–1945 – Dreams and Nightmares* (Hambledon Press, London, 1994).

—— (ed.), *Imperialism and Nationalism in the Middle East – the Anglo-Egyptian Experience, 1882–1982* (Mansell, London, 1985).

Wilson, Trevor, *The Myriad Faces of War – Britain and the Great War, 1914–18* (Polity Press, Cambridge, 1986).

Wyllie, James, *The Influence of British Arms – an Analysis of British Military Intervention Since 1956* (George Allen & Unwin, London, 1986).

Young, Hugo, *This Blessed Plot – Britain and Europe from Churchill to Blair* (Macmillan, London, 1998).

Young, John, *Britain and the World in the Twentieth Century* (Arnold, London, 1997).

—— *Britain and European Unity, 1945–92* (Macmillan, Basingstoke, 1993).

—— (ed.), *The Foreign Policy of Churchill's Peacetime Administration*, 1951–5 (Leicester University Press, Leicester, 1988).

—— *Winston Churchill's Last Campaign – Britain and the Cold War, 1951–55* (Clarendon, Oxford, 1996).

Zametica, John, *British Officials and British Foreign Policy, 1945–50* (Leicester University Press, Leicester, 1990).

Ziegler, Philip, *Wilson – the Authorised Life of Lord Wilson of Rievaulx* (Weidenfeld & Nicolson, London, 1993).

Articles, pamphlets and reports

Adamthwaite, Anthony, 'Britain, France and the Integration of Western Europe', in Michael Dockrill (ed.), *Europe Within the Global System, 1938–60 – Great Britain, France, Italy and Germany – From Great Powers to Regional Powers* (Universitaetsverlag Dr. N Brockmeyer, Bochum 1995).

—— 'Britain and the World, 1945–49: the View From the Foreign Office' in Joseph Becker and Franz Knipping (eds), *Power in Europe? Great Britain, France, Italy and Germany in a Postwar World, 1945–50* (Walter de Gruyter, Berlin, 1986).

—— 'Overstretched and Overstrung: Eden, the Foreign Office and the Making of Policy', *International Affairs*, Spring 1988.

Ashton, Nigel John, 'A Microcosm of Decline: Britain's Loss of Nerve and Military Intervention in Jordan and Kuwait, 1958 and 1962', *The Historical Journal*, vol.40, no.4, 1997.

Bell, Philip, 'A Historical Cast of Mind – Some Eminent English Historians and Attitudes to Continental Europe in the Middle of the Twentieth Century', *Journal of European Integration History*, no.2, vol.96.

Boyle, Peter, 'The British Government's View of the Cuban Missile Crisis', *Contemporary History*, Autumn 1996.

Brinkley, D. 'Dean Acheson and the Special Relationship – the West Point Speech, December 1962.' *Historical Journal*, vol.33, no.3, 1990.

Burgess, Simon and Geoffrey Edwards, 'The Six Plus One: British Policy-Making and the Question of European Economic Integration, 1955', *International Affairs*, Summer 1988.

Burk, Kathleen, 'Britain and the Marshall Plan', in Chris Wrigley (ed.), *Warfare, Diplomacy and Politics – Essays in Honour of A. J. P. Taylor* (Hamish Hamilton, London, 1986).

——Great Britain in the United States, 1917–18 – the Turning Point', *International History Review*, April 1979.

Cable, Sir James, 'Interdependence: a Drug of Addiction?', *International Affairs*, Summer 1983.

Caccia, Lord, *The Roots of British Foreign Policy, 1929–65* (Ditchley Foundation Lecture, Ditchley Park, 1965).

Cairns, John, 'A Nation of Shopkeepers in Search of a Suitable France', *American Historical Review*, June 1974.

——'Great Britain and the Fall of France – a Study of Allied Disunity', *Journal of Modern History*, December 1955.

Callaghan, James, *Challenges and Opportunities for British Foreign Policy* (Fabian Tract No.439, London, 1975).

Callahan, Raymond, 'The Illusion of Security: Singapore, 1919–42', *Journal of Contemporary History*, April 1974.

Chamberlain, Austen, 'The Permanent Bases of British Foreign Policy', *International Affairs*, July 1931.

Coker, Christopher, *Who Only England Know – the Conservatives and Foreign Policy* (Institute for European Defence and Strategic Studies, London, 1996).

Darwin, John, 'An Undeclared Empire – the British in the Middle East, 1918–39', *Journal of Imperial and Commonwealth History*, May 1999.

——'British Decolonization: A Pattern or a Puzzle', *Journal of Imperial and Commonwealth History*, January 1984.

——'The Fear of Falling: British Politics and Imperial Decline Since 1900', *Transactions of the Royal Historical Society*, Fifth Series, vol.36, 1996.

Davis, Richard, 'Mesentente Cordiale – The Failure of the Anglo-French Alliance . Anglo-French Relations During the Ethiopian and Rhineland Crises, 1934–6', *European History*, October 1993.

——'Why Did the General Do It? De Gaulle, Polaris and the French Veto of Britain's Application to Join the Common Market', *European History*, July 1998.

Deighton, Anne, 'Britain and the Creation of the WEU, 1954' in A. Deighton (ed.), *WEU, 1954–97 – Defence, Security and Integration* (European Interdependence Research Unit, St Antony's Oxford 1997).

——'Britain and the Three Interlocking Circles' in Antonio Varsori (ed.), *Europe, 1945–90 – the End of an Era?* (Macmillan, Basingstoke, 1995).

——'British Imperial Memories and the European Question' in *Memory and Power in International Relations* (Cambridge University Press, Cambridge, forthcoming).

Dockrill, Michael, 'The Foreign Office, Anglo-American Relations and the Korean War, June 1950–June 1951', *International Affairs*, Summer 1986.

——'Restoring the "Special Relationship" – the Bermuda and Washington Conferences, 1957' in Dick Richardson and Glyn Stone (eds), *Decisions and Diplomacy – Essays in Twentieth Century International History* (Routledge, London, 1995).

Douglas-Home, Sir Alec, *Britain's Changing Role in World Affairs*, (David Daves Memorial Institute, London, 1974).

Dutton, David, 'Anticipating Maastricht – the Conservative Party and Britain's First Application to Join the Common Market', *Contemporary Record*, Winter 1993.

Ferris, John '"The Greatest Power on Earth": Great Britain in the 1920s', *The International Historical Review*, November 1991.

Feske, Victor, 'The Road to Suez: the British Foreign Office and the Quai d'Orsay' in Gordon Craig and Francis Loewenheim, (eds), *The Diplomats, 1939–79* (Princeton University Press, Princeton, NJ, 1994).

Folly, Martin, 'Breaking the Vicious Circle – Britain, the United States and the Genesis of the North Atlantic Treaty', *Diplomatic History*, Winter 1988.

Frankel, Joseph, 'The Intellectual Framework of British Foreign Policy' in Karl Kaiser and Roger Morgan (eds), *Britain and West Germany – Changing Societies and the Future of Foreign Policy* (Oxford University Press, London, 1971).

Furedi, Frank, 'The Political Management of Colonial Emergencies, *Journal of Imperial and Commonwealth History*, September 1993.

Gillespie, Paul (ed.), *Britain's European Question – the Issue for Ireland* (Institute of European Affairs, Dublin, 1996).

Grant, Charles, *Can Britain Lead in Europe?* (Centre for European Reform, London, 1998).

Grayson, Richard 'The British Government, the Channel Tunnel and European Unity, 1948–64', *European History*, July 1996.

Greenwood, David, *The Economics of the 'East of Suez' Decision* (Aberdeen Studies in Defence Economics, Aberdeen, 1973).

Hill, Christopher, 'Britain's Elusive Role in World Politics', *British Journal of International Studies*, October 1979.

—— 'The Influence of Ideas in British Foreign Policy' *Contemporary History*, Summer 1996.

Hopkins, Michael, 'Focus of a Changing Relationship: the Washington Embassy and Britain's World Role Since 1945', *Contemporary British History*, Autumn 1998.

Hopkins, Tony 'Macmillan's Audit of Empire' in Peter Clarke and Clive Trebilcock *Understanding Decline-Perceptions and Realities in British Economic Performance* (Cambridge University Press, Cambridge, 1997).

Howard, Michael, 'Britain's Strategic Problems East of Suez', *International Affairs*, April 1966.

Jong-yil, Ra 'The Special Relationship at War: the Anglo-American Relationship During the Korean War', *Journal of Strategic Studies*, September 1984.

Journal of Contemporary History 'The East of Suez Decision', Winter 1993.

—— 'The Role of the British Embassy in Washington', Autumn 1998.

Kent, John 'The Egyptian Base and the Defence of the Middle East, 1945–54', *Journal of Imperial and Commonwealth History*, September 1993.

Kerr, Sir John, 'My Job: Bringing the Foreign Office Into the New Millennium', *Journal of the Royal United Services Institute*, February 2000.

Kissinger, Henry, 'Reflections on a Partnership – British and American Attitudes to Postwar Foreign Policy', *International Affairs*, Autumn 1982.

Lapping, Brian, 'Did Suez Hasten the End of Empire?' Contemporary Record, 1/2, Summer 1987.

Larres, Klaus, 'Integrating Europe or Ending the Cold War? Churchill's Post-War Foreign Policy', *Journal of European Integration History*, vol.2, no.1.

Lawler, Peter, *Moral Vision and British Foreign Policy* (University of Manchester, Manchester, 1996).

Lindley-French, Julian, 'Paying for the Privilege – Why an Ethical Foreign Policy Needs an Increase in Defence Expenditure', *Journal of the Royal United Services Institute*, October 1999.

Lloyd, Lorna, 'Britain and the Transformation from Empire to Commonwealth – the Significance of the Immediate Post-war Years', *Round Table*, no. 345, 1997.

Louis, William Roger, 'American Anti-Colonialism and the Dissolution of the British Empire', *International Affairs*, Summer 1985.

—— 'Harold Macmillan and the Crisis of 1958', *Proceedings of the British Academy*, London, 1994.

—— and Ronald Robinson, 'The Imperialism of Decolonisation', *Journal of Imperial and Commonwealth History*, no.3, 1994.

Ludlow, Peter, 'The Unwinding of Appeasement' in Kettenacker, Lothar *Das 'Andere Deutschland' im Zweiten Weltkrieg* (Ernst Klett Verlag, Stuttgart, 1977).

Manne, Robert, 'The British Decision for Alliance with Russia, May 1939', *Journal of Contemporary History*, July 1974.

Martel, Gordon, 'The Meaning of Power: Rethinking the Decline and Fall of Great Britain', *The International Historical Review*, November 1991.

Mills, William, 'The Nyons Conference – Neville Chamberlain, Anthony Eden and the Appeasement of Italy in 1937', *International Historical Review*, February 1993.

Morphet, Sally, 'British Foreign Policy and Human Rights – From Low to High Politics' in David Forsyth (ed.), *Human Rights and Comparative Foreign Policy* (United Nations University Press, Tokyo, New York, Paris, 2000).

Neilson, Keith ' "Greatly Exaggerated": The Myth of the Decline of Great Britain before 1914', *International Historical Review*, November 1991.

Nicolson, Harold, 'Modern Diplomacy and British Public Opinion', *International Affairs*, September–October 1935.

Northedge, F. S. 'Britain as a Second Rank Power', *International Affairs*, January 1970.

—— *Freedom and Necessity in British Foreign Policy* (LSE, London, 1972).

Ovendale, Ritchie, 'Macmillan and the Winds of Change in Africa, 1957–60', *Historical Journal*, vol.38, no.2, 1995.

Palliser, Sir Michael, *Britain and British Diplomacy in a World of Change* (David Davies Memorial Institute, London, 1975).

Rawnsly, Gary, 'How Special is Special? The Anglo-American Alliance During the Cuban Missile Crisis', *Contemporary History*, Winter 1995.

Report of the Committee on Representative Service Overseas (Plowden Report) (HMSO, London 1964, Cmnd 2276).

Reynolds, David, 'Churchill and the British "Decision" to Fight on in 1940; Right Policy, Wrong Reasons' in Richard Langhorne (ed.), *Diplomacy and Intelligence During the Second World War* (Cambridge University Press, Cambridge, 1985).

—— 'Eden the Diplomatist, 1931–56 – Suezide of a Statesman?' *History*, 240.

—— 'Rethinking Anglo-American Relations' *International Affairs*, Winter 1988/9.

—— 'A "Special Relationship"? America, Britain and the International Order Since the Second World War', *International Affairs*, Winter 1985/6.

—— '1940: Fulcrum of the Twentieth Century?', *International Affairs*, April 1990.

Rifkind, Malcolm, 'Peacekeeping or Peacemaking? Implications and Prospects', *Journal of the Royal United Services Institute*, April 1993.

Robbins, Keith, *Britishness and British Foreign Policy* (FCO Historians Occasional Papers, no.14, 1997).

Ruane, Kevin, 'Anthony Eden, British Diplomacy and the Origins of the Geneva Conference of 1954', *The Historical Journal*, March 1994.

Schroeder, Paul, 'Munich and the British Tradition', *The Historical Journal*, vol.19, No.1, 1976.

Sharp, Paul, 'The Place of the EEC in the Foreign Policy of the British Government, 1961–71' *Millennium*, 1983, no.2.

Shlaim, Avi, 'Britain, the Berlin Blockade and the Cold War', *International Affairs*, Winter, 1983/4.

Shonfield, Andrew, 'The Duncan Report and its Critics', *International Affairs*, April 1970.

——'The Pragmatic Illusion – On the British Formula for Muffling Public Purpose', *Encounter*, June 1967.

——'The Pursuit of Prestige – a Guide to British Post-War Policy', *Encounter*, June 1957.

Steiner, Zara 'The Fall of Great Britain' in Geir Lundestad, (ed.), *The Fall of Great Powers – Peace, Stability and Legitimacy* (Oxford University Press, Oxford, 1994).

Vital, David, 'The Making of British Foreign Policy', *Political Quarterly*, July-September 1968.

The Strategic Defence Review (Cmd. 3999, London, 1998).

Wallace, William, 'British Foreign Policy After the Cold War', *International Affairs*, July 1992.

——'Foreign Policy and National Identity – the UK', *International Affairs*, January 1991.

Wallach, Jehuda, 'The Sea Lion that Did Not Roar' in John Hattendorf and Malcolm Murfet (eds), *The Limits of Military Power – Essays Presented to Professor Norman Gibb* (Macmillan, Basingstoke, 1990).

Warner, Geoffrey, 'The Impact of the Second World War on British Foreign Policy', in Brian Brivati and Harriet Jones (eds), *What Difference Did tha War Make?* (Leicester University Press, Leicester, 1993).

——'The United States and the Suez Crisis', *International Affairs*, April 1991.

Williams, John, 'ANZUS: A Blow to Britain's Self-Esteem', *Review of International Studies*, October 1987.

Wilson, Keith 'The Foreign Office and the "Education" of Public Opinion before the First World War', *The Historical Journal*, Vol.26, No.2, 1983.

Wilson, Trevor, 'Britain's "Moral Commitment" to France in August 1914', *History*, October 1979.

Young, John, 'Churchill's "No" to Europe: the "Rejection" of European Unity by Churchill's Post-War Government, 1951–2', *Historical Journal*, no.4, 1985.

Unpublished

Faughnan, Sean, 'The Politics of Influence – Churchill, Eden and Soviet Communism, 1951–57' (Cambridge University, unpublished PhD thesis, 1993).

Kane, Liz, 'Tilting to Europe? Britain's Response to Developments in European Integration, 1955–58' (Oxford University, unpublished DPhil thesis, 1996).

Royal Institute of International Affairs, 'Britain in the World', conference proceedings, 29 March 1995.

Thornhill, Michael, 'Britain and the Egyptian Question, 1950–2' (Oxford University, unpublished DPhil thesis, 1995).

Index